Black Coffee in a Coconut Shell

Black Coffee in a Coconut Shell

Caste as Lived Experience

Edited by
Perumal Murugan

Translated by
C.S. Lakshmi

YODAPRESS | SIMON & SCHUSTER

First edition published in 2018

This edition published in 2023

1 3 5 7 9 10 8 6 4 2
Simon & Schuster India
818, Indraprakash Building,
21, Barakhamba Road,
New Delhi 110001.

YODA Press
79 Gulmohar Enclave
New Delhi - 110049
www.yodapress.co.in

Printed and bound in India by Replika Press Pvt. Ltd.

Simon & Schuster India is committed to sourcing paper that is made from wood grown in sustainable forests and support the Forest Stewardship Council, the leading international forest certification organisation. Our books displaying the FSC logo are printed on FSC certified paper.

Identifiers: LCCN 2018036151 (print) | LCCN 2018038166 (ebook) |
ISBN 9789352808397 (Web PDF) | ISBN 9789392099847 (ePub 2.0) |
ISBN 9789392099830 (pbk.: alk. paper)

ISBN: 9789392099830 (PB)

MIX
Paper from responsible sources
FSC® C016779

Contents

Translator's Preface

Marked Bodies, Marked Minds

I belong to a generation that went to school immediately after Independence in the late forties and fifties. Among other songs, Bharathiyar's 'There are no castes, little girl' and his assertion that there are only two castes, woman and man, made deep impressions on our minds and we grew up with the notion that in order to do away with caste we only had to deny its existence and assert our own casteless status. Those were idealistic times. It was not long before we realised that dealing with caste and its ways of marking bodies needs more than assertions and denials; it needs confrontation and overcoming.

In one of my Journey stories a woman makes a strong gesture of anger against an old man who insists on knowing her caste before drinking the water she offers when he is thirsty. There are others in the compartment he does not ask for water for he knows their caste. When the old man almost chokes on a betel nut, one of the other passengers helps him out. He is a doctor. He tells the woman: Madam, you might feel compelled to show that you do not believe in caste. I don't. Even though I don't believe in it, it still stays sticking to me. I just have to keep dusting it away as I go. I should not allow it to make me, or the others who are close to me, lose self respect. That is all I care about....

The essays in this book are about living, loving and dying with caste as an indelible marker. They are not just sad stories about the oppression of caste; they are also about existing with caste and being inextricably caught in caste. There are times when caste protects you and gives you security in the form of a goddess or god that belongs only to you; it becomes a group solidarity you can fall back on even when it limits you in many ways and includes you and excludes you in specific ways. Caste is also a quietly sleeping demon within you which comes out and shocks you in the most unexpected moments when you use language you never thought you would, like it happens in the case of P. Ezhilarasi in this book. In a moment of anger, she names a lowered caste forgetting that one of the women present, who is like a mother to her, belongs to that caste.

There are times when you wonder what caste is all about. Like when you are lovingly given black coffee in a coconut shell when the lady who serves the coffee belongs to a household that has regular utensils and many cows and no dearth of milk, or when your dream as a small boy is to sit in the swivelling chair in a salon and the salon owner tells you he cannot cut your hair because he will lose upper caste customers, or when the mother of a friend wonders whether to serve you inside the house or outside or whether to serve you on a steel plate or a leaf. Caste enters schools, colleges and universities and it gets into friendships in a way that can hurt. It can affect the way you see a woman and the way you love. Some essays in the book talk about it with deep pain like when the family refuses to accept the woman from another caste R. Rajasekaran brings home. Sometimes punishments a caste can impose may put fear in one, of the opposite sex. Like the fear instilled in the mind of M. Natarajan by the incidents in his caste group where anyone who is considered immoral is forced to commit suicide or killed. The threats that nothing can be hidden for even if a person hides a 'misdeed', the day after that person's funeral they would inspect the grave and if a dog had shat on the grave, that was a sure indication of the immorality of the dead person.

Some deal with matters of caste and love with a bit of humour. M. Venugopal speaks of pursuing love undaunted by caste and how every time he failed. He writes about his final attempt of proposing to a Brahmin woman who tells him that she was an

Iyengar and that this would never work and that they should remain friends. To hell with women, he decides and finally marries someone from his own caste. The irony is that his attempts to marry women from another caste for altruistic reasons or for reasons of love are stymied because of caste but the names of all the women including the one he finally marries happen to be Vetri, success!

The essays in this book talk about what Perumal Murugan, the editor, refers to as the omnipresence of caste similar to what is seen as god's omnipresence. They talk about the pain of identity and the anger of being in an identity as much as they talk about helplessness, inability and personal limitations in dealing with caste. The personal experiences are frank and directly spoken, honestly and with no holds barred. They clearly map how caste makes its insidious way into language, gestures, family, love and death and how its tentacles have extended into the politics of the nation.

Translating these essays has been an important experience and meeting the authors and my discussions with them added so much to my knowledge of life and politics in Tamil Nadu. Working with my friend Perumal Murugan and staying in his house with his students has been a great experience. This was a house a little away from the main roads of Namakkal which he had bought and two of his students stayed there and occasionally guests were hosted there. The night I reached, I went off to sleep and woke up to the sound of something being ground. I went to the kitchen to see his students trying to grind some horse gram with a large vessel. 'What are you doing?' I asked. 'We are going to make horse gram kuzhambu for you because you are diabetic. Horse gram is good for diabetes,' they said. And so the diabetic diet continued on the days I stayed there. Perumal Murugan, the other authors who came to discuss and answer my queries, and the students were all good cooks and made some great breakfasts with finger millet dosais and lunches with diabetic recipes of sambar and poriyal. My job was only to teach them to make ginger tea for making tea was something they could not master. Finally it was decided that in the plot next to his we would build another house in the Kerala style and that I would spend my old age there reading and writing! So the benefits of this translation work have been many.

My friend, poet and writer Charanjeet Kaur, read my initial drafts and was kind enough to edit them for me. I thank her for her time and patience. I thank Kannan Sundaram of Kalachuvadu Publications for involving me in this work when I told him I would love to translate this book. My relationship with my publishers and editors has always been tumultuous and this one with Yoda Press has also had its share of tumult. Arpita Das has seen it through despite the personal tragedy of losing a dear father, not giving up even when it seemed impossible. My thanks are due to her and her team at Yoda Press.

Mumbai **C.S. Lakshmi**
9th September 2017

Introduction:
The Buried Treasure I Found

Perumal Murugan

In 2005, we began a series of meetings under the name Koodu Aayvu Santhippu (The Nest Research Meetings) on our terrace, where we could meet and discuss various subjects. Our great desire for a house had just then been fulfilled and we had bought the house. When I saw the terrace the first thing I wanted to do was to have meetings there. Writers like to speak as much as they like to write. Moreover, when I was in PSG Arts and Science College in Coimbatore during my postgraduate studies, I was a coordinator for a year in an organisation called Sinthanai Mandram. My job was to arrange one meeting every week. Choosing the space, arranging the programme and the speaker, sending circulars and getting the audience and all that I did there had trained me well.

Apart from that I am a writer who had also been trained by my having been part of a left movement for a few years. There is a general opinion that leftists are incessant talkers. There would be meetings of lower committee and higher committee, room meetings, meetings in auditoriums and several such meetings. If one had worked for half an hour it would take half a day to talk about it. So this general opinion is not very far from the truth and my own attitude towards meetings is proof of that. If I see a place I would immediately start calculating in my mind how to conduct a meeting there and how many people it could accommodate. That is how our terrace meetings began.

For the first meeting some 15 people came. Then the number of participants increased slowly, and then, at least 45 to 50 people began to attend every meeting. One month the number rose to 65. That was the month I had returned from my trip to South Korea and spoke about my experiences.

We felt that 50 people per meeting was fine. It was not a meeting in an auditorium. It was the terrace of my house. The meetings should not invade the privacy and the running of the household. Initially, we offered tea to everyone. When the numbers increased, we collected a small contribution from each one and offered tea and biscuits. Then it progressed to dinner at night. Since the Koodu meeting provided an opportunity to meet friends and converse, many came with enthusiasm. Some wanted to share happy events of their life by offering a celebratory dinner to Koodu friends. This continued and now we don't have meetings without dinner. The meal is normally according to the choice and convenience of the host. Now people have to book the dates on which they want to offer dinner in advance. I am happy that happy occasions have increased.

After Koodu was formed, a parallel meeting came to be organised a day before the Koodu meeting. A hotel room would be booked and many would come to correct the papers of research students and also discuss them. Many were able to get their PhD degrees with this kind of help. The quality of the dissertations also improved. It also brought to an end the calumny that students who worked under me for a PhD would never be able to complete it soon. While the Koodu meeting would be for three hours or so, the other meeting associated with it, where all of us met in the hotel room, took place for two full days. When I say all of us, I mean teachers, including me, postgraduate and graduate students, writers and some special invitees.

I have no doubt that Koodu has made it possible to build friendships, to improve relationships, to help one another and to progress. It was not as if we planned it that way. We never plan in a big way for meetings. According to the needs of a given month, it would be casually planned. Initially, only research articles were read out. Computer printouts of the papers in the form of a book were distributed among those who gathered for the meeting. That is why the nomenclature 'Research Meetings' got stuck to our activity. Taking into consideration the kind of inconveniences such a term created, we changed the way the meetings were organised. We added some poetry reading, book reviews, and some talks on specific subjects to the activity of reading the research articles in the meetings.

Special invitees also participated at times. When writers came to Salem and Namakkal we tried to bring them to our meetings too. The list of such writers who came is rather long: Prapanchan, Pa. Jeyaprakasam, Anand, K. Mohanarangan, Jeyamohan, K. A. Gunasekaran, Ka. Vai. Palanisamy and Pavannan. When professors were to attend a seminar or had to come for the viva-voce of students, we used to ask them to come a day earlier and participate in a Koodu meeting. V. Arasu, Ka. Poornachandran, Pa. Madhivanan, Ka. Kasiappan, Ma. Venkatesan, Va. Krishnan and Ira Iraman attended the Koodu meetings when they had come for other commitments. Writers who are locally placed in areas like Salem, for instance Balamurugan, Santhiyur Govindan, A. Karthikeyan, Ve. Babu, Agacheran and Pa. Raja, continue to participate in the Koodu meetings. Those who live far away, like Ankarai Bhairavi, Pudugai Sanjeevi and Manya, have come very often just to attend Koodu meetings.

We don't ignore local players in our area too. There is hardly a meeting without Po. Velsamy; Na. Pa. Ramasamy, book collector and rationalist; and Ma Murugan, who has retired from the Postal Department and is an astute reader of books. Avid readers Sarvarasu and Satishrajan have also participated in Koodu meetings. The role played by our friends and students is a very important one. They are there to arrange all the meetings. To list them will be an impossible task. Pa. Nallusamy, Mu. Natarajan, Na. Arulmurugan, C. Chandran, A. Chinnadurai, V. Rajiv Gandhi, Re. Mahendiran... the list could go on.

The Koodu meetings also had some other interesting outcomes. Homeopathy doctor Govindaraj spoke about that system of medicine once. It was followed by his visits every month in which he treated people. A few people turned to homeopathy medicine entirely, along with their families. We also did sale of books. If anyone showed interest in buying the reviewed books, they would be made available in the next meeting for purchase. In book sales one month we made ₹7,000. The sale of books would be, at least, a thousand rupees. The participants not only got introduced to new books and magazines, but they also read them and discussed them. Some took up creative writing. Ira. Prabhakar (Dheeran), Pe. Suresh (Senchadaiyan) wrote stories which got published in magazines like *Uyir Ezhuthu*. When G. K. Ramasamy, who runs the magazine *Padigal*, came to speak in a meeting, we got introduced to his 70-year-old friend, Ma. Venugopal. Every month he would enquire about the meeting and participate enthusiastically. Like a young boy he also became interested in writing and has started writing short stories. One of his stories also got published in *Uyir Ezhuthu*.

At the end of two years we decided to get out of the terrace and thought that we would have a special meeting in an auditorium. We chose the books published by Kalachuvadu Publications and arranged for a one-day seminar. Neidhal Krishnan took part in that meeting and wrote about it in the *Kalachuvadu* magazine. Koodu organised a two-day seminar on poetry in collaboration with *Kalachuvadu* Trust in Mohanur Subramaniam Arts and Science College. In the same college, Koodu organised, with help from Kavya Publications, a one-day seminar on the subject 'Gods of Namakkal'. The papers read in that seminar have come out as a book with the same title.

In order to meet regularly and exchange views we needed a name for our group and we have called it 'The Nest' but it is not exactly an organisation. We have no president, secretary or any other official positions. All those who come for the meetings are members. If some cannot come for some meetings we don't bother them either. Since, in a way, I am the motivating force for everyone to come together, sometimes I am called the coordinator. This responsibility is because the meeting place happens to be the terrace of my house.

It is eight years since the Koodu meetings have begun. We don't feel compelled to have a meeting every month. So there have been small gaps and sometimes a long time lapse between meetings. In all, 49 meetings have been held in eight years. The next was the 50th one. We decided to make it a special meeting. We thought bringing out a book would be something special and that is how this book has been written.

In one of the editorial board meetings of *Kalachuvadu,* when we were discussing future plans, I had suggested a series under the title 'Caste and I'. We wondered if it would be feasible to commission such articles from individuals. My friends asked me to write the first one. I thought I would write and start the series but it kept getting postponed. But the thought that many must write on the subject kept simmering in my mind. There were many titles suggested for the book to be published, associated with the 50th meeting. I put forward the title 'Caste and I' and everyone unanimously accepted it.

It is very easy to structure how many essays could be written on one subject. The essay has to be experiential. It has to detail incidents. That was all that was needed. This sounds very simple. But there were so many problems we had to face before the essay reached us. First, we had to prepare ourselves mentally. In one's mind one always thinks that talking about caste is akin to using abusive language with swear words that centre around women's body and society's notion of morality of women. But in everyday life we think of caste at some moment or the other; talk about it. And incidents related to it do happen. But there is a certain hesitation in speaking about it in the public sphere. We had to make a lot of effort to make people overcome that hesitation. As a result, the first essay we received was that of Nallusamy. To me it appeared to be a good beginning. All this trouble was for people to open up and write with no holds barred.

Despite all these efforts, some could not write. It was not that they did not know how to write. But there was that hesitation—the fear that writing about caste may lead to this or that problem. Even though they were told not to be afraid even before they had begun to write—to write whatever came to their mind and that, wherever they felt a particular point may lead to trouble, that portion could be removed—some could not allay the fear. Those who exorcised the fear of retribution submitted good essays. There were some who, after writing the essays, said that they would use a pen name. So, there is a lot of fear in talking about caste in the public sphere. We were very clear in our minds when we decided that no essay would be published under a pseudonym. The notes on the author of each essay have hence been given perspicuously. These are also aspects of being open.

Experiences of caste differ in nature. In the book, different aspects of caste domination have been spoken about. Some take the form of complaints and some others are filled with guilt and regret for having had the mentality that accepted caste and having gone along with it. Some said that they felt light after writing it. There are essays which have tried to find consolation in writing about caste; there are others which have tried to justify various actions. There are some which have turned first-person accounts into third-person accounts, out of timidity or fear, and the authors have hidden themselves in these third-person accounts. There are some which are like testimonies. Some are autobiographical in style. Some are incomplete because of lack of training in writing. What I feel greatly relieved about is that although given total freedom, there is not a single essay that supports the caste system. This gives me, at least, a little hope for the future.

The locales and the incidents in the essays are different. They made me cry, sigh and laugh when I read them. My intention is not to categorise these various incidents and put them under scrutiny. I think this would be a useful documented source for researchers and those who are active in the eradication of caste since nowhere has caste been spoken about in the public sphere with such explicitness as in this book.

The book does not deal with all the castes but there are significant records of different castes. There are different pictures in the essays about Dalits, other minority castes which keep themselves aloof, and about dominant castes. The views of the authors regarding caste have been brilliantly expressed. But one is still left with the feeling that there is so much more to say. People of different castes must speak. They must talk in the public sphere about their feelings, talk about incidents in their life, being true to their own conscience. I hope this book will provide the inspiration for it.

I had the illusion at first that putting together the essays would be easy. But more than the difficulty of getting the essays were the difficulties of time and energy connected with editing them. Only a few essays which seemed rough hewn have been rejected. Otherwise each essay, when it arrived, brought the joy of excavating some buried treasure. The person with whom I shared this joy and also exchanged ideas with was my wife P. Ezhilarasi. My dear students Pa. Nallusamy, Re. Mahendiran and Pa. Kumaresan were always available to deeply discuss the essays and also type them in to create a soft copy. Another good student who showed great interest in the project was A. Chinnadurai.

My friend A. Ira. Venkatachalapathy read some of the essays and opined that this would be an important book. Poet and fiction writer and the present editor of *Kalachuvadu*, Sukumaran, encouraged me saying that caste has not been spoken about so openly anywhere else. Their many suggestions were very useful. To Kannan of Kalachuvadu Publications, who agreed to publish it when I mentioned such a book and Thanga Akila and others of the Kalachuvadu office team who took a lot of interest in bringing out the book, my thanks are due.

Namakkal **Perumal Murugan**
19 October 2013

A Relentless Voice

N. Arulmurugan

Although it is a village that is linked to us by blood, Malappatti which is in the lower half of Modakkur village in Aravakkurichi Circle, Karur district, remains alien to us. Perumal Nayakkar known as Thoonga Nayakkan was one of the descendants of the Telugu speaking Vadugar community that lived here. He had four sons and two daughters.

The family was steeped in poverty, not knowing where their next meal was going to come from. The eldest son was put to work in his own brother's farm and the second son began to work in Perumal Nayakkar's paternal uncle's farm. One of his sons was a defiant one and never paid heed to his words. Yes, the son who quarrelled with him and went away to Andhra with a group of Muslims from Pallappatti was none other than the third son Nariyandu. He returned to Tamil Nadu from Andhra as Narayanasamy. When he avoided Malappatti and married Siththappatti Lakshmi and began to live in Jegadabi, my entire ancestry got transformed.

My sister and I were born in Jegadabi which had brought about such a historical turning point. This place which is part of Thanthoni local self government union in Karur district remains my only permanent address. This union has many small villages. Bommanathupatti, a village with absolutely no amenities, is one of the villages of this union. My father bought some land here on the advice of his friend, one Kothampattiyar. Since the land had been bought we had no other choice but to come there to take up farming. My younger brother and sister were born here.

My father sold the house and land in Jegadabi and also brought his second brother from Malappatti. How what began as a joint family later got split into two families due to fights over property, is altogether a different story. We had no blood relations in the village we had migrated to. Narayanasamy, my Appa, became Narayanan.

Our childhood and growing up years in Bommanathupatti were not happy or peaceful. The entire village was under the control of the Thottiya Nayakkar community. Rajakambala Nayakkar and Kambalathar (or Thottiyar), as well as Kambili Nayudu, are Telugu communities which are all part of one of the branches of the Kapu/Balija communities. There were supposed to be nine different Kambalathar, and the Thottiya Nayakkar community people of the village generally went around boasting that Rajakambalam was the best of the nine and that they belonged to it.

There were some unwritten laws they laid down. Whoever went past their living quarters was not supposed to remove their footwear till they crossed the village limits. They were not supposed to tie the loose turban people wore on their heads while crossing their living quarters. If one was riding a cycle back to the village, as soon as one reached the village limits, one had to get down and push the cycle and not ride the cycle while going past their area.

Our house is on the west of the village in the farm. Other communities lived outside the limits of the village. Appa used to give a cycle for use only when we had to go and recruit people to work in the farm. Initially, we were the only family to own a cycle in that village. Whenever I went out to get farmhands I used to push the cycle. Once the hiring of farmhands was done, I would look around and, if no one was there, I would ride my bike quickly past their quarters. Sometimes I could hear someone shout '*Adhi Orraa?*' (Who is that?).

Appa often took the road through the Porani village. That road ran by the pond that was to the north of our farm. We were the first ones in the village to go to school. We had to walk three miles every day to go to the school in Jegadabi. While returning we used to walk through the fields of Kothappattiyar. Appa and Kothappattiyar, who were friends, parted ways and became enemies when they had a misunderstanding over some issue. So we had to change our route. After that we took the route that was to the west of our house, through Manjanayakkanur village. This village also belonged to the Thottiya Nayakkar community people but they were not very strict. Also, they did not get along with their community people in our village. Gradually they turned a blind eye to our wearing chappals and riding a bike.

Their houses had mud walls with roofs thatched with corn stalks, millet stalks or palmyra or coconut leaves. They had neem-oil smeared heads with tufts with a pin stuck in them. The men wore a regular turban or a loose and casual turban which would be in any of the vivid colours like light red, blue or green. There was a fetid smell when one went near them. They did not bathe regularly and looked at us strangely when they saw us bathing using Lifebuoy soap.

Where marriage was concerned they strictly maintained the tradition of avunculate marriages where a girl marries her maternal uncle. An old man will marry a little girl and an older girl may marry a small boy. Child marriages were common. There were also situations where an older girl waited for a maternal uncle to be born! When people from other villages, who may also have some avuncular claims, heard of such girls they would come and kidnap the girls overnight. A search being launched for them and their being caught and the case being brought to the village panchayat was not uncommon.

The marriage was only a customary formality. The girls would then cohabit with men of their choice from the same caste and live their lives. If the husband found the slippers of another man outside his house, he would leave and not enter the house. A man in a relationship of this kind was called a *vankankkaaran*, a clandestine lover. Our farmhands indulging in a conversation would blurt out all the stories of clandestine relationships. My mother knew exactly who was with whom.

People of that community did not allow others not belonging to their community to enter their house. When Korrai, wife of

Manavala Nayakkar, who owned the other half of the farm land, gave birth to a baby girl, there was no one around. Their house was just a stone's throw away from ours. There was just a field between both the houses. I vaguely remember that it was my mother who rushed to help when she heard her loud cries. After that incident, they became a little lenient.

This baby girl who was born after two children, Mondi and Kutlan, was named Monnai. Manavala Nayakkar's brother Jeganadha Nayakkar was the one who settled all the issues in the village. There was an official Nayakkar who was supposed to do this but Jeganadha Nayakkar was the one everyone went to in matters of dispute. Killankundi was his son, whom he had not sired.

In the entire village there were only some five or six names like Jagga Nayakan, Jonama Nayakkan, Perumal Nayakkan and Ranga Nayakkan that were used for naming. Jeganadhan's son would be Jonaman and his son would be Jeganadhan; his brother would be Perumal and his son would be Jonaman; Jonaman's brother Jakkan would name his son Jeganadhan. It would continue this way and a lot of confusion was created with this custom of naming the grandson after the grandfather. So instead of the given names they would be called Konaiyan (the one who walked twisting his body to one side), Mottaiyan (the bald one), Oola Sevvan (one with pus-filled ears), Guvvan (skinny), Chinnakkalai (young bull), Gunnasu, Barri and Dhorri (one like a hole) and these would become their real names.

During elections their actual names would be in the list. The teachers and agents who would come looking for them to cast their vote would be at the end of their tether by the time they managed to identify the correct person. Even then sometimes a wrong vote would be cast and some excuse or the other would be made to legitimise the vote.

Some of the young men would take up jobs in faraway farms and would come to the native village only during festivals or fairs. When I was in school, Kutlan, who was my age, and his elder brother Mondi were working as farmhands in a place far away. Some of the boys, sent out on a yearly contract, would run away from the farms and come back. The landowning Kaundars would come time and again to get the advance money back. The Nayakkars were known to be sorcerers and sometimes the landowners would avoid coming to look for the escaped farmhands to get the advance money back.

Porani Mariamman's temple festival was a common one for all the villages around. But the Nayakkars would claim that the first *poojai* or ritual worship should be by them. In the three days of the festival they would harass without end the Reddiyars who would take up the task of conducting the festival.

The Nayakkars were adepts at sorcery, casting a spell, black magic using collyrium, giving metal plates with secret chants written for burying in the house, armlets and amulets, herbal medicines, being able to say where a lost thing or a person may be by applying collyrium on a betel leaf and seeing visions on it, predicting with shells, and making things disappear. Appa used to reassure us saying that their black magic will do us no harm for our god Madurai Veeran at Malappatti would protect us.

Their buffalo with a chain of small bells around its neck was never tied up. Its nose also would not be pierced like it was normally done. It would wander about grazing freely on anyone's field and no one could dare object. They would not bother to tether their cattle and allow them to feed on our harvest. They would not only stop farmhands of other castes from coming in but would also stop people of their own caste from coming to do agricultural work. At times we would call farm workers to sow, weed or for harvesting. They would come the first day but next day, when we would reach our fields, a shock would await us. There would be no farmhands. They would have been threatened by the Nayakkars. Sometimes, even while they were working, there would be arguments and they would drop their work and leave. Appa and Amma would go and negotiate with them and only then the workers would come.

Irrigation was mostly well-irrigation. Half of the well was supposed to be ours. The next quarter of the well was Jeganadha Nayakkar's and the other quarter belonged to his wife's brother. We took turns to do the irrigation and at times they would start doing it out of turn and when questioned they would argue with crooked logic. During rainy seasons, water that would collect in their high-level lands would be directed to flow into our low-lying lands. Vegetables that were kept ready to be taken to the market would be plucked off. If one was not careful, they would walk away with bundles of peanut plants set aside to be sorted out. They would have no qualms in picking up huge quantities of agricultural products that were spread out in the fields to dry, as if it were their harvest. Coconuts would disappear from the trees. The thief would never be caught. One could only feel upset and frustrated. We considered this an endless ignominy we had to face for the work we did with our blood and sweat on our own land.

They would pretend to be friendly and warm. '*Kandhukadu seppitha nessa undra*' (When these people say something, it will be right) they would say. But they could not tolerate our progress in life. They would grumble with jealousy, '*Konga banikichoodra etha kozuppu*' (Look at the impudence of this fellow from the Kongu region!) or '*E vooru kongkodu iita mana voorna ochi itta pathakaththaada*'(Who knows from which part of the Kongu region this fellow is, he is doing well here, in our village). They had long dogs as pets. There were times when at night we got scared seeing the black dogs and would come running back home. They used to go rabbit-hunting at night. If the rabbit entered the fields to be harvested, they would give it chase with their dogs, urging the dogs to catch it, shouting, '*Ore... kunthili... petra... petra...*' (Hey, there's the rabbit... catch it... catch it...') and run all across, stamping on the field. The dogs would go looking for the rabbit and destroy the entire harvest crop. In the morning when we would come to the agricultural field it would look like a battlefield. The sight made our gorge rise and Amma would let out expletives as if she were spitting them out from the depths of her belly.

We went along with them and against them and life went on. We constantly faced days with no peace. Then there was the property fight and division of property. Appa's elder brother, our uncle, sold off his share of the property secretly to Thottiya

Nayakkar without letting his younger brother, who had brought him from their ancestral place, know about it, and left the place. Appa grew dispirited.

The struggle went on till 1993. When an entire community is against you it is difficult for a single family to deal with it. When I took up a job, I could not bear it anymore. I got the courage to tell my father that we did not belong here and that we must leave. We repurchased the land Appa had sold off at Jegadabi. The fertile land at Bommanathupatti that we had nurtured with our sweat, we sold it to those villagers at rock-bottom price, the kind of price one would sell cattle meant for the slaughter house. Kothampattiyar, the friend who later became an enemy and who had brought Appa to that village, also could not put up with the whole thing for long. A few years later, he also sold off his lands and other properties to the villagers and came back to Jegadabi.

A school was established in the village only much after we left the village. When it was newly established, the teacher would find it very difficult to keep the students in the school. The students who came in the mornings, would run away for hunting if they found a dog, a rat or a rabbit. Since their mother tongue was Telugu, it was almost impossible to teach them Tamil. One of my friends, Ramachandran, who was posted as a teacher there, would tell us tales about his experience. It seems Monnai, the daughter of Manavala Nayakkar, now works in the school as a helper in the mid-day meal programme for school children. It also appears that the dominant castes who oppressed other castes, maybe due to ignorance, have now changed a little.

In later years, I had to come away from my region due to my job and stayed in Namakkal district for six to seven years. I had the opportunity to meet a scholar of that caste and had the good fortune to be able to read many different books and also think about various matters. That has been one of the ironies of my life. Now I understand that the Thottiya Nayakkar community in Bommanathupati of my childhood was in a stage of transition, not yet fully out of its tribal context. That a family that was part of its language and part of the greater community the language extended to, could not cope with the caste domination and had to leave the village, makes one realise the torment that even a totally different kind of caste domination is capable of inflicting.

My job takes me to different places. Wherever I go, I still hear the voice of one dominant caste or the other. The suffering of my childhood is so deeply embedded in my mind that a shiver runs through the body. Over a period of time, however, the suffering has given me strength and the support of many other castes. In rising against caste domination, I have become twice the person I am in strength.

******

Caste in Folk Theatre

K. Anbazhagan

Many take part in *koothu*, the folk theatre, because they come from a family of traditional folk theatre performers and have learnt the art or because they are interested in the art or because it can fetch them an income of thousand to two thousand rupees for a night's performance. But those who are traditional folk theatre performers outnumber others. Those who belong to many different castes like Parayar, Thombar, Vannar, Sakkiliyar, Vanniyar, Gounder and Kuravar are folk theatre performers. The descendants of Thombar and Parayar castes are able to learn this profession without much effort. In other castes, this profession may last perhaps just for a generation and then end. The reason for this is the caste issues that crop up during performances.

Near Bavani is the Nayakkar village Kuchanur. During every annual temple festival, there would be a koothu performance in that village. Koothu performances are also organised whenever an elder of the village passes away. The koothu performers would be offered food on a street away from the village. The performers must take a banana leaf with them and then go and sit for the meal. Water would be offered in an old traditional brass measuring cup or in a tin used for washing up. Even if one is filled with revulsion one would have no other choice but to drink the water. They would not touch the things used by the performers. After eating, the performers would have to pick up the leaves and tin or old brass measure, take them far away from the village, and throw them.

While performing, if they felt thirsty, they would have to sit with both palms cupped together right on the stage and water would be poured from a tin held above. Even though Gounders and Vanniyars also perform, the villagers prefer artistes from the Thombar community. It is the women who normally decide who should be invited to perform. Even the men grumble, saying, 'Only when artistes from the Sakkiliyar community come and perform do these women feel thrilled.' They may be fed sitting on the road but when men who enact the roles of women performed on stage, the women of the Nayakkar community would offer them their jewels and request them to wear them. Once the performance was over the performers would return the jewels. The performers have more female admirers than male. Whatever the caste restrictions, these women's love for art would manage to scuttle them.

Near Thuraiyur is another Nayakkar village, Kottaiyur. Those who go to perform there would have to hold their slippers under their arm as they entered the village. Normally, performers would cover their heads with towels to cover the long hair that they grow. One can identify them as performers when you see their heads covered thus. This towel would have to be removed and tied around the waist. The rich and influential men of the village would be seated in a row and the performers would have to touch their feet and offer respect and only then enter the village to perform. This has been so for many years. Some artistes who do not want to touch the feet of some men in a particular village would avoid going to that village to perform.

Some 15 years ago, a group from Elimedu went to a particular village to perform. The usual group of men were seated in a row and told the artistes to touch their feet and then go into the village to perform. The artistes categorically said that they were not in the habit of touching anybody's feet before the performance and began to go back with their trunks. They were then called back and these self-respecting artistes were given a proper feast and asked to perform near the temple.

Tharamangalam is a Nayakkar village. When a koothu took place there, some of the admirers pinned currency notes on the artistes, a normal way of showing appreciation during performances in villages. The influential people of the village took great objection to that saying there was definitely a higher and lower status where caste was concerned and that lowered caste artistes should not be touched and have currency notes pinned on them. They brought those who had pinned the money on the artistes to the panchayat. These individuals were excommunicated from the village. Those affected appealed to the special cell of the Chief Minister. A small incident got politicised and finally a compromise was reached. The village does not allow koothu performances anymore.

When I was studying in college, due to my interest in koothu, I once went during the Wednesday Fair to a village of Kongu Vellalars to watch a koothu performance. A Gounder had asked for the koothu performance. I went along with the artistes to his house to have my food. I wondered as I ate if they had allowed the koothu performers into the house because they did not know about their castes or if they were truly above caste prejudices. While eating, the artistes asked for some water to drink. The person who had invited them asked which caste all of them belonged to. They replied saying there were many castes among them, like Sakkiliyars, Vannars and others. They were given water in steel tumblers. There were no plastic cups in use those days. The people in that house told me it was the fate of the koothu artistes to be asked such questions; you are an educated boy, why do you subject yourself to these indignities and come and watch koothu, they asked me? The performers then finished eating and went to the place of performance.

As they began putting on make-up, they needed a tumbler to mix the various pastes. A friend and I went to the same house where we had had food to ask for a tumbler. When we reached there, we saw the lady of the house pouring water and washing the room where the artistes had eaten, because lowered caste people had sat there and eaten. She was yelling at her husband saying he should have first asked about their caste and then allowed them in. 'How can you invite them in and feed them without checking about their caste?', we heard her shout. The tumblers used by the koothu performers were thrown out. We took one of them and gave it to the artistes. We decided not to speak about the incident to the koothu performers. After that even if I went to watch a performance I avoided eating with them as far as possible.

That night's performance was 'Nala Chakravarthi Koothu', the story of King Nala and his wife Damayanthi. When Saturn appeared on stage to separate Nala and Damayanthi with his trickery, many in the audience came and touched the feet of the person who was playing the role of Saturn. The woman who had washed the floor where the performers had eaten also came and touched his feet, despite knowing that the artiste was from the Sakkiliyar caste. The one she saw as someone from the Sakkiliyar caste in the morning seemed like a god to her by night during the performance.

Yet another incident in a village near Tiruchengodu—I don't remember the name of the village. There was a temple festival for which a koothu performance was going on. There was no stage. The performance was taking places in the fields. So when artistes sat down and performed, those seated at the back could not see. People from different castes had gathered there. When famous koothu actors perform, people come in cars and mini-autos in great crowds to watch them. The performers get excited only when there is a large audience. When there is a huge audience, there will be a crowd of people standing surrounding the audience. Those seated in the back rows would not be able to see the performance properly. As the performance was going on, an old man was heard saying aloud, 'Who is that standing? Those at the back are not able to see.' Pat came the reply, 'We will continue to stand. If you want, you go sit elsewhere.' Many voices rose in unison. 'It is not meant for only your viewing; we must also see it.' With this back and forth going on, a big crowd gathered. The koothu performers stopped performing. Many grumbled aloud that because of all of them the koothu performance had to be stopped. 'Which village are you from? Why are you creating trouble here?' they were asked. 'So, only if we tell you our names and our village, you will allow us to watch the koothu, is it?' they replied and the villagers could make out that they did not belong to the village and were outsiders. The villagers had been patient all along thinking that they may be guests of someone in the village. But when they realised that they were not related to anyone in the village, they assumed that they were of a different caste. Everyone got up and thundered,'If you don't tell us the truth about yourselves, we may have to call the police.' 'Have we committed some murder that the police must be called?' they answered. Some of the youngsters challenged them to try and commit a murder. A small problem became a caste issue and a fight, and finally ended in real murder. The koothu performers ran helter-skelter and disappeared from there.

Ponnugounder of Tuthipalayam was a famous koothu performer. It was said that once, after he got married, his wife locked him up inside the house on the day of the koothu performance. He became restless in the house. He opened the thatched roof and escaped from the house and came to the place of performance. He did not want the art of koothu to end with him and so he used to get hold of boys going for farm work from the Arunthathiyar street in his village and teach them koothu. Normally only one or two would have a good voice in a group. But every person he chose has a resonant voice even to this day. His group was famous in Salem and Namakkal area. They would go in a bullock cart to perform. And his words were much respected.

Everyone in his group except Ponnugounder was from the Arunthathiyar caste. Chellamuthu from his group was from the Vannar caste, the washerman community. He had a wonderful voice and could act very well and hence was part of the group. Ponnugounder was getting old and often no one paid heed to his words. At one point they were performing 'Karuvattu Koothu', a story of the fishing community, which they had newly introduced and were performing very successfully everywhere on continuous invitations from villages. All the villages around knew about their group then. Chellamuthu was an important reason for their success. During one performance, he was sleeping before the commencement of the play. Someone in the group said, 'Wake up that washerman fellow who is fast asleep. It is time for the performance.' Chellamuthu heard that. He left the group saying he had been addressed by his caste identity. With no one to do the main role the group did not last long. The group that Ponnugounder had put together with great effort died right before his eyes and caste was the reason for it. Many efforts were made to bring together the scattered group and they did come together on his death day but soon the group broke again.

The koothu groups these days have performers of several castes. Chettipatti Chinnavar does the main role and he guides many. His walk, expressions and dialogue delivery is followed by many. He belongs to the Vanniyar caste. If artistes from the lowered castes perform with him, his make-up material would be kept aside and no one was supposed to touch it. The villagers would give a pot of water to the performers, but artistes from other castes wouldn't be allowed to use that water. Everything was kept separately for the performers from other castes considered lower than his. So even good artistes were not willing to perform with him.

Kannantheri village near Konkanapuram arranged for the play 'Karna Motcham', Karna's Salvation, carefully choosing good artistes from many different groups. The village spent five lakhs and slaughtered 25 goats and fed everyone who came for this grand occasion. Chettipatti Chinnavar was playing the role of Arjuna. Periya Madhu from Nallur belonging to the Parayar caste was to play the role of Karna. He was famous for playing the role of Karna. The most important scene in the play which everyone was waiting for was the meeting between Karna and Arjuna. In the dialogue with Karna, Arjuna would abuse Karna. Arjuna looked at Karna and said, 'You don't know who your parents are. You who are born into a degraded clan and a lowly caste, do you dare think of ruling the universe? How can you think of battling with me?' I don't remember the entire dialogue. Karna replied, 'I am the one who knows; and you are the one who does not know.' I thought the dialogue with quick repartees were part of the koothu. I got to know only in the morning from what people around me were discussing that these were indirect abuses, between two artistes, based on caste. I came to know that after this Madhu avoided acting with Chinnavar. Only then could I understand how deeply he would have been hurt by those dialogues.

Koolipatti Subramani was from the Gounder community. In the village Padarai in the Arunthathiyar street, he was playing the role of Arjuna in the play 'Arjunan Thabasu', Arjuna's Penance. A palm tree would be cut and its leafy part would also be cut off and ritual obsequies would be done and the tree would be planted where the performance was to be held. This palm tree was referred to as a post, i.e., it became a metaphor for the penance itself. The actor would climb the post and would climb down only after Krishna's (Vishnu's) mount, the Garud, the celestial kite, appeared. Since kites are almost extinct, this koothu is rarely performed. If the kite does not appear the actor playing the role of Arjun would have to stand on the post for even 10 hours. Nowadays, the actor would just point his finger at a distance and say, 'Look there,' and when the audience's attention is distracted he would quickly climb down. Subramany also got down from the post thus and many came to touch his feet. He reviled them saying, 'How can those from Sakkiliyar caste (cobblers) come and touch me?' This annoyed many. 'In the first place, getting off the post when the celestial kite had not appeared, itself was wrong. They are worshipping you as a god. So what if they touch you? Does their touch stick on you?' they asked him. 'Isn't there something called caste difference?' he asked them. 'You came to perform knowing it is a village of the Sakkiliyar caste. The money we give is sweet; our touch is bitter, is it?' Many voices rose to counter him. He could not reply. It is not just Subramany; many others behave like him. They take the help and money of people from lowered castes but do not accept them.

Caste discrimination exists even among artistes. Since koothu performers from the lowered castes are insulted by the so-called upper caste artistes, koothu performers mostly form groups of their own caste. However, many times, there is also the compulsion to put up with caste discrimination. Art never seems to rise above caste.

*****

Discrimination

M. Ananthan

I belong to the Arunthathiyar community. My village is Manjanayakkanur in Bommampatti village in Namakkal District. I came to know about caste at the age when I began to understand life around me. As a child I heard many stories from my grandmother. Arundhathi's story was one of them. And the story went thus:

Arundhathi, who belonged to our caste, used to go daily to Thottanna Nayakkar's house to herd goats. Thottanna Nayakkar's son fell in love with her and they eloped. They were caught and brought back and questioned. But Thottanna Nayakkar's son firmly stood by his decision and said that he would only live with her and began to live in the Arunthathiyars' village.

Grandmother spoke highly of our caste. Even at that age when I did not know what caste was, I was made to feel that I was different because of my caste. I studied in the Local Self Government Union's Primary School which was in the street of the Nayakkars in my village from 1995 to 1999. At that time, there were only students of my caste in the school and those of the Nayakkar caste. We used to sit together in class. Some of the Nayakkar caste boys among us used to tell us, 'You cannot touch us. You are Sakkiliyars, cobblers. We would be polluted if you touch us.' These were not mere words. They would also sit far away from us. We could not take any liberties with them, nor freely address them in familiar terms like *dei* like we would our other friends. In case we made the mistake of calling them *dei* before their parents, it would lead to a big fight.

If my caste friends or I felt thirsty, we had to ask the Nayakkar boys for water. Only when a boy from their caste would scoop the water from the pot and pour it out for us could we drink it. We had to cup our palms and stand before them and drink the water as they poured it into our hands. After lunch break, we had to wait for them to come and pour water on to our plates to wash them. They would first wash their plates and only then pour the remaining water for us. It was not as if there was any dearth of water in the village. In the past as well as now there has been no water scarcity in the village.

When people of our caste addressed them we had to say 'Saami', the respectful way of addressing a superior, or say 'Thevarae' referring to their superior caste. There is another irritating factor that has been continuing for a long time and exists even now. Those from the Nayakkar caste would call an older person like my father or even other elders of our caste 'vaadaa,' 'podaa,' which is considered disrespectful when not used among close friends or relatives. From small boys to older people, everyone of their caste would address our elders in this manner. Those from my caste would go when called thus, without any protest. I have got into arguments sometimes with my Nayakkar friends over this.

As if all this was not bad enough, the Nayakkars used their caste and power to completely alter a situation in the village. My ancestors had been living for many years in a village that was a mile away from the present village where we stay. There were 25 families of our caste living in that village who had set up homes for themselves. All of them had got together and dug a well. The well never lacked water and they began to cultivate the land around the well, which was convenient for irrigation. Once the Nayakkars got to know this, they cajoled and threatened my ancestors and made them migrate to the present village and settle down here.

Where we live now used to be the cremation ground of the Nayakkar community at one time. To this day the well dug by my ancestors is used by them for irrigation. As a symbolic gesture to assert that the well belongs to us, during temple festivals water is brought from that village and used for rituals by us. The ancestral village is now known as Pinankukkadu. The amazing thing is that Netti, my grandfather, wrote away his fertile land there to someone who offered a well-cooked meal with mutton. Such generous gestures have also happened.

In the year 2000, when I was studying in the sixth standard, I went to the saloon in a nearby village Sangamanayakkanpatti. 'Come, thambi, sit down,' the saloon owner said, addressing me in familiar terms as a younger brother. I swiftly went and sat in the swivelling chair. For a long time I had wanted to sit in that chair and have a haircut and have fun turning the chair around. I thought I had finally got what I wanted. The saloon owner began to converse with me. 'Thambi, what is your name? Which is your village? Whose son are you?' I happily answered him. 'Hey, A Sakkiliyar boy, are you? I can't cut your hair. If I give a haircut to those from your caste, no one else will come here for a haircut. Go elsewhere for a haircut,' he said and made me get up from the swivelling chair. My haircut remained half done. It was only two days after I came home that the rest of the hair was cut.

Kumar, a young man who lived behind my house, fell in love with a Nayakkar woman who lived nearby. She was a married woman with three children. When everyone came to know about this they excommunicated the two of them from the village. And they declared that no one must have anything to do with the two of them and their relatives. Whenever I saw this woman's children, I would feel upset.

When anyone from the Nayakkar community would enter our village, our people could not remain sitting. We had to stand up. This custom exists to this day. When we collect water from the drinking water tap, that place would be sprinkled with water and cleaned before they fill water in their vessels.

My father's name is Muthusamy, but everyone called him Chinna Paiyan, small boy. During the temple festival and others, my father and some other elders of the village would be invited by the Nayakkars to play the parai drum, a frame drum played with two sticks. If anyone died in the Nayakkar caste my father would go and play the drum, go to the cremation ground and burn the corpse and stay all night at the cremation ground. During such occasions, they would often use abusive language with him for some reason or the other. I continue to fight with my father for going on such occasions.

There is an unusual wedding custom among the Nayakkar caste. A person from the Sakkiliyar caste would have to come and put a pair of slippers on the bride or the groom. This custom is supposed to bring the Nayakkars honour. The person from the Sakkiliyar caste who would come to put the slippers on would be treated with respect, given a new dhoti and a sari, plied with a feast of a meal, and sent away. Caste does not seem to be a hurdle where this custom is concerned. I have not yet understood what this custom means exactly.

When I was a little boy my mother would go to work in the fields of the Gounders nearby. She would take me along. They would give us lunch in the afternoon. They would make us sit on the dirt ground away from the house and feed us. Water would be given to us in a coconut shell. When they gave me something they would drop it into my hands from above. But my mother would be asked to wash their vessels. They would take the washed vessels inside the house. There was no discrimination where the vessels were concerned.

Life goes on while I still try to understand the patterns of discrimination.

******

Of What Use?

N. Ranjan

It was my mother who told me which caste I belonged to. Till the fifth standard I studied in the local school. My mother admitted me into the Government High School in Pottireddypatti. She told me then: Thambi, if the teacher asks you which caste you belong to, don't use the respectful suffix and say Pall*ar*, say Pall*an* instead; only then will you get some educational concessions. I don't remember if I had heard my caste being mentioned before that. It is only after she said this that the name of my caste got deeply imprinted on my mind.

When I was a small boy, if there was a wedding in a house in the village, no one in the entire village would cook the previous night. Everyone would head towards the house where the wedding celebrations were on, to be served food. As a part of the celebrations, a new film would be shown on TV, courtesy the local cable operator. One could identify the houses which had TVs easily on such nights. Whenever a new film was shown we would carry a mat or a gunny bag and rush to reserve our seats. The older people in our street, normally, did not go to the next street to watch a film. But when a film was screened on a specially installed large screen on public grounds in the village, they would go. Only the very affluent could afford to show films on large screens. Those with small means and from lowered castes would find even TV screenings a big expense.

Once we went to the house of a person from the Arunthathiyar caste to watch a film. Dinner was going on and they said that the film would be shown only after dinner got over. My friends and I sat down for dinner. The brinjal *kuzambu* was very tasty. One of the women serving food saw me and said, '*Yaetti, idhi Oguru kodukku di*' (Hey, this is the son of Oguru). And the other one said, '*Idhi Angayi kodukkudi*' (This is the son of Angayi). I could make out that they were referring to Angayi Athai's son Balamurugan, who had accompanied me. I can still remember the taste of that brinjal kuzambu and the term *kodukku*, a Telugu word for son.

My mother came to know about my eating at the house of the Arunthathiyars. Maybe the women who served the food had told her. Or maybe some 'solicitous' person who always enjoyed carrying tales had told her. Whatever it was, my mother scolded me the entire day for going and eating in an Arunthathiyar household. As I studied further, I had friends from many castes. Their coming home for food and my going to their house to have food became an accepted practice. After that whoever spoke to me about caste got thoroughly chastised by Amma. I won't say that she has entirely changed but I must say, she has changed quite a lot. Otherwise, she would not have told me to marry a girl of my choice from any caste, would she?

There is something else that has been bothering my mind for quite some time. I was very good at the game of Coco in the sixth standard at Pottireddypatti. So they made me the captain of the junior team. I was not only the captain but I was also a good player. And we won many times. Normally, when the school kids won in any competition, their names would be announced the next day in the morning assembly; that would normally begin with a prayer, and the winners would be honoured with a prize before the entire assembly. If it was an individual competition, the name of the boy who had won would be called out and he would be congratulated. If it was a team victory, the captain would be called and congratulated and given the shield. The shield would be kept in the Headmaster's room. In the Coco game at the sports competition held in Varagoor, our team and the team of Varagoor Government School had reached the finals. It was a stiff competition.

We had played three times and our scores were equal. So they decided that they would decide the winner by the time it took for the players of one team to touch a person in the other team. Whichever team managed to do it in the shortest time would be declared the winner, the judges decided. We managed to touch a player in the other team in 16 seconds. But they took 36 seconds to touch a player in our team. We won the game. I was thrilled, thinking I would be called the next day before the entire assembly and congratulated. Next day, I stood ready for the team captain's name to be called out. But they called out the name of Parameswaran. My heart broke. This happened a few times when we won games. I would be the captain of the team when we played, but he would be the 'captain' when congratulations were due before the assembly. Now I realise that caste was the reason for this.

When I was doing my Master's in the Tamil University in Tanjavur, there was a tough competition between me and a friend of mine to get the highest marks. She belonged to one of the dominant castes. But we were like siblings; it was as if she was my elder sister and I was her younger brother. She was older than me and resembled my elder sister. Hence this feeling. But in the eyes of some teachers only our caste was visible, and not us as individuals. Even if I did better than her in the exams, since these teachers graded us, I would be given proper marks in grammar but in other subjects we would be given equal marks or she would be marked higher. The teachers were keen on giving her the highest marks. In the final exams in the scientific Tamil paper, she was told the questions over the phone. She certainly would not have asked for them but the teacher must have volunteered to give her the questions. She told me about this through a friend of hers. So she got the highest marks in the final exams. I came second. I don't know if the teacher ever felt guilty about revealing the questions to her, but my friend, who was like my elder sister, did feel guilty whenever she referred to those marks she got. Teachers like these affect the life of students.

I was doing my graduation when I got to know her. She was a little handicapped. When I was doing my MPhil in Tanjavur, I got her admitted to do her Masters in Lexicography, which was my field of study. She invited me to come to the college where I had done my graduation. She told me that she had to get some certificates and that she was unable to lift some heavy bags and needed my help. I went to the college to help her with the bags. She came late. I asked her why she was late. She said, 'Ranja, my younger sister has put us to shame, *da*. She has run away. And what is more, she has run away with an SC (Scheduled Caste) boy, *da*.' I jumped out of my skin. Her sister was only a schoolgirl then. If she had referred to her sister's young age, that would have been okay. I could have accepted her being upset over the matter. She knew I belonged to one of the lowered castes and yet I can't understand how she had the heart to refer to the caste of the boy her sister had run away with. She did not even seem to show any regret for talking to me thus. How can such people call themselves friends?

When I was about to complete my MPhil, I had applied for the Rajiv Gandhi National Research Fellowship. The UGC (University Grants Commission) offers this scholarship and it is meant for Scheduled Caste and Scheduled Tribe students. Nineteen students who had applied got the fellowship. I was one of them. The scholarship meant for us would be sent to the university but to get it from the university would be a great struggle. There is no history of students getting their scholarship on time. It would take six months to one year to get it in our hands. Wonder what they did with the interest accumulated for this period. When we would send the request for the amount, it would take them a couple of months to process the application. But when it came to their salaries, the files moved very fast. Any enquiries made would end in a fight. I was considered a rowdily behaved student. When we complained to the professors in the department about the administration, they would instead ask us, 'Why do you go and fight with them?' What could they do, they also had to fear the administrators. Otherwise important letters meant for them might never have reached them. Indeed, not just students and researchers but even the academic staff could not displease the administration. This is the current situation in most educational institutions.

The administrative staff would not even address us by our names. Whoever received this fellowship would be addressed as

Rajiv Gandhi: 'Come on in, Rajiv Gandhi' they would say when they asked us in. When they would say that, they would be burning with jealousy because the fellowship amount we received was more than their salaries. And they behaved as if it was their own money they were handing out. I gathered from their various conversations that many of the computers in the office were bought with our fellowship money.

I completed my PhD nearly two years ago. I have not yet been given the transfer certificate. They argue that our entire fellowship amount has to be first given and only then they can give the TC. What kind of oppression is this! If we owe some money they could refuse to give the TC. But I have been given a No Dues certificate saying that I owe nothing in terms of fees or any other payment or anything else to the university. Despite that they refuse. They have not returned the library deposit to me either. They say that too can be processed only once the TC is given. It is now confirmed that I will never get my fellowship amount, transfer certificate or for that matter, the library deposit amount.

Once I completed my PhD I went for an interview, for the post of an Assistant Professor in Tamil, to a college run in the name of a great philanthropist in Hosur. It was a well-known college. They had three vacancies in the Tamil Department. Some 30 applicants had turned up. Some of them were friends I had met during the 30-day Sangam Literature Workshop which was held in Bharathidasan University in 2008. The interview was conducted at three levels: selection through a written test, grades given on the basis of certificates, and competency in teaching. Six of us were chosen, although there were only three vacancies. Of the six, I was the leading candidate. Friends there conveyed this news to many others and congratulatory messages were pouring in. Many went back disappointed. When one of the professors working there came and told me, 'Ranjan, your interview stands out among the interviews given by everyone today. Congratulations.... You can stay with me when you join', I felt that the job was assured for me. Apart from what he had said, there were other things also that made me feel confident about landing the job. Of the six, I was the only one who had a doctorate and had also successfully cleared my NET exams. The person who stood second among those shortlisted for the job was a young woman who only had an MPhil degree. The third person had an MPhil and NET selection. The remaining three were boys.

Of the six, the third boy, the sixth and I belonged to the Scheduled Castes. The remaining belonged to dominant castes. We were told that whichever three were called by the secretary would be the selected candidates. All of us kept our certificates ready. I stood there with not only educational certificates but also extracurricular activity certificates like sports, drama, etc. I was excited, nervous, happy and afraid all at once. But the Secretary called out the name of the girl who was the second candidate. She was the one who had asked me to keep all my certificates ready. She could not have known that what was going on inside the room was a different kind of a politics—caste politics. The three people from the dominant castes got the jobs. What we from the lowered castes were left with was pain and grief.

The fact was that the main qualification needed for an Assistant Professor's job was belonging to the dominant castes, something which the three of us did not have. I brooded over this and pretended that I was happy to be born in this caste when actually I was sad. Who will know about this pain that is rooted in my mind? I can't even begin to count the number of youngsters moving about with this unbearable pain in their minds. Only time can tell if the burden of this pain can ever become less.

Recently there was a public viva-voce in the Folklore Department of Tamil University. An Associate Professor from the Bharathidasan University was the external examiner. He demonstrated to us how one should act in a cultured and sophisticated manner. He explained that, for example, he would not ask researchers under him about their caste directly. That would not be cultured behaviour. But indirectly he would ask them about their various relatives and find out about their caste. Let someone's caste be revealed naturally or let it not be known at all. But to insist on knowing a person's caste and go through all this trouble of finding out about the person's relatives to know his caste, is really distressing.

Whenever I have been affected by caste, it was mostly in educational institutions. When educational institutions that are supposed to build knowledge have such an attitude, of what use will it be to blame others?

*****

Only Son of the Family

R. Rajasekaran

I belong to the Vanniyar caste. I married my classmate who belongs to the Nayar community from Kerala. Wondering how my family would accept this inter-caste marriage, we came home with trepidation. They had come to know about my marriage and the house looked as if death had befallen it. Slowly relatives began to pour in as if to offer condolences. Since they got into groups and started talking I was terribly scared about what was going to happen. I was talking to my wife confidently, hiding all my fear. The crowd of relatives decided to send the girl back overnight to her parental house. They forced my wife to abide by what they said. My wife began to cry saying, 'If I go home they won't accept me. I have no other option but to commit suicide.'

She was very firm about being with me and not leaving me ever. I also began to cry, saying I would die if she left me. My family could not care less about my tears. My anger was of no use. One of my relatives said, 'He will cry now. But if we send the girl away and get him married to someone else, he will be perfectly okay.' I was very sure that if anything like that was forced upon us I would give up my life. Since I was the only son of the family they were a bit afraid and changed their decision to send the girl away. It was only on that day that I understood why when a Vanniyar marries an Adi Dravida it invariably ends in suicide.

In Kerala, the Namboodiris are considered upper caste. Next to them are the Nayars, and the Ezhavas come below them. Seen in this context, my wife's family considered anyone from any caste from Tamil Nadu as inferior to them. They had also heard of the honour killings Vanniyar indulged in, their dowry demands and about their dishonesty in money matters. Judging the situation from this point of view, they had sent out people to hunt us down. Fortunately, we did not fall into their hands. Had we been caught, our life together would not have been possible. They reached our house a day after we reached home. Since we had had a registered marriage and my family had finally approved of the marriage, they left my wife with us.

In the house of death, relatives come for a whole year to offer condolences. Similarly, people began coming to our house. Whoever came home, my parents would embrace them and begin to cry. Every day passed this way. The first two months of my marriage I spent sitting on the pyol outside the house and crying. My wife's people were confident that she would not be able to live long under these circumstances and that she would return home. My father changed his views and became understanding but my mother never changed. She would tell all the visitors, 'Even if he had married a farmhand of our caste, I would not have minded. He has now gone and brought some riff-raff.' More than me, my wife was hurt by these words. They almost stopped inviting relatives for any festive occasion in the house. My wife's family invited only her for family functions.

Since our basic needs were taken care of and we were happy, my father began to come around. But my mother continued to grumble: 'They must have thought, good riddance. They don't bother at all about her. Even if we marry a girl from a poor family for some auspicious or other occasions, some coconut or fruits would have come from the girl's family. Even that is lost now.' My wife would tell me, 'What can I do? Your family does not like my caste, and my family does not like yours.' I began to hate the caste system much more then. One of my relatives used to go to Kerala often on business. He came home once and saw my wife and told my mother, 'This girl is from the Nayar community. She would be a very responsible person in the family.' It was only after that that my mother began to speak properly with my wife.

That is the story of my inter-caste marriage.

*****

The Ugly Face of Caste

P. Rajeskannan

In all spheres of society caste has pierced its sharp nails. Caste keeps revealing itself directly and indirectly depending on the circumstances. Schools, colleges, work places are where caste shows itself indirectly. In temple festivals, marriage celebrations and funerals, caste reveals itself nakedly.

Where schools are concerned, before the times when private school buses arrived to take school kids to faraway schools, school education was normally in a school near one's village. All the students knew from where every student came and who their parents were. 'He is from Ambedkar Street,' 'He is a boy from the Pallar Street,' were normal comments indicating the caste of a student. In colleges, even as they fill up the forms they get to know the castes, and friendships are formed based on that.

In offices, different kinds of efforts are made to find out about the caste of a person. When one joins an office most of the initial conversations would always be efforts to identify the new entrant's caste. Once one says that one is a bachelor still, the next thing they would say will be: 'We know an educated girl from among our acquaintances, what caste do you belong to?' If it is education that is being discussed they would definitely ask, 'Under which quota do you come?' If one says in general BC, MBC or SC they would begin asking about the sub-castes of those groups. Or they would mention the name of a person known to them and ask if you were related to that person. Or it can be a more direct and somewhat shocking question: Which community do you belong to?

During weddings, temple festivals and funerals, when they get together they will spend their time glorifying their caste or talk about how the lowered castes are coming up and ridicule their progress. One is prepared for caste being an important factor in these situations. What I would like to share here are unexpected situations when I was caught in the terrible clutches of caste.

I belong to Periyeri near Thalaivasal in Salem District. There are two groups of Vanniyar living in this district known as Arasu Vanniyar and Padaiyachi. My family belongs to the Arasu Vanniyar group. I completed my entire school education staying with my grandparents, at Kongavalli near Aathoor. In government high schools, every now and then there would be squabbles among students based on caste. Once an inter-school kabaddi competition took place. The final round was between our school team and the Dhammampatti school team. The boys in our team were all Dalit students. So the non-Dalit students of our school cheered the rival team and stood by them. The next day this became an issue and the result was an outbreak of fisticuffs and it went to the extent of the school being closed for an unspecified period of time.

An incident that occurred when I was in the eleventh is one that fills me with persistent feelings of guilt and shame. A boy from another class next to ours would come often and talk to his friends in our class. Since he was a Dalit the other students did not like this. One day, during the recess, that boy came to our class, chatted with his friends and left. Some non-Dalit students who were outside rebuked him and came towards the first row where I was sitting. They told me to tell the teacher that I had lost the money kept in my notebook. I agreed and went and told the teacher that I had kept thirty rupees in my notebook and that it was lost. Immediately those students stood up and mentioned the name of the boy from the other class and said that he came often to our class and that this should be settled one way or the other, else they would boycott the classes. Some students went out and called the other students to come out also. With the intensity and stubbornness of that age, they even argued that that Dalit student must be rusticated from the school.

The class teacher felt that things were going out of control and so he approached the Headmaster. The next day the parents of that Dalit boy were called and questioned. Four of us were called into the Headmaster's room. Till the end, I insisted that I had kept money in my notebook. The Dalit student also kept insisting that he had not taken the money. The students who had asked me to say I had lost the money said that since he came to the class he must have taken it. At this point one of the officials in the office told me that if I had really kept money in my notebook I should swear by it. Until then I had insisted that I had kept the money in the notebook but I stood hesitantly without taking an oath. All the others said that if it was true that the money was lost I should take the oath. I got scared and began to cry and pointed to the boy who had asked me to say that I had lost the money. He immediately pretended to faint and got out of that situation. The Headmaster, teachers and office workers admonished me severely and warned me. Whenever I saw that Dalit boy later I felt a terrible sense of guilt and inferiority and I feel it to this day.

During my school days I was friendly with Bhaskar, a Dalit boy, and we used to spend a lot of time with each other, even going for tuitions together. His father was also a Science teacher in our school. We had to go for tuition classes at seven in the morning. The tuition teacher lived some three kilometres away. Bhaskar lived a kilometre away from my house. I used to go cycling and would pick him up on the way. If I gave him a pillion ride, Thatha, my grandfather, would get annoyed and scold me. So the cycle carrier seat was removed and one of us would ride the bike while the other would sit on the bare triangular metal rod. We were friends throughout the years from the ninth standard to twelfth standard.

This happened when I was in my first year of college after the twelfth. Bhaskar had joined the BPharm course in Salem. He came home on Diwali. I was watching the TV. Before that whenever he would come, he would not enter the house. That day when he came home, Paatti, my grandmother, was bathing near the tub in the front portion outside the house. So Bhaskar came in and sat next to me and we chatted, and watched TV. Paatti had gone for her bath just a little before he arrived but seeing Bhaskar come into the house she quickly finished bathing and came in and said angrily, 'Go out, the two of you; I have to change.' We became anxious and got out and went directly to the bus stand on his cycle. Afraid that I would be scolded or even beaten if I went back home, I wandered around and went back home only at night. Thatha and Paatti did not speak to me. I woke up the next morning and went back to my village. I returned to my grandfather's place only three months later.

Thatha and Paatti at least belonged to an older generation. But I unexpectedly came to know through an incident that things were not very different at my parents' place either. I had failed in a subject in my graduation and remained at home for a year. On Pongal, two college friends came to see me. One was a Dalit from our own village and the other was a Gounder caste friend from the next village. They had come to my house many times before this separately. If the Gounder friend would come, he would come in and chat with everybody and then leave. The Dalit friend would normally stay in the verandah or somewhere outside and we would chat there. My parents would ask him a few formal questions about his studies. But this time both of them arrived together. In the beginning they both sat in the verandah and chatted. My mother came out and spoke a few words and went in. Normally the Gounder friend would be invited in and offered food and the Dalit friend would be offered only tea outside the house. We had just finished the Pongal ritual obsequies before they came. So we had to offer them Pongal.

My mother was a bit hesitant. She called me in and asked me where the food should be served. I pointed to the dining table and told her, right here. But Amma did not want to serve food to the Dalit friend inside the house. Nor did she want to serve food to the Gounder friend outside the house. She was standing at the entrance confused about what should be done. I brought water for them to drink and invited them for food. The Gounder friend washed his hands and took the pot and went inside the house. The Dalit friend washed his hands and hesitantly continued standing outside. Seeing this, the Gounder friend said, 'It is breezy here outside. Let us eat here,' and sat on the bench outside. My mother quickly brought banana leaves and spread them on the bench and served them food. I stood quietly watching them eat. More than the joy of meeting friends on a festive occasion, seeing the ugly face of caste agonised me and the feeling lasted for a long time.

******

Of the Soil

P. Ezhilarasi

Among the professional service castes, Kuyavar (potters), generally referred to as Kulalar, are an important community. In spoken parlance, a Kuyavar is referred to as Kosavan. They make pots for daily use with clay, terracotta figures and brick tiles and perform similar jobs related to the soil. Today, terracotta figurines and brick tiles are made even by other castes. But making clay pots using the wheel is something only the Kuyavar do. People from other castes do not have the patience to deal with clay. That is why Kuyavan consider themselves the descendants of Brahma who creates lives that are temporary, and think highly of themselves and their profession.

Although they think highly of themselves, other castes consider them idiots. One of the insulting abuses even today is, 'He is an absolute Kosavan.' Kuyavar are known by different names in different places. In Tamil Nadu, they are known as Udaiyar, Pathar (jewellers), Velaar, Setukkarar and so on. In Vellore district, we are known as Udaiyar. I used to feel that it sounded impressive. But a time came when I finally stopped showing off about being 'a girl from the Udaiyar household'.

Once when my brother went to his friend's house they asked about his caste as it is normally done. He said he was from the Udaiyar caste. Ramasamy Udaiyar known as Saaraya (liquor) Udaiyar was very famous then. But he was not from the Kuyavar community. Maybe they knew his caste, so they asked my brother what exactly our profession was. He replied that we were potters. 'Oh, so you are Udaiyars of the soil?' they said in a tone of ridicule. It was only when he returned and narrated this to me that I realised that we were not moneyed Udaiyars known as Ponnudaiyar (a term also used to refer to the Agamudaiyars who are Mudaliyars) but only Mannudaiyar, Udaiyars of *just* the soil. Some children are, in fact, named Mannu, soil. It directly refers to the caste. Even today, however, I identify myself as Udaiyar without any specification and escape my real identity.

After marriage when I came to the Tiruchengodu area some people asked me about my caste because I wear a nose-stud. The Gounder women of this area do not wear a nose-stud. They know therefore that a woman wearing a nose-stud must be from another caste. I used to reply that I was from the Udaiyar caste. 'What kind of Udaiyar?' they would ask again. 'They call us Udaiyar. I don't know anything more,' I would answer and end the conversation. I could have said Kosathi, the female form for Kosavan, but Kosathi also had the other derogatory meaning of being an ignoramus.

From very early times, the professional life of Kuyavan has always been one that was dependent on others. To this day, in rural areas, that is the kind of lifestyle that is followed. In earlier times when there were no money transactions and barter system was the norm, they gave pots in exchange for *merai* or grains. A village would be set aside for a family of potters. Only that family would make the necessary clay utensils for that entire village. There would be demands throughout the year for pots for regular household use, for festival times and for marriages. In return they would be given grains by the villagers. These grains given in barter were known as merai. During harvest times when potters say, 'I am going to get merai', it would mean they were going to get their share of grains.

One village per Kuyavan family meant the entire village with all its castes including the Dalits. The privileged classes were referred to as *samsari* (farmers or cultivators), *kudiyaanavan* (farmers including farm labourers) and Nayakkars. The Dalits were referred to as people from the *cheri,* a separate colony within the village where the Dalits lived. People of the Pallar, Parayar and Sakkiliyar caste were included in this. Where professions are concerned, the Navidhar (barbers) and Vannar (washermen) who were part of the Dalit community had their own living spaces like the Dalits, but the Kuyavan did not have a separate place like the others. In every village *Kosatheru*, the street where the Kuyavar lived, was in the middle of the village and the *cheri*. Being at the end of the village was convenient for them to collect soil from the lake and set up brick kilns. Since they also traded with the Dalits, the derogatory reference 'He is just a Kosavan' may have been coined. Perhaps in order to escape from this derogation, they grouped their different identities as *gotras* or lineage. And during marriage ceremonies, the groom wore the sacred thread, the dhoti in the Brahmin style worn during traditional ceremonies, followed the *Kasi Yathirai* ritual of Brahmin weddings where the groom goes on a symbolic voyage to Kasi renouncing the world until the father of the bride requests him to return and marry his daughter, and the bride wore the traditional nine-yard sari of the Brahmin bride known as *madisaar*. In temple rituals and funerals also the Kuyavar followed the Brahmin conventions.

In caste hierarchies, only those placed in the middle level are deeply attached to their caste and have unshakable faith in their caste and also deep hatred for the oppressed castes. They look upon themselves as superior castes and actively spread the customs and habits of the so-called superior castes. They act as if they are the people who give practical shape to the attitudes of the superior castes. They do this to improve their own image and they are the ones who use the most oppressive measures to control the Dalits. This may also be seen as an act of self defence so that the Dalits don't begin to think that all the castes, other than the so-called higher castes are one and the same. Where caste groupings are concerned, those castes that exist in an environment where they live close to the Dalits are the ones who exclude them and harass them. Indeed, one can see Kuyavars taking similar stands when it comes to Dalits.

Even in present times, many Kuyavar families are in a condition where they aver that all that they need for living well, with no dearth for food, is to have one village each for all Kuyavar families. I have known my mother to say this: 'More than the samsari, the merai that the cheri people give is always more. You need enough intestines to eat the amount they give.' It is so even to this day. Last week my maternal uncle said that when he took the traditional mud pots known as 'Salung karagam' for a cheri-family wedding, they gave him the money due to him and also a generous quantity of pulses, tamarind and chillies. Thus, although there is an everyday life dependence on them for basic necessities, the Kuyavar treat Dalit differently. In their family functions they make the Dalits stand outside the rear door of the house, they sprinkle water and purify the things the Dalits give them and give the Dalits food in broken pots. This is not unusual even now.

Once in an auspicious function of the family in my paternal uncle's house, some Dalit friends had come home to eat. One of my brothers stopped them and asked them to come to the back door. My father admonished him saying, 'In which era do you live? Can an educated boy utter such words? Even if we behave this way, you are supposed to advise us. Instead, you are speaking this way.' But many of the relatives did not appreciate what my father said. They grumbled saying everything was okay for him.

My father was a follower of the Dravida Kazhagam (Dravidian Organisation) an off-shoot of the Self-Respect Movement which E. V. Ramasamy Naicker, respectfully referred to as Thanthai Periyar, had launched. When he passed away, my elder sister arrived with a lot of grievances of her own. The grievances seemed to outweigh the loss of a father. 'The wretch, the *kammanatti*, look at him all stretched out. What did you do for me, *da*?' she shouted, speaking abusively and adding disrespectful suffixes to her words. All of us gathered there were shocked. After a while, my paternal uncle's daughter, my elder cousin, and head of the joint family, who came to know what my sister had said, came in and yelled at us: 'What does she mean speaking like that? Why did you let her in?' Pat came a reply, 'This is a funeral ceremony. Parayar and so many such castes come to such places. Let her also be like one among them.' The moment the angry reply was uttered, I realised I had spoken it. By then my father's body was being carried outside and laid on the wooden plank there. The person who had taken the responsibility to supervise everything was none other than Ponnamakka, who belonged to the Parayar caste.

At that moment, my own words cut me to the quick. What words had I uttered? Would Ponnamakka have heard them? After I got married to someone from a different place, every time I came home she used to come and speak to me with affection, more than a mother would. 'So dear, everything going okay?' she would ask with concern coming from deep within her heart, in a tone that could melt anyone. I felt guilty that my words referring to caste would have alienated a person like her. I also remembered what my father had told my brother, 'Are these words uttered by an educated person?' These may be words commonly spoken but I felt deeply affected that I had spoken them. Along with the sorrow of my father's death, I carried with me the distressing memory of this happening on that day. I understood only then that the roots of caste are very strong and go very deep and that education and wisdom were two different things.

Caste feelings are very strongly embedded in the minds of the educated. Even though they may be educated, they enquire about the caste of the visitors to their homes and treat them accordingly. When they know a visitor is a Dalit they don't allow him to enter the house and make him stand far away from the house, on the street, and finish chatting with him there itself. One of my fellow professors was speaking angrily about one of his students thus, 'Forget about him; he is a Kosavan after all.' I was sitting next to the professor. He must have known about my caste. He was the kind who was interested in finding out such details about others. I felt then the pain of being abused in the name of caste.

Many lopsided traditional values are still being followed. Many values regarding caste are part of them. To move away from them one has to realise oneself and only then there would be clarity of mind. Even though I was born into a family that had great faith in the Dravida Kazhagam and Marxist ideas, and I had moved with many different friends and had friendships of many kinds, that there was caste even within me is something that shocked me. Someone from the Parayar community is the daughter-in-law of our joint family now. We are bonded by this marriage and live as relatives after this marriage in the family. And whenever I remember now the words that I had uttered the day my father died, I feel as if I had spat on myself.

****

In Which Ganges Do We Bathe?

T. Kalaichelvan

I belong to Kumaramangalam. It is a five-mile distance on the road from Thiruchengodu to Namakkal, and a place where big *zamindars* used to live. The zamindars owned a lot of land here. Dr P. Subbarayan was from this zamindar lineage. He was the Chief Minister of the Madras Presidency during the British times. After him, his son Mohan Kumaramangalam was known in the world with the name of his native place suffixed to his name. Kumaramangalam became famous then. In English pronunciation, Kumaramangalam got elongated as Kumaaramanagalam. Both Mohan Kumaramangalam and his son Rangarajan Kumaramangalam did not marry women from the Gounder caste that they belonged to. They married women from outside their caste, from different regions.

Rangarajan lived in the northern part of the country but he won the parliamentary election from Salem and Tiruchi constituencies and came to Tamil Nadu often when he was a Member of Parliament. He learnt to speak Tamil. Once in a while he used to come to Kumaramangalam. The entire village would gather to meet him. He used to meet the people at the Eswaran temple, a temple built by his ancestors. The place where his ancestors stayed is now totally dilapidated. Rangarajan did not discriminate between one caste and another and moved freely among everyone. The day he came to Kumaramangalam, a meal was assured for everyone. He had married a north Indian woman. Despite belonging to the Gounder caste which is considered an upper caste, his family members went against caste restrictions and had inter-caste marriages; yet they were highly respected among the Gounders. This may be because they lived outside Kumaramangalam and were rich. Their own lands were later given to the people and the government. In the land given to the government, one portion was a wasteland near the water body. Some realtors separated this land from the rest and sold it off. But it was named Subbarayan Nagar. Due to their good efforts some 300 or more houses were built there.

At present most of the people in our place manage their lives running the looms. They work day and night six days in a week. They buy things for their basic needs at the Tuesday Fairs. The rest of the money is spent on films and liquor. If they need money before their payment is due they go to the loom factory owner and take a specific amount as a 'mid-term' loan.

There are many castes living in Kumaramangalam but they live separately in specific areas. In the centre of the village live the Mudaliyars, in the south the Gounders, and after them the Dalits, and in the east the Nadars, and after them, the Dalits. East of the centre towards the north is Subbarayan Nagar. This Nagar is where there is a confluence of many castes like the Nadar, Arunthathiyar, Parayar, Pallar, Mudaliyar, Gounder and Kuravar. The Mudaliyars outnumber the others. There may be just one or two Gounder families. The rest of the castes are present almost in equal numbers. All of them visit one another for family functions. When there is a wedding they share the work. No caste discrimination is observed here. The only exceptions are the pig-rearing Kuravars. They do not mix with others or visit others. Their dwellings are also in an isolated part of the village. This area where they live was a thorny forest to the north east of the village. It was also a place used by women as an open toilet. There was always a foul smell around their living quarters. The smell was repelling. So, no one really wanted to visit them.

Kuravars who did not keep pigs were unlike these others who reared pigs. They were very sociable and attended the functions in the houses of others and invited them to their own family functions. One Anjali among them had once decided to slaughter a pig as an offering to their clan god and invited everybody for a feast. Many of us from different castes had gone to her house to take part in the feast. Anjali was famous for singing dirges during funerals. Her dirges had the quality of melting even the most stone-hearted. A funeral without her dirges would be incomplete. How could her feast be ignored? And how could one attend the feast and come away without eating? Even women who did not much care for pork went for her feast and honoured her.

Except for this area, in the rest of Kumaramangalam, caste is a very important part of daily life. I used to visit a friend of mine in Kumaramangalam often. He would always refer to people in our area as, 'oh, that boy from Sakkiliyar caste' or 'oh, that boy from Parayar caste'. He was a Mudaliyar himself. When it came to boys from his own caste he would say, 'oh, our boys, is it?' He was not an exception. The entire village apart from our area was like that.

In school the intelligent students would be friendly with other intelligent students, and there would be no caste discrimination or the effort to keep Dalit students away. One could easily be friends with them. They were friendly and not fussy about things. As a student I knew nothing about Dalits. I know now; especially now when I am trying to gather information about Dalits. Among my current friends, many are from the Gounder caste. My friends don't believe in caste discrimination. They have been so liberal since school days. But their parents were different. I had heard about the hurtful incidents of caste but had not really confronted them myself. I did my MPhil from Anna Government Arts College in Namakkal. Perumal Murugan was my guide. He suggested that I take up the topic of weavers in Tamil novels. He told me that in the novels I would take up, many were from my own community. Tho. Mu. Si. Ragunathan's *Panjamum Pasiyum* (Drought and Hunger) dealt with Mudaliyars; M. V. Venkatraman's *Vaelvi Thii* (Sacrificial Fire) spoke about the Saurashtras, and Soothradhari's *Amman Nesavu* (Weaving for the Goddess) had Devanga Chettiyars as subject. He told me to write about the condition of the weavers in these three novels and the caste-based harassment they faced. It is then that I realised my caste identity as a Mudaliyar. My mother always used to refer to some finance minister or chief minister as belonging to our caste. I used to tell her, 'Of what use is it to us that he belongs to our caste?'

I also faced an incident based on caste. On a holiday, all of us were playing cricket. I was thirsty and I went to a friend's house to drink water. A large tumbler was kept in the courtyard of the house. Since it was right in front of me I picked it up and walked to the steps to go in and drink water. My friend's mother saw me through the window and came rushing. '*Dei*, stay right there... stop...stop...don't come in' she shouted. I did not know what to do. Since she suddenly rushed out screaming I was taken aback. 'What happened, Akka?' I said. 'Go... go out...' she said. I was about to cry. She had always been very affectionate and I wondered what had brought about this change. Had I done something wrong? I thought for a while. I could not think of anything I had done wrong. I always went in and drank water; what had gone wrong this time? I stood near the steps staring blankly. My friend's mother came near me and said, 'Go stand near the gate.' I walked towards the gate. 'Stand right there *da*, and throw that tumbler in that corner,' she said and brought water in a small water-scooping vessel and said, 'Here, hold this.' I extended my hand. She poured water on my hand and grumbled, 'What is this habit of touching things that Sakkiliyars touch? Sprinkle the water on your head three times.' I did what I was told. 'Go now,' she said after that. I could not make out anything. It did not occur to me to ask her either. I was dying to get out of that place. I went back to play without drinking any water.

At present, many of my friends are Dalits. I am very friendly with them. I go to all their houses to have food with them. They are like my brothers. If these others know that I eat at their houses, which Ganges would they expect me to go and take a dip in to accept me?

******

Futile Whimpering

K. Kasimariyappan

I belong to Pungavarnatham, in the Kovilpatti area, highly populated with Nadars. Since we wanted to set up a shop and do business, we shifted to Sivanthipuram in the Ambasamudiram circle. Many different castes like Pillai, Thevar, Konar, Chettiyar and Achari lived in streets of their own there. Even though they were not related by marriage they would address one another as Mama (maternal uncle) and Chinnaiya (paternal uncle). One must appreciate the fact that Pichikonar gave us a shop and place to rent in Nadusivanthipuram where there was not a single Nadar. His son Paramasivan was my childhood friend. We used to go together to the backyard to answer calls of nature.

I got admitted into Kamarajar School in Class I. I vaguely remember reading the Nallathambi lesson in Tamil about a good, obedient boy who went to school regularly with neatly combed hair and properly folded collar. Pichamma teacher was rather proud of me as a student. The school was near Pacheri. There was a huge banyan tree too. A Sudalaimadan temple. A large space to urinate. An old granny who sold *javvu mittai*, a sticky, pink toffee that one could chew forever. One could see Pacheri Ravi's house from the school.

It was only after I reached Class X that I found out that Nadars were inferior to Thevamar or Thevars, in terms of caste. Our next door neighbour, Umaiyammal, used to address my mother as Ponnamma. There were a lot of 'endearing' exchanges during street fights. The women fighting on the streets used to be told to go sleep and lie flat on the back with a Pallappaya, Parappaya, Chanappaya or Sakkilipaya (men from Parayar, Chanar and

Sakkiliyar referred to derogatorily as *paya*, fellows). Maybe lying flat with these people would harm the genitals of these women, I used to think. I did not know much then. My genitals were also not of adult size yet.

Malaiyammal, who belonger to the Thevamar caste, ran a tea shop in the village. I used to love her idlis. Even Saravana Bhavan cannot match her idlis, soft as foam at the centre. The tea, however, was not as good as the sambar and chutney served with the idlis. Her husband used to make the tea. Malaiyammal's son and I had a fight once. He called me names and so did I. Before we got into fisticuffs the women around there came and asked me, 'How could you abuse him?' No one accepted my answer that he had abused me and so I had responded with abuses of my own. When Sandanammal told me, 'He can abuse you. But how can you abuse him?' I could not quite get the logic of that statement. Malaiyamma's son and I remained friends later.

Appa's shop was situated in front of the well at the crossroads. It was like any other village shop. He used to sell cigarettes, bidis and betel leaves. There was no limit to the constant harassment he had to face at the hands of drunken Thevamar who used to come that way. They would throw vegetables kept for sale on the ground, demand money for drinks and go about threatening Appa and he would confront them with a sad face. He would speak falteringly. His face would crumple. He would not get angry. 'Why don't you confront them boldly?' I would ask him. 'I am alone. He has many goons,' he would say. He was a slave to all this for more than 30 years. Sekkadiyan, Mookkandi, Murugan, Komu were some rogues around the village. They died early due to alcoholism and other reasons. Not that their deaths mattered. Thevamar women gave birth to many sons, so there was no dearth of fights!

'Oy, Nadarae, Kandha' were the general ways in which my father was addressed. Being addressed as Annachi was very rare. Ayya's name was Kandhasamy. He had a neat handwriting. He had studied up to Class VI. He could do all the calculations in his mind without writing them down. He died in 2000. He worried a lot about his daughters. But for that, he could have lived longer. 'Kandha…' Muthachiammal used to call out to him. In response Ayya would say, 'Yes, Amma.' My maternal grandfather Kuzandaivelu used to get irritated. 'What is all this Kandha and Thondha? Can't she call you Kandhasamy?' Only in the nineties did I begin to get answers to my grandfather's questions—it was the politics of names.

Kuzandaivel Thatha was rather tall. When he sat on his haunches to eat he would look like a preying eagle. He would walk all the way from Pungavarnatham to Ettaiyapuram with a head load of *vatral* (rice or sago crispies) to sell. He would perform tricks like bringing out sweets from his thumb. I also learnt that trick from him. When he got dismissed after a strike, he thought he could make a living selling *javvu mittai*. On his way to Ettaiyapuram, there were many thickly populated Nayakkar villages. From wells full of water, women would scoop out water in buckets and pour it from above into his cupped palms. It was humiliating, of course. One's clothes would get wet. Water would splash on the face. Any protest would be severely dealt with. Even the dogs would endlessly bark. Maybe they recognised people of other castes. When Thatha could not bear it anymore he threw the weighing scale at the dog and killed it one night, and threw its body into the well, and returned to the village, without anyone being the wiser. Not a word was breathed. Had word got around, they would have killed him. He calmly went past the women vomiting after drinking the 'clean' water with the dog's body soaking in it. I did not have his courage and strength. Maybe I was more like my father.

In the southern part of the village there were many Saivapillaimar. They were also in the Madatheru, the street where there was a Saiva mutt. Periyanayagam's father was a clerk in the Harvey Textile Mills. He was the brother-in-law of the trustee at the hill temple. He could recite the 108 words of praise for god and do it with a mic in his hand without referring to a book. There were many who worked in the mill. To be a writer (as clerks were known) in an office that paid them the wages was a very important job. Periyanayagam studied in the Welfare School and I studied in St Mary's School. He was a good student. My ambition was a job in the mills, a Raleigh cycle, a bath in the river, a paratha without omelette at the Sardar's stall once a week, a tiled house without smoke stains and a cot without bugs. The days of mills, Raleigh cycles, paratha-making Sardars and smoking firewood ovens are over now. Only the Thamirabarani river flows still.

Periyanayagam was very fond of me. He did not know many words of abuse. His abusive words were limited to idiot, pig and bull. I used to go to his house to play. He would climb on the terrace and pluck guavas for me from the tree. His father used to ask me to wash my feet and come into the house. Lakshmanan also used to come with me. His father Rajathevar was the village functionary who guarded the crops from getting stolen. I knew about birthdays being celebrated only when I attended Periyanayagam's birthday celebrations. I collected some money from the shop and from home and bought him a pen as a birthday gift on one occasion. His mother had prepared payasam, milk pudding. She placed a leaf in the place in between the outside toilet and the backyard door and served me the payasam there. Lowered caste guests who come for a feast would normally be served on leaves. After eating, the guest was expected to fold the leaf and throw it away. It hurts me now to think that like a dog, I ate whatever was served, wherever it was served.

We used to go as a family to attend the Pongal festival of Pungavarnatham Mariamman temple which used to fall in Panguni, the last month of the Tamil calendar around mid-March to mid-April. All the Nadars who had gone out for a livelihood to the cities and their relatives would come in great crowds in cars and buses. We would spend our time watching people donning the *Alivesam,* smearing the slush at the lake all over the body and going around the place swirling the bunches of neem leaves in their hands, pouring turmeric melted water on one another, piercing one's side with a rope and eating *olaikozakkattai,* rice balls mixed with jaggery and dried ginger powder, wrapped in palm leaves and steamed. Nadars who sit bound to their shops morning to night would wait the whole year for Panguni Pongal.

The annual exams coincided with Pongal. When I was in class X or XI everyone went for Pongal to the village. I could not go due to the exams. Saraswathi Akka next door had promised to take care of me. She belonged to the Thevar community. I used to address her husband as Anna, elder brother. Their house was the only one in Sivanthipuram that subscribed to the *Kumudam* magazine. I used to go and sit inside and read it. They believed I was a good student and did not mind my reading the magazine. I would have no problems sleeping at night also. Akka and Anna would sleep in their home and I would sleep at my place. I did not have to go to their house for using the toilets or for baths. I would take care of all that on my way to the men's bathing area in the pond known as *Arasankitangu* because it was near the Peepal tree.

The morning after my family left for Pongal, the coffee was brought. Akka cooled it properly and gave it to me with love. It is only when it is cooled that one can drink the coffee pouring it from above into the mouth; hot coffee would have to be sipped putting one's lips to the edge of the coffee tumbler. I drank the coffee lifting my face and pouring it into my mouth. I had to look for a leaf for the food to be served. No shop was open. After a while the food arrived in a plate. It was one of those porcelain plates painted in white and blue colours. They must have really searched for it. 'Actually, this is the plate Anna used to eat in before. He doesn't use it these days' Akka explained. I had no problem in digesting coffee poured from above and food from a porcelain plate.

Nadusivanthipuram was the main town or the kasba as it was known. There were other villages around like Keezhasivanthipuram (situated at the lower side) and Melasivanthipuram (situated at the higher side). On the eastern side of the canal at this end and near the main road where the buses used to ply, there were large groups of Nadar houses. Ayya used to have his hair cut in upper Sivanthipuram. I also used to go for my haircuts there. The hair clipper would hold the hair behind the head tight. In the Nadusivanthipuram kasba there were also saloons meant for those who were not of the Nadar caste. My school friend Balasubramaniam's father, Sethu, was a barber. He was a great supporter of the Dravida Kazhagam. His was a thatched house situated a little higher than the road. His house was separated only by a small wall from his friend's house, whose father was a washerman. The familiar smell emanating from professional washermen's houses of steam mixed with soda was a pleasant one. Balu used to make us all laugh with his pranks and stories. His sister's husband had a shop opposite the Perumal temple on the uphill road after the butcher's shop.

I used to see Anandan when we would go near the pond for our morning ablutions. Anandan's testicles used to hang like a beehive. He suffered from hydrocele. They say that if you hold one leg of a boy and pull it hard it would lead to hydrocele; the testicles would swell with water. Wonder who pulled his leg? He would bow before the Thevamar addressing them as Ayya. On his shoulder hung the cloth he used to wipe the shaved faces of his clients. He would never wear a shirt. When I was in the tenth standard I wanted a stylish haircut and I went to him. 'Have a haircut this time. But don't come again. If someone sees you here I would get abused,' he told me, meaning the dominant caste people may object. I should have returned without a haircut. But it is only after one has gone through a bad experience that it registers that one could have done this or that to avoid it. One does not think about these things. Later, I only went to Murugesan's saloon where he gave haircuts exclusively for Nadars. He was my school friend. He was hesitant about calling someone like me, in trousers and having a regular job, by name. I persuaded him to address me without the respectful suffixes.

When I was studying in Azvarankurichi, I began to address a boy from the Pillaimar caste as Mappillai, son-in-law, a friendly way of addressing someone. He remains a Mappillai for me to this day. In Madurai University, I found two more friends to address as Mappillai. Kachaikatti Natarajan used to call me Mappillai and call Manivannan Anna, elder brother. He was from the Parayar caste. He was fond of a girl from the Konakkamar community and considered her his elder sister. How she let him down is another long story. Silukuvarpatti who fell in love with Parameswari and got married to her also calls me Mappillai to this day. He does not have a permanent job. Being with him is a great pleasure. All we need is a quarter.

Temples like the Murugan temple and the Alankari Amman temple have caste-based taxes. Around mid-February to mid-March, which is the month of Masi in the Tamil calendar, the traditional small wooden chariot with the god's image in it, known as *chapparam*, would be pulled by each caste group, referred to as *pattarai*, in the name of the hill temple god Murugan. Pattarai is a different term for caste. Sometimes women are abused as *palavatrai*. A palavatrai is someone who sleeps with men from different *palavattarai* castes, which really is a comment on her character. The different palavattarai castes would, according to their caste hierarchy, address one another as Maman (maternal uncle), Chinnaiya (paternal uncle) or Mappillai (son-in-law). I addressed everyone as Akka or Anna. I never used the relationship terms Mappillai or Machaan. Machaan is a mutated version of Maithunan, which really means brother-in-law, husband's brother. Persons with whom a physical relationship, referred to as *maithunam*, is not ruled out, are called Maithunan or Maithuni, the female form of the word. Addressing a lowered caste person as Maithunan or Machaan would give them a higher status with possibilities of a relationship that allows physical intimacy. Not using these terms of address was perhaps due to a sense of caution. In the present times, once people grow older, everyone becomes Sir or Madam.

Nandini and Shanthi were two girls in the university, whom I addressed as Akka. When I studied in Madurai, Chandra was my classmate. She used to write poems. They were very precise and forceful poems. My friend Saundar and I have been to their house near the incomplete northern tower of the temple known as Mottaikopuram, in Madurai. Both of us were from castes ostracised by the Saiva Pillaimar. However, Chandra's mother used to serve us food with a smile. She is no more but the food she served is still fresh in my memory. Another friend was Amirtha. Her full name was Amirthavalli, similar to the character of a princess Kumudavalli in one of the novels we had studied, written by Maraimalai Adigal. Amirthavalli was from the Kambam area. Since her name kind of matched that of Kumudavalli of the novel, we used to call her the princess from Kambam. She did not get a good job and I heard that her marriage had also not worked out well. She was of the Pillaimar caste. Her mother was wonderfully affectionate. The dried lotus-stem fries that I ate in their house, I never saw anywhere else. They served me food in the inner quarters in these Pillaimar households.

When I studied in Azvarkurichi, Ganesh, a Brahmin boy from Kadaiyam, studied with us. He was fascinated with catching snakes. His mother was a teacher. I saw *kolu*—a decorative doll arrangement—normally done during the Navarathiri festival being done for the Sivarathiri celebration only in his house. I remember sitting right inside the house and having snacks. 'How did they allow us in? I am surprised,' I told Thirumalaichamy, who had come along. He said they would wash the place afterwards. That was the first Brahmin household I saw.

Professor Sethu Pandian was a warm and friendly person in the university. His house was in Avaniyapuram. He had invited me home once. In a hurry to wash my hands, I put my hand into the pot where water drained from rice is kept for the cows, by mistake. The professor guffawed. On another occasion when I referred to my caste, he said, 'Oh, I thought you were a Paraiyan.' Looks like caste is written all over one's face.

Professor Puranachandiran had invited me to take part in a seminar on Dalit ideology to be held in Bishop Heber College in Trichy. Writer Imaiyam, who was also a participant, ridiculed Tamil teachers when he spoke. A separate table was arranged for meals for special invitees like Dr Christodas Gandhi, an IAS officer and others. It was a table meant only for them. Po. Velsamy, a critic, pointed this out to me. My paper was well appreciated. One of the professors who was my colleague, and who had heard about my paper, praised my paper, assuming that I was a Dalit. The cat came out of the bag when I told him my caste. His face fell. Another professor in Palayamkottai, who knew that I was working on Dalit ideology for my PhD said, 'One of my boys is also working on a similar topic in the university.' A very supportive gesture. In a few days, the truth was out and our friendship slackened a bit.

I did my PhD in Palayamkottai at St. Xavier's College. My friend Manohar and I were active participants in seminars. We would tear research scholars to bits. Manoharan was researching novels by the writer Samuthiram. He was a Dalit. I had also chosen Dalit writing for my research. Manoharan was a friend who accepted me completely. He was very handsome and extremely fair. And he had a bright, smiling face. We would spend the whole day in the room meant for PhD researchers. His wife always prayed for that room to come down! He is active in teachers' movements these days. We are not in touch as much. I remember going with Manoharan to invite Su. Samuthiram for a departmental seminar. He was staying at the Tourist Home in Tirunelveli then. We travelled with him in the official government vehicle. It was afternoon. There was a lorry going ahead, carrying dried fish and I told the driver to overtake the lorry. 'Not necessary,' Samuthiram said, 'the smell of dry fish won't hurt.' He asked us about our research. He said, 'You look like a Dalit and Manoharan looks like a BC (Backward Class).' Since I had a large nose and dark complexion, people were never sure of my caste. A professor, who is my colleague, says that the caste of a person can be identified by that person's looks. I don't have that talent.

As soon as he entered the seminar room, Samuthiram asked, 'Is that Sivasu who runs the *Melum* magazine here?' And he referred to Sivasu Sir with the singular disrespectful form of address. People were shocked. Sivasu Sir was not there that day. Samuthiram thundered continuing to use the singular disrespectful term: 'He says what I write is rubbish. He should call it rubbish after reading it. Is it right to say so without reading? Let him come face to face with me; I will handle him.' He also spoke about a Nadar who had been breastfed by a Dalit woman.

While I was a student at the St Xavier's College, a Dalit poet came to the Folklore Department for his field work. I had met him in the Art and Literature Association meetings before and knew him well. He used to come to our room. He was very much into poetry then. A Nadar girl from my neighbouring village was doing her MA in Folklore. She used to travel in the same train with me. I knew her elder brother. The poet and the girl fell in love. Once her family came to know about it, they stopped her education. The poet began to write poems accusing us for her being stopped from coming to college. I am not against love. But my caste was enough to accuse me. The poet does not know that for the past 15 years or more I have been feeling guilty for no fault of mine. I am not sure if the poet waged a struggle for his love as much as his struggles for the many causes in his poems. Just because someone belongs to a lowered caste, that person should not make unreasonable accusations against people of other castes. How can that be right? I could not prove my innocence in his court. Another Dalit poet told me not to make much of it and forget about it. Poets don't realise that poems have a way of finishing off an individual. Only those accused without a reason know what it feels like.

My father, who had spent more than 30 years of his life in Sivanthipuram, died of a heart attack. There were women from other castes who shed tears on his death and I was moved by that gesture. When caste Hindus (a term that is used for dominant subcastes or endogamous groups that fall within the caste system) die in Sivanthipuram, they are normally buried or cremated in the Kalyani *thurai* (steps leading to the river in different parts of the river bank with different names) of the river Thamirabarani. Kasamuthu Thevar's son Sankaran and others suggested that my father who had spent all his life in Sivanthipuram should be buried in Kalyani *thurai* of the river. Sethu Thevar, however, did not agree: How could a Chanar fellow be buried there? I could not bear to see my friends protesting against him. My father had never paid the taxes or membership fees to the Nadar trade association in lower Sivanthipuram. But he had to undertake his final journey in the vehicle brought by the Nadars to be buried in the soil that belonged to the Nadars. Reality does hurt a lot.

My father who gave up his sleep and his life for a little profit, used to open his shop anytime at night to bring out ginger and garlic or any other herbal medicines for the people in Sivanthipuram. The local gods Alankari Amman, Sappani Madan and the hill temple Murugan were offered fruits from the bunch he had carried on his shoulders and their faces shone with the oil he had poured out for people offering worship. Had the Nadars to whom he had paid no taxes refused to offer land for burial, where would I have gone? These responsibilities were emotionally entwined with my flesh even if I had rationally risen above them.

Whenever one goes house hunting, we can see the ugly grin of caste. In colleges, the caste groups in majority get together for secret conversations, plotting to capture power. It is scary. When loud sloganeering rises with hands raised above heads tied with ribbons and eyes red with liquor, one's peace is ruined. Young people go in hundreds of vehicles shouting slogans. There are processions for Ganesh Chaturthi and protest marches of caste groups. Watching them, one is terrified.

To say that it needs only a hundred young people to build this nation is empty talk. To say that students have no caste is an idealistic statement. It is not the truth. There is revenge and anger on the faces of the young lions who have been driven by the commands of their castes. When a girl of one's caste is humiliated there is a passionate outburst which does not happen when women of other castes get degraded. Could educational degrees transform people who have come out of a caste-ridden society? The teachers and the textbooks are not really against caste.

When caste is discussed and my caste is mentioned, I am not able to get over the feeling that I belong to that caste. I would have no objection to my son marrying a girl from another caste. The rootlets of caste may have gone from within me, too, as an impact of social psychology. My mother does not enquire these days about the caste of those who come to my house. She feeds everyone. She washes the plates in which they eat. When young girls in the village used to call my mother by her name, not using a relationship term, she did not mind it. But she would address them with respect. She also wanted to call those considered 'inferior' to her by their names. In our family, all the marriages have been within caste. However, I saw to it that in the marriages of my generation, caste was not mentioned. I don't have friends who believe in caste. When Kamaraja Nadar was discussed I would even hesitate to take his side thinking it might be seen as a caste stand.

There are so many incidents based on which one can even write a novel. Nadars also have their sorrows. My wife has not seen any humiliation based on caste. My son, who studies in a city school, does not think about caste much. But he is ashamed of his dark complexion. His ears are now attuned to the song sung in the village: *Nadar Ayya Nadaru, Naadu potrum Nadaru…* Nadar Sir, he is Nadar, the Nadar the whole country praises… the song being sung for one or the other political leader of the Nadar community. I pray to the non-existent god that his heart does not get attuned to it.

It is not necessary to end an essay with a moving poem or touching lines. So I end this with futile whimpering.

******

Pollution and Untouchability

V. Krishnan

Everybody gets affected by things happening around them. Pleasant or bitter, whatever the nature of the events, they remain unforgettable. The incidents may have been experienced personally or they may be those that affected others which one has been witness to. How strong the impact of such incidents could be depends often on the person's stand regarding caste. This kind of impact goes beyond the divisions of dominant caste and oppressed caste. But the chances of scars, borne by those who have experienced oppression, remaining permanent, unhealed scars, are more. It is possible that the experiences of the dominant castes would be more in the nature of other castes singing their praises or being obedient towards them.

Without taking a position of dominance or oppression, what I try to narrate here are what I have felt about incidents that happened around me, incidents that I still question constantly in my mind.

I did my school education in Kulithalai, my grandfather's place. There were three *agraharams* where only Brahmins lived. One of them was Vaikanallur Agraharam. The Peengan Kottai Store (Porcelain Fortress Tenements) had the postal number 2 and seven families lived in it. I don't know how it got the name Porcelain Fortress. The houses were in two opposite rows situated facing north and south. They were one room tenements with a large hall and a kitchen with a front door, and a back door directly opposite the front one. There was a courtyard in front of the doors of each house, with a well in the backyard. A Portia tree behind the well and 10 or 20 coconut trees surrounded by thorn bushes completed the backyard.

The thorn bushes were open toilets for women and children at night. For men, it was an open toilet in the day. Outside the house there would be two large *pyols* on two sides as extensions of the house. When one opened the front door and entered the house there would be two pyols there as well, on both sides. The large 16 by 10 feet pyol facing the north had no doors and the wall was only half covered with a roof. That 'room' would be dark with no cross-ventilation. There was no way a breeze could enter that space. Outside that room was a space to stand the cycle and space for cast-off broken wooden chairs and benches, for the entire store.

This 16 by 10 space was the one that first affected me. One of the customs of the Brahmins was to segregate women for three days of the month when they had their periods. In a way, unlike other castes, Brahmin women could use these three days for rest, without any household work. However, they had to stay in a segregated place, which was like a dark room, with no light and air. In the Peengan Kottai Store, in this room inside, facing the north, on an average, barring a few days, there would be some-one or the other. At times, there would be four or five women there at the same time.

In this state of segregation, how these women were given food from their respective homes was pitiable. They would be given a plate and a tumbler or a brass mug for drinking water by their families. When the food was brought, the woman having her period must place the plate and the glass on the floor and stand at least five feet away. The food would be dropped on the plate from two feet above. The rice and kuzhambu would be given as if they were being given to a beggar with a dangerous contagious disease. The food would be given only after the elders of her house had finished eating their meals. She would be given only those pickles which were nearly getting over, the ones one could throw away or discard as waste, for if she was given pickles from full jars, they would get contaminated. This applied to all other food also.

The women would never get food when they were hungry or at the right time. If it was a ritual day when death rituals were being performed for a dead ancestor, the woman could eat lunch only in the evening. If this was the kind of deplorable condition regarding food, the conditions regarding sleep were no better. They were not given mats or pillows. They would use either a wooden plank or a brick-shaped wooden piece as a pillow. Two old saris would be given to them, to be spread as sheets and used as covers. In the day, there was a different path to leave the house and they would only use that path. In the night, they could not come out of their room and go directly to the backyard. They would have to walk through the front passage of the north-south facing houses. All the seven houses would close their doors when they went past. Ten feet ahead of them, their mothers or sisters would walk holding a chimney lamp or a torch. They believed the Vedas prescribed such purity practices.

I don't know about women from other castes and their condition during monthly periods. But when women from Brahmin households got their periods, at least four or five neighbours would come to know about it. No household members of their families would come close to them. Due to this, there have been instances of young girls segregated during their monthly periods being harassed by some young rogues. Maybe during their periods Brahmin women had no household work to do. But for those three days, their life would be hell.

No one could go close to the Brahmin women in their periods. If, by mistake, someone went near them, they had to have a bath pouring water over their heads. Children or small boys who would accidentally go close to them would be asked to remove their clothes and be made to wear fresh clothes. Hence, they would put on new clothes, as yet unwashed, on small babies. New clothes supposedly did not carry any pollution. Little kids would also move about naked. Since the women with periods were kept far away, the word for which is *dhooram* in Tamil, the days when they are to be segregated are known as *dhooram naal*, days to be kept far away, and the term for periods itself is *dhooram*, and the pollution of that period is referred to as *dhooram naal thiittu*, pollution of days when kept far away. I used to ask my Paatti and Periamma often why women who had their periods were treated this way. They used to answer: it is like that; our elders have stipulated it. I could never understand it then. When I grew up, I understood that the condition of Brahmin women was worse than that of women of other castes. I have often told my friends about the customs of Brahmins and told them to change the high opinion they have of the caste.

The incident I am going to narrate happened when I was studying in class IX. The teacher who taught us science was a Brahmin woman. She was a spinster. She was an excellent teacher. When she took biology classes and taught us about lungs and kidneys, she would get the parts of animals from the butcher's shop and touch them with her fingers and explain it to us without any qualms. She would demonstrate by keeping the lungs close to her mouth and blowing into them. If it was plants, she would ask us to bring lots of leaves, plants and flowers. Once I took a whole lot of leaves, plants and flowers and gave them to her. When I came back home after school my neighbour came and asked me if I had had a science class that day. I told him, yes, there was a science class that day. Immediately, he went and told my grandmother to ask me to put my clothes in the wash and have a bath. When I asked him the reason, he said it was because of the pollution of segregation days. After that, whenever one of the neighbours asked me if there was a science class I used to lie to them, saying that I had not gone near the teacher or that I had worn new clothes. These notions began to change only in the nineties when they began to say that coming near women during their periods was not polluting. Also, if you did not actually touch a person, you would not be polluted, they began to say.

I have learnt from some of my friends that there is a general belief that the customs and habits of Brahmins are laudable. My friends are mostly non-Brahmins. In my friends' circle I am the only Brahmin. So my friends tend to speak very highly about Brahmins. They would not accept it even if I told them that they were not right. Their praises, in fact, induced me to critically view the Brahmin way of life and its unsavoury aspects. One look at the way Brahmins eat and at their kitchens would be enough to change one's views regarding their clean and devoted ways of functioning.

While serving food for people seated on the floor, the serving vessels with food would be kept on the floor, and if someone walked across, the dust of the feet would most likely fall into the open vessels. But no care would be taken regarding this. The person serving food or the one eating would sneeze without covering the mouth, least bothered about anything falling on the food spread around. If they had a cold they would blow their nose with the left hand and wipe it on the floor or the wall. There are times when I have been unable to eat or have left half way through the meal after seeing all this. Once you serve rice, kuzambu and *poriyal*, the vegetables, if one had to serve buttermilk or pickles one had to wash one's hands or at least touch water because rice and other things were considered polluting.

Apart from salted food like chapatti, poori, fried snacks, all other food that sticks to the fingers, is considered polluting. Pickles are not considered polluting. To remove the polluting effect of these food items, the person serving the food would have to dip the fingers in water or just slant the tumbler of water kept nearby and pour out some water and place the fingers on the spilt water. With all these efforts to remove pollution, eating would not be a very pleasant experience. Only the cooking oven would be neat and clean. There would be cobwebs dangling from the roof, ready to fall any time. Sticking to the chimneys would be oil-smeared cobwebs. In the seventies and eighties, most Brahmin households had such kitchens.

Pollution rituals related to death have also given me no end of problems. If close relatives passed away, pollution rituals would be observed for 10 days. Depending on how close the person who died was, the number of days of pollution would be reduced to three or to just one day. For very distant relatives, it was enough to have a bath on hearing the news of death. The one observing one-day, three-day or ten-day pollution would have to remain segregated from the rest of the family. If children or someone else touched that person by mistake, they would have to have a bath. Children would have to change clothes. There are also strict rules about offering condolences when someone passes away. If the body has not yet been removed one can go to the house of the dead on any day of the week. But after cremation if one had to visit the house to offer condolences, it had to be on a Thursday or a Sunday. But if these days fell on two-digit dates then the visit had to be avoided. By the time all these calculations were done and the visit to the house of the dead would be planned, the family would have got over the death. Only the elders in the family are to go to offer condolences. The others cannot. Due to these rules, I have missed offering condolences to my close friends when someone close to them has passed away. There have been instances when my parents have been ridiculed for offering condolences much after the event. During my college days, I flouted these rules, and I still do.

I have also been deeply affected by instances when I was considered 'polluted' after eating in non-brahmin households. Near my grandfather's house was a timber shop and they would do *pooja* on Tuesdays and Fridays and distribute *prasadam*, the offerings, of roasted gram and sugar. I would stand, along with my friends, to receive the prasadam. It was fun eating with my friends. Once the shop had acquired a new timber cutting machine and they did pooja and distributed tamarind rice to everyone. I eagerly partook of the food along with my friends. I must have been hungry that day for I asked for a second helping. Of the seven families that lived in the store, one of them was that of a relative. The relative chastised me severely for eating in the timber shop and forced me to have a bath. A bath is supposed to do away with the pollution of eating in a non-Brahmin place.

When I got a job as a teacher in a college, a colleague reminded me of my Brahmin status in a different way. I had gone to his house along with other colleagues and he said: You don't have to worry about eating at my place. My mother is like all of you. She observes cleanliness rules very strictly. She does not eat meat and can't even bear the smell of meat. She would even put the vessels in which meat has been cooked far away from the other vessels.

I grew up in an agraharam (my grandfather's place) till tenth standard. I came to live with my family when I was in the twelfth. Appa worked in the Public Works Department and we lived in official quarters. There was no caste discrimination in the quarters and we were all friendly with one another. But since I had come from an agraharam I was seen as someone with all the traits of having grown up in an agraharam. Even my close relatives could not accept that I carried no traces of an agraharam upbringing in my daily habits. In the quarters, I had no Brahmin friends. It was, therefore, possible for me to carry on in my usual way.

Eight years after my marriage I came to know about an incident related to my engagement. In my speech and habits I did not carry my Brahmin identity because of living in the quarters and the friends' circle that I had. Many of my friends tell me so. My wife is the same. This happened before my engagement. My maternal uncle's friend worked in my college. Enquiries about me were made of him. He had some doubts about me, for my language was not Brahmin nor were my other habits. He came and spoke to me in a friendly way and patted me on my back and ran his hand over my back to check if he could feel the sacred thread inside the shirt. Since he could not find it, he went to the Employment Register to make sure of my caste.

Addressing girls and women, regardless of their age, with the disrespectful suffix *di*, washing a tumbler after offering water to a person who is not Brahmin, an old father-in-law washing his young son-in-law's feet during marriage ceremonies, humiliating poor Brahmins who come to take part in death rituals, cooking in a wet sari for annual death ceremonies, not attending to calls of nature until the Brahmins have eaten and if forced to go to the washroom then bathing again, taking spurious medicines to postpone or bring the monthly periods earlier, when a woman is unable to participate in auspicious or inauspicious functions, publicly having to declare that she was having her periods—all these are experiences which have pained me no end. It is these experiences that have taught me to respect and understand the feelings of others around me.

*****

Ugly Grin

P. Gunasekaran

There was a Panchayat Union Middle School in our village. I studied in that school till Class VIII. I belong to the Udayar caste. There were many Udayar teachers in the school. Most of the students were also of that caste. The math teacher belonged to my caste. When someone could not do a math problem correctly, he would beat up the lowered caste students really hard and students of my caste would be beaten lightly. Caste discrimination was strong even among teachers. During lunch time the teachers of my caste would sit at a distance from teachers of other castes. The flag hoisting on Independence Day was always done by someone from the Udayar caste. It is so to this day.

A new math teacher was appointed when I was in Class VII. He was a Gounder. Most of the teachers in that school were middle-school teachers and each one would teach two or three subjects. The new teacher taught math as well as social science. He would teach two lessons in a class meant to cover one lesson. Reading out the lesson in one breath with no pauses was his way of teaching. All the students were afraid of him, no matter which caste they belonged to. At least two students got beaten in his class every day. He never touched the girls.

I used to speak very softly and often got beaten for giving answers that he could not hear. One of the students whom he had beaten wrote some ugly things about him on the school compound wall when he completed his Eighth. The rest of the students saw what was written with charcoal on the compound wall, felt quite elated and kept talking about it. Finally, it was found that the student who had written it was of the Gounder caste. Many students affected by this teacher plotted that they would put a handful of sugar in the petrol tank of his TVS 50—the petrol tank would blow up and he would die, was what they thought. But for some reason, that plan was never carried out.

To this day, Gounders have remained those who dominate me. Around the same time that I was getting beaten by the Gounder teacher, my mother would chastise me, comparing me with kids in the Gounder households. Our field was surrounded by those of the Gounders. The young people of the Gounder household would come and work on their fields and my mother would point them out to my younger brother and me, saying: Look at the Vellala kids. Look at the way they work, looking like newly sprouted onions bunding the fields, setting up the boundaries and grazing the cows. This act of hers continued even after we grew up. Even now my mother has not given up this exercise in comparison and ridiculing. Once she said: Look at how discerning the Vellala boys are. If you ask them to just cut something, they would come back with bundles; and if you tell them to bring bundles they would just cut and return. And look at the two of you. I did not answer her and kept quiet. But my younger brother joked saying, 'The Vellala boys can't do what is told, is it? If they are asked to just cut, they should only cut, why are they bundling it and bringing it?'

Since we were surrounded by the Gounders, there would often be disputes over land. Once they bribed those in the police station, and we were threatened by the inspector there that he would see to it that we wouldn't be able to work anywhere. A group of them came and attacked my father, hurried to the police station to complain against him and admitted themselves in the government hospital. Every time they attacked, they 'took care' to prepare the police station for it, and so our side of the incident never got heard. The police took a written statement from us that we would not get into any squabbles with the Gounders in the future.

I completed my Eighth and had to go for my Ninth to the Government High School at Senthamangalam. There were boys from the Pallar and Vanniyar castes in class who took dominant positions threatening other caste boys. Some of the students would even threaten the teachers. The caste of a person could be guessed when the name of that person's village was mentioned. Each village or street, stood for a particular caste. The teachers would ask the students only the name of their village. Senthamangalam Ward I meant Pallar, Janganapuram Pudhur meant Udayar, Gandhipuram meant Gounder, Pallipudhur meant Padayachi, Gandhipuram Catholic Church meant Parayar, Senthamangalam Market Street meant Chettiyar, Kollar (Blacksmith) Street meant Achari and so on. When some students would merely say Gandhipuram, the teachers would enquire which Gandhipuram they were referring to: Gandhipuram Fort or Catholic Church, they would ask. If a boy said Senthamangalam, 'Where in Senthamangalam?' would be the question that would follow.

When I was in Class XI, some of the students started brewing illicit liquor. They were of the Pallar caste. Some of them would fill the illicit liquor in lorry wheel tubes, bring them from the brewing point to sale point, and then come to school in the morning riding their TVS 50s. They would be so tired that they would fall asleep in class. They would explain that they had to do a night job. Pallars were also adept at stealing. They would target those who came for the market fairs and steal cycles and the TVS 50s. Once something was lost everyone would know that the lost object would be in Senthamangalam Ward I, where the Pallars lived. Some people would have to buy back their own vehicles, after paying four to five thousand rupees.

Students from our village would go for private tuitions and return home only at eight at night. Two boys in Class XI lost their cycles. Everyone said that the bikes would definitely be there in Pallar Street. But the cycles were not to be found. In the school campus, there was a shed with a thatched roof to park the cycles. But the inner tube valves and mouths would be removed and thrown away by miscreants. They would deflate the tires or puncture the tires with compass instruments. All this would be the handiwork of Pallar and Padayachi students.

After Class XII I joined the Arinjnar Anna Government Arts College for my graduate course. I found out that the perversity of caste was more deeply rooted in colleges. There, the teachers never asked the students their caste, but the students themselves formed caste groups. There were instances of upper caste students attacking lowered caste students outside and inside the college campus. They would only want someone from the Gounder caste or some other backward caste to win the student body elections. The lowered caste have never taken part or won any elections so far, as far as I know. The elections would normally take place on a Friday and how many heads would get broken on election day could be anybody's guess.

A day before the elections, the student contesting the elections would gather as many students as possible and take them to one of those wedding halls and literally lock them in. The voters (students) would be shown blue films, given alcohol and a mutton feast. The next day they would all be taken in private vehicles and dropped near the college hostels. The annual student body elections had already taken place before I joined the first year of college. In the second year, I got locked up along with others in a wedding hall situated in the foothills of the mountains known as Nainamalai. They said we had to spend the night there. I never used to carry my lunch to college. I was carrying only a notebook that day. I gave the notebook to my friend and told him I would just go out to a restaurant, and I caught the bus to my place and came home.

I came to know later that the person who had locked us up in the Nainamalai wedding hall was a contestant who belonged to the Minnampalli Udayar caste and that he was a third year Economics student. They said he had the support of a political leader of the Udayar caste. Finally, he lost the elections by a small margin. Those counting the votes were hit on the head with hockey sticks and students from the lowered castes were attacked on that occasion.

There were regular instances of students from my village attacking Dalit students and Dalit students organising protests in the college against such attacks. When I was in the second year, those from my caste attacked a lowered caste student in the third year. When questioned, they said that he had ragged a first year Udayar student and they were enraged that he had dared to do so. Near the entrance of the college, with students standing around, the first year student slapped the third year student. Next, I took part in the protest organised in the college by the lowered caste students. The students from my place saw this and stayed away from me and avoided talking to me. They even stopped interacting with me in the village.

Most of my classmates were from the Gounder caste. They first found out who the girls from their caste in the class were. Then they further traced the sub-groups they belonged to and began to get interested in girls who did not belong to their subgroup, because marrying within your own caste sub-group was not allowed. Ultimately, only one such love affair ended in marriage. Students of one group of the Gounder caste would sit together in class, go out together and watch films together.

After my graduation, I worked for two years in a Xerox shop in Salem. It was my friend Prabhakar who had got me the job. The photocopying shop owner was a Reddiar. Knowing that I was an Udayar, he asked me to manage the shop. There were three shops in Salem, and I supervised them along with the manager. There were many girls of the Arunthathiyar caste working in the shops. If any mistake was made in photocopying, Reddiar would scold them saying, 'Does paper grow on trees? If you waste paper like this, will your father make up for the loss?' And he would deduct the money from their salaries for the paper wasted and account for it saying that the money was deducted against the advance taken by them, when they would have actually taken no advance. When he admonished the girls, he would be more stern with the Arunthathiyar girls, while gently admonishing the others, as if he was advising them.

I worked in the photocopying shop for two years and then joined a university to pursue my postgraduate studies. There was one professor who showed keen interest in knowing the caste of the students. He would ask any student to stand up in the class and ask him which caste he belonged to. I expressed my distress over this to the Head of the Department. A week later, the professor came into the class and made me stand up and asked me, 'What is your caste?'

I said, 'BC.'

'I don't know what BC is. Please explain properly,' he said.

'Udayar,' I mumbled.

'What do you mean by Udayar? Which sub-group among the Udayar?' he asked further.

'Malayaman,' I answered.

I understood that he was asking me specifically because I had complained that the professor wanted to know all the caste details of students. He asked me these questions that day in a tone that indicated that he would ask questions about caste affiliations directly and that I could do nothing about it. Finally, the entire blame fell on me for the professor's behaviour. My friends went around telling others that I had said that the professor was dealing with the students on the basis of caste and that he was playing caste politics. He began to threaten the students in the class: I will finish you off. I am the one who is going to correct your papers. I will see to it then. Once you complete your studies, wherever you go for jobs we will be in your selection committees. We will deal with you then. And he kept his threat; he failed some students. I was greatly affected by this. I came first in the first semester but in the following semesters I was pushed down to second place. Finally, I could only come second in the university. The caste prejudices among the educated are much more dangerous than the caste prejudices among the uneducated.

The school in my village has now become a High School. The Middle School I studied in has become a Primary School. The High School is run from another part of the village. I got an opportunity to function as a Junior Assistant in the High School for some time. Actually, I worked more in other offices as a replacement than in our school. When I used to share my experiences in other offices with teachers they would mention someone's name in one of the offices and ask me if I knew him. If I said yes, they would say at the end of the conversation, 'He is one of us.' Whoever one spoke about, finally it would end in stating that person's caste. If one was going to an office on work, they would refer to a person working there and give details about his appearance and finally say, 'He is one of us. You go ahead; you will be taken care of.'

Whenever my friends came home, my father would be eager to know about their caste. While my friends would be eating he would sit right in front of them and ask, 'You are Udayar, aren't you?' If they shook their head, he would ask, 'Gounder, is it?' He would tirelessly question them until he got the answer to his question. This used to upset me a lot. When some friends complained to me, 'Your father will not let go till he knows about our caste. He sits right in front of us and questions us....' I felt very bad. My younger brother fought with him often on this score. If he failed to find out about the caste of the visitors, my father would ask me about their caste. 'What does it matter which caste they belong to? How will that help you?' I would tell him.

After college, one or two friends who used to come home even stopped visiting me. These days my father and I just speak over the phone. If I am getting ready to attend some function in a friend's place, my father asks, 'Which community does that boy belong to?' However happily one was getting ready to go, that one question would kill all the joy.

It is not that this kind of atmosphere exists only at home. Wherever I go this seems to be the pattern. When I did field work for my PhD, I had to go to a Panchayat Union office. When I went there one of the officials asked me the usual questions about why I was collecting these details, where I was studying, what I was studying and so on. And these questions were inevitably followed by the question, 'Which place do you belong to?'

'R.P. Pudur,' I said.

'Is it the R.P. Pudur in Namakkal?'

'No, the one in Senthamangalam.'

'You are Udayar then, isn't it?' he said immediately.

'Hm...'

'Do you know the person who was Chairman there?'

When I said I knew him, he took me to the computer room itself to get me the details I needed and told the girl sitting at the computer to give me all the facts and information I needed. He also gave me names of persons in other Panchayat Union offices, and told me that I should mention that I was from Pudur, and also give his reference, and I would get all the information I needed.

Even if I deny my caste identity or hide it, the way things are, those around me constantly identify me with my caste in the way they speak and act. At every stage of my life, caste seems to flourish and it stands before me and follows me around with its ugly grin.

*****

A Kind of Pain

P. Kumaresan

Human beings can live without food in this society but not caste; society will not allow it. That is why everyone needs a caste identity. There is a myth that today's younger generation doesn't bother so much about caste. That is not true. Caste identity is actually formally registered in school. My caste name, Agamudayar, is in my school register.

My school education began in a school in Kumbakottai in Rasipuram Circle, Namagiripettai Panchayat, Namakkal District. Students from Koraiyaru, Kattappuliyamaram, West Kumbakottai, Thaneerpandhalkadu and Maraiammankoil villages came to study in our school. The teachers would identify some students as 'red ink students.' When I was in Class III this terminology got imprinted on my mind. The Principal would call the 'red ink students' from each class to his room and talk to them. The teacher would enquire who the 'red ink students' were to give them free textbooks, uniforms, shoes, notebooks and bags. When the students would stand up, he would tell them that books were to be given the next day and that they should come without fail. When higher educational officials were to visit the school the 'red ink students' would be warned not to be absent on that day. The midday meal organiser would come in the afternoons and count the number of 'red ink students'. I was not given textbooks and notebooks. I used to feel terribly disappointed about that. At those times, I used to feel that it would have been better had I been born a 'red ink' person.

The 'red ink students' had to write the annual exams with pencil. Dull students were separately coached by the teachers. Sometimes, they would be asked to rub out the wrong answers and right answers would be given for them to write. As far as I know the 'red ink students' never failed. The reason why they were called 'red ink students' was because in the attendance register there would be a section on caste and the names of SC/ST would be marked in red ink. The other students' names would be marked in dark blue ink. But they were never referred to as 'blue ink students'.

Most of the 'red ink students' came from Mariammankoil. Buses would not stop here, mostly. The buses would stop only at my village, Thaneerpandhalkadu. The students would get off here and walk to Mariammankoil. Everyone had got used to this. Old and feeble people were greatly affected by this. Some of them organised a road strike a few times to protest. Finally, some buses began to stop at Mariammankoil. One had to clearly say Mariammankoil-Thaneerpandhalkadu stop for getting tickets to Mariammankoil and state Thaneerpandhalkadu-banyan tree stop for Thaneerpandhalkadu.

More than 135 Dalit families stayed in Mariammankoil. They hold a temple festival in the Tamil month of Masi, which is the eleventh month in the Tamil calendar and which falls on 12 February and lasts till 13 March. A temple tax of ₹1000 to ₹1500 would be collected from each household. Nobody was exempt from the tax. Since it was an annual festival, they would not hesitate to spend the money, even though it meant a big cut in their income. Both sides of the street would be grandly decorated with colourful electric lights. It would brighten up the street for a week.

Next to the bus stop was a Mariamman temple. But there were two deities in that temple. One was Mariamman and the other was Madurai Veeran. During the temple festival pooja, more importance was given to Madurai Veeran. On the festival days, there would be many entertainment programmes like the *kuravan-kurathi* dance-dialogue programme. Kuravan and his spouse Kurathi are actually names of men and women from hill tribes who wander for a living and the programme would have bawdy dialogues. There would also be dance programmes with men and women dancing to film songs with sexual innuendos. A large audience would gather for dance programmes. The district administration has now banned such dance programmes. The audience would not only enjoy the show, but also shout and whistle in between. Although the temple was a Dalit temple, other castes would also come and do pooja on annual festival days. On other days, they would stay away from the temple.

In the Tamil month of Chithirai which is from 14 April to 13 May, a temple chariot festival is normally held for the Mariamman temple in Namagiripettai. People from Thaneerpandhalkadu, Kumbakottai, West Kumbakottai and Koraiyaru would carry pots of water and pots decorated with flowers known as *poongkaragam*—which are normally carried on the heads during temple festivals, when people have taken a vow—and come for the Mariamman temple chariot festival. West Kumbakottai village is situated a mile away from Thaneerpandhalkadu, on the road towards the north. During temple festivals, the villagers would dance with a *kumbam*, a ritual pot, on their heads and hence the name of the village. The village was also known for the poongkaragamritual that it undertook. To the west of West Kumbakottai there was a hill at the foothills of which was a temple. Water would be taken from the temple pond and filled in the kumbam pots and the flower decorated poongkaragam pots would also be kept ready at the temple. Then they would be brought to the centre of the village and the dance would be performed. There would also be other kinds of entertainment.

A lot of youngsters would come to see the kuravan-kurathi dance. Among them there would be more outsiders than youngsters who belonged to that area. They were supposed to watch the programme quietly. They were not to whistle or shout. If they indulged in such activities, they would be forcibly removed. But youngsters from farming communities had no such restrictions. I began to look at my caste critically when I witnessed such incidents. I could make passionate speeches about caste on stage and win prizes, but in my own village I was not able to speak against it. The dominant caste to which I belonged was my handicap in this matter.

I did my post-graduation in an old and well-known university. We were 20 students in our class and we were different from one another in 20 different ways. We could not be close friends for we were all restricted by the way we were brought up and the way we had been educated. There was a group whose job was to find out the caste of each student in the first six months. Questions regarding caste would not be direct but there would be a string of questions: How much scholarship did you get in your BA, where are you staying now, which writer do you like, what is the admission fees that you have paid for MA and so on. Once they got replies to these questions they would guess the student's caste. 'Do you like Periyar and Ambedkar?' was a question that not only one's classmates, but also students who were doing their doctorates, would ask. This was also another way of identifying Dalit students.

I am a regular reader of literary magazines. I was once reading *Dalit Murasu*. A girl in my class noticed it and asked me the next day, 'I thought you were a Gounder; are you an SC?' I did not answer her immediately, but looked at her, wondering what the need for such a question was. I really could not make out her intentions then. 'Why do you want to know?' I asked her. 'You are dark; and you also read *Dalit Murasu*. That is why I asked,' she said. Only then did I understand what her question was all about.

Many students who studied there were keen to know your caste and the sub-group of your caste. By the end of the first year there would be so much caste affiliation that they would form different caste groups and discuss caste. A classmate of mine would address the others as, 'Sakkili Karthi, Padayachi Vel', i.e., prefixing their castes before their names. Some of my friends and I told him that he should stop this as we found it abhorrent. It was only then that he stopped addressing people in this manner.

I spoke about the despicable state of caste in an elocution competition. I won a prize. A fellow contestant told me: However much you speak and write, can you feel the pain of a Dalit? You cannot. Your thoughts don't come from real experiences.' It was like a slap in my face. Since then a guilty feeling has taken hold of me. I could clearly perceive that I was born into a dominant caste and that I have also been a part of caste oppression. A kind of a pain, a guilty feeling, continues to haunt me.

*****

A Wedding Feast with Mutton

S. Gopi

There are Pallar and Parayar in the village Pavithiram in the Erumappatti Union in Namakkal District. They are referred to as 'Pavithirathaan', belonging to Pavithiram, and this is their only identity. I belong to the Parayar caste myself. My family had not taken up the caste profession and had gone into daily wage labour work. My family arranged my marriage even though I was doing my research for PhD.

I wanted to celebrate my marriage in a grand way, just like the dominant castes do. My parents were also not against it. I wanted to book the marriage hall in advance the first opportunity I got. There is a wedding hall in Navalappatti, which is near our village. I went with a government school teacher to book it in advance. The teacher was not a Parayar. The owner of the wedding hall was a Reddiyar. I told the owner, 'Ayya, we are coming from Pavithiram. My friend is a teacher in a school in Varakur for the 11th and 12th Standards. We want to rent the wedding hall.' He asked me, 'What do you do?' I said, 'I am a research scholar in a university.' And I added, 'I am the one getting married. I belong to the Parayar caste. Will you rent out the wedding hall to us?' I did not beat about the bush and asked him directly, right in the beginning. The teacher looked askance at me. It was as if he was telling me: 'Where is the need to mention your caste these days?'

I continued to talk to the owner: 'There is one more thing. We will serve a wedding feast with mutton. Let me know if you have any objection to that.' The owner said, 'What does it matter to which caste you belong? This is our wedding hall and we can rent it out to anyone we choose.' He added, 'Just last week a goat was cut here. We are not bothered about all that,' he firmly reassured us. The teacher who had come along looked at me, indicating that the advance needed to be paid. I found out all the details about the various payments to be made for different services. I gave an advance of a thousand rupees to the teacher and the teacher handed it over to the owner.

The owner also gave us a guided tour of the wedding hall. Then we prepared to get back and on the way we were full of praise for the anti-caste stand taken by the owner.

The wedding preparations were on. I got a call from the wedding hall owner. The call, I felt, indicated the heights of human civilisation that we had reached in the 21st century. 'The date for which you have booked the hall, has already been booked by someone else. Please come and take your advance back,' he said over the phone. 'Why do you say that? I told you clearly about the date. If you say this now, what can I do? The wedding date is close and I cannot get another wedding hall at such short notice. Why are you doing this?' I asked him but the call was cut off even as I was talking. I called him two hours later and asked him what exactly the matter was. He said the owner had objected to mutton being served. 'Please find another wedding hall,' he told me. And he continued to give disconnected explanations. I rang up the teacher and bemoaned the owner's attitude. He was a more mature person than me. 'Let it go,' he said, 'What has happened has happened. Go book another wedding hall immediately, for the wedding date is close. There is no point going and meeting him now for we wouldn't, then, be able to celebrate the wedding the way we want to. You have not spoken to anyone, isn't it? Only we know about this. We will deal with him after the wedding.' My anger subsided somewhat for the time being.

I spoke to my family and we booked another wedding hall and the wedding was celebrated just the way I had planned. A month after the wedding, I went with my wife in a car to get the advance amount back. We met the proprietor of the wedding hall. He had warmly welcomed us the first time we had met, but now his clean-shaven face got twisted, as if to ask, 'What is it?' 'Where is the advance?' I asked him. He got a bit perturbed and said,

'Come tomorrow.' 'I am not asking you for a loan. Give back the advance, you stupid cunt,' I said. He did not respond to my abuse. His house was at a distance from the village. 'I don't have the money now. I have given it to the owner. If he comes, I will get it from him. You please go,' he said. I raised my voice and yelled at him: 'When you took the advance you said you were the owner. And now you act as if the owner is someone else. I must get my money back right now. Otherwise, you mother-fucker, there is going to be a murder here.' It looked like he was thoroughly scared. He went in to get the money without a word.

His wife came out and said, 'Is this the way to talk? You are not talking like an educated person.' 'How else can one speak after what your husband has done? You please go in, Madam. What did I say when I gave the advance? I told him about my caste and I also said clearly that mutton would be served at the wedding feast. He agreed to everything and then 10 days before the wedding your husband rings up and says, book some other wedding hall. What were we supposed to do?' I asked her. Her husband came and said, 'Thambi, no need for unnecessary words. Take your advance and go. My brother is the owner. What could I do?' 'Look here, when I gave the advance, I told you everything. Why didn't you say then that you would consult the owner?' I asked him.

We continued to argue and our arguments reached such heights that we could not climb down. When he could not argue anymore he went inside the house and locked himself in. I hurled the choicest of abuses at him to let off steam and got out of there. On our way back, my wife and I bore the humiliation along with the money he had given us and grumbled about the oppressive ways of caste and people.

I could guess what had gone on in the mind of the wedding hall owner from this incident. Why did he agree to give the wedding hall and later tell me to look for another one? Where was the need to say that non-vegetarian food should not be served and that the hall would be available only if vegetarian food was served? In a caste-ridden place like Navalappatti, if a person from a lowered caste celebrates a wedding grandly, the news would spread all around the area. The so-called upper castes would hesitate to use the utensils used by the Parayar community. He may have feared that those considered upper caste may refuse to book the same wedding hall in the future. Why the stress on vegetarian food? Normally meat was not cooked for wedding feasts in our region. So everyone would get to know about this unusual wedding. People would want to know who had celebrated the wedding in this manner. They would come to know that a certain person of a particular caste from a certain village had celebrated the wedding in this manner and the news would spread like fire. Hence the stress on vegetarian food and the need to say that they would not allow a wedding where mutton was served as part of the wedding feast. One can see the mind of a person who believes in the Hindu Sanatan dharma here.

There is one more thing and an important one at that. It is the notion that if a Parayan wants to serve meat in a wedding, his caste economic status would definitely allow him to serve only beef and that would have driven them to take such contrary stands. Whatever the government and governmental organisations plan for the upliftment of oppressed castes, caste oppression is present all over, omnipresent like god.

*****

Empty Pride

Govindaraj

Ever since I became aware of things, caste has adhered itself to me. Even as a kid when I used to go out to play I was warned not to play with Gounder boys. The boys from Gounder households had to be addressed as Periya Gounder, Senior Gounder and Chinna Gounder, Junior Gounder.

I belong to the Navidhar (Barber) caste. They are generally referred to as Maruthuvar, practitioners of medicine or as Hindu Maruthuvar, Hindu practitioners of medicine. They are also known as Nasuvan, Ambattan, Chakkara Kathi, Kudimagan and so on. The terms change from village to village. They are supposed to be descendants of a Vaisya woman and a Brahmin and they are considered experts in the Siddha system of medicine. The Navidhar women have been traditionally midwives who have served all the castes in that capacity. But our caste-profession is basically removing hair from the body by shaving or cutting hair. There have also been weavers and other professionals from my caste. They have taken up many jobs like tending to sheep, agents who arrange sale of cattle in cattle fairs for a commission, mill workers and so on. They got into whatever jobs were available. Among the Kongu Gounders, no ritual can take place without a Navidhan. From going to invite the entire village till the last ritual, the Navidhan plays an important role. Along with shaving and cutting hair, the knowledge of medicine comes naturally to them. Although I was born in a city and I grew up in a city I have felt the rigidity of caste whenever I have visited villages.

My Periamma, maternal aunt, lived in Poosaripalayam. Whenever I visited her I was told not to address anyone by name. I could not use friendly terms like '*Daey*' '*Vaada*' '*Poda*' used among friends, for they were considered disrespectful. I could not just walk into the neighbours' homes. Periamma would keep warning me about all this. She used to sell vegetables in fairs. Periappa was the *Kudimagan* of the entire village. Kudimagan, literally meant son of the community, but it indicated in reality that he took care of the shaving and cutting of hair of the entire village as Kudimagan, another name of his caste. Periappa used to go from farm to farm to cut hair. When there was a village festival, or during weddings Periappa and Periamma would go and get food, called *Oor Sappaadu,* which was given by the village. It used to be very tasty. I still remember the onion sambar from houses where weddings were taking place.

When I think about certain things I am surprised. My father's name was Subban. His friends used to call him Lame Subban. He had corns in his feet and so he walked with a limp. Corns are the bonus you get when you herd goats. My father had herded goats when he was a small boy. In my school certificates, he had signed his name as Subban. It was only when he was 67 and we went for some astrological consultation that I got to know his full name. His name was Balasubramanian and it was reduced to Subban. Shortening names is a practice in all castes. For example, if we take the name Ramasamy, among the Panchamar, the fifth group outside the four varnas referring to the Dalits, a person with that name would be called Raman. Among the dominant castes like Gounder, Thevar and Pannadi the person would be called Ramasamy. Among the Brahmins and similar upper caste people, the person would become Ramaswamy. We can see this happening to many names.

Appa's father was Apparu, grandfather. His name was Raman. My father took a decision not to follow the caste profession and went to work in a mill. He never touched a barber's knife in his life.

A scholar has said that the word Navidhan means someone who shows his proficiency or skill, through his '*naa*' meaning the tongue. Yes, a quality associated with the profession becomes the quality of the caste. My community people wander around a lot. They serve people. Comrade Karl Marx says that the skill in a job becomes the characteristic of a worker. The skill to use one's tongue is now seen in all professions, including the real estate business. The barber community has this skill. Due to the nature of their work they made themselves an important part of the society; they could not be ignored or kept away. They took part in auspicious and non-auspicious occasions of every family in villages and they became knowledgeable about rituals connected with such occasions. They continue to play an important role in the rituals of Kongu Velala Gounders. During weddings 'auspicious felicitation' is an important ritual. This auspicious felicitation has been written by the famous Kamban who wrote the *Kamba Ramayanam*. That is why there is a story that Kamban was a Navidhan, a barber, by birth.

It may amuse you when I say this but I was considered good looking as a child and as a young person! When I was around six or seven I would pester people with all kinds of riddles. This earned me many friends and enemies. My relatives encouraged these riddles. Aunts and uncles would fondle and pamper me. Those who could not answer my riddles would tell me on my face, 'This Nasuvan is trying to be over smart.' I don't remember making much of it or taking it to heart those days.

In my youth, when I was working in a company, I was an avid reader of La. Sa. Ra (La. Sa. Ramamrudham) and I had become a devotee of beauty like him. Some young girls used to approach me then and ask me, 'Which caste do you belong to?' 'I am a Nasuvan, my girl' I used to tell them. 'Don't jest in this way. You do this all the time,' they would say flirtatiously. Such loving whimpering faded away slowly when the truth about my caste came to be known. The banter would ultimately end in them addressing me as older brother, 'Anna, do you have a holiday tomorrow?' All this is what that great genius Manu left for us. I have experienced how it crushes all budding love and affection; I still experience it.

It is true that in a city caste is not obvious. But it has become a subtle part of city life. People maintain a certain attitude until the caste of a person is not known and change their attitude with ease once the caste is revealed. From my youth, I have never approved of the ways of society. My intention was not to obviously oppose it but when I did not follow certain rules it came naturally to me to oppose them. When I was young most people would ask me my caste and many times I lied about it. In the villages they would ask, 'Are you a Chakkara Kathi?' and in the cities the question would be, 'Are you a Maruthuvar?' The essence of both the questions is the same.

As a homeopathy doctor, I was invited once to attend to a patient suffering from cardiac asthma. His daughter told me that they were celebrating the coming of age ritual of her daughter. 'Appa is serious. Please save him for three days. We will feel relieved only after the ritual is complete,' she said. I went to the son's house with whom he was living, and began to gather details about the symptoms. There was the smell of urine all around the cot. Nearby there was a spittoon filled with sand, and a walking stick. The daughter-in-law had put on a grumpy face. The son knew what his duty was. I was assessing the atmosphere. When I was asking the patient questions, he asked me in a slurred voice: 'Are you a....Mu...ll...iy...ar?' I could not get him and looked at the son. He explained to me that he was asking if I was a Mudaliar. I lost my cool. 'Why, will you take the medicine only if I am a Mudaliar?' I asked him. He gestured with his hand to say no. 'It will be convenient if you are a Mudaliar' he said slurring. I tried to detach myself from that atmosphere and think dispassionately. Even on his deathbed this man was caught in the grip of caste. What kind of caste madness was this! I would not kill him with medicine, obviously. I gave him the homeopathy medicine Arsenicum Album. He saw his granddaughter's coming of age rituals to his heart's content and passed away five days later.

When I was a small boy most of my relatives were supporters of the DMK (Dravida Munnetra Kazhagam), Dravidian Progress Federation. In fact, our caste was so closely associated with the DMK Party that it was generally known as 'Nasuvan katchi', Barbers' Party, at one time. One of my uncles in Kongu Nagar was a staunch supporter of DMK. When he ran a lottery ticket business I won the first prize once. The person who handed over the prize to me was the then MLA Duraisamy, so close was the association with the DMK Party. The people of Tamil Nadu have been hearing for a long time Kalaignyar Karunanidhi's opponents referring to him as a Nasuvan. I am not bothered about the truth or non-truth of that statement. What is obvious is that such statements are made to assert someone's inferiority.

The poet Inquilab once wrote: If someone asks you your caste, tell them the name of your caste like a slap on the face. After I read that even if someone begins a casual conversation and asks me about my caste I would tell them loud and clear: 'Nasuvan.' 'Oh, sorry Sir, I just asked casually,' the person would try and make excuses. In weddings and funerals, caste continues to renew itself in many ways. Unless we rid ourselves of these rituals and the ignorance in pursuing them, one can't even dream of anyone shaking the roots of caste.

I used to cringe when someone asked me my caste when I was a young person. But now I don't allow it to affect my inner emotions. It is true that my caste identity prevents me from getting some good opportunities. But I firmly stand by the belief that my actions will take me beyond caste. Caste cannot be cut at the roots by opposing it. It will continue to return in many different forms. People must learn to live by ignoring it. It should be dried of its juices. And that would be possible only if every individual stands aloof from participation in caste.

This essay would remain incomplete without mentioning what Bhagwan Osho, whom I respect a lot, said: If that Manu comes before me now, I will set aside my wisdom and grace and shoot him.

These are the words of a great thinker of our society. Caste stands in the way of many things that must bloom naturally. I have found out how to overcome it. Hence, I stand away from it. Not just today, but always.

*****

The Deep Pain of Identity

S. Sathiskumar

I had no interest in either the caste system or its intricate layers nor did I have any specific views regarding it. The question deep in my mind, that why should one take an interest in something as hateful as caste when it often hurts and agonises, is the reason for this attitude of mine. There was also the pain within me of being cheated by the rousing poems of some poets and the falsehood of the line 'There are no castes, little girl', by Bharathi.

I constantly feel the frustration that whatever heights I reach struggling and battling with obstacles, there will be the enlarged image of 'Vannan', washerman, that will stick to my body despite the heights I will scale. However, when I sat down to write about the Vannar community, there were some thoughts that were in the depths of my mind and I would like to record them here in this essay.

In *Periya Puranam*, a classical text which is believed to have been written in the twelfth century, there is the story of Thirukurippu Thonda Nayanar. Through this story we come to know about the origins of the washermen community. In ancient literature and in rock inscriptions there are many references to the Vannar community. I have also heard from my grandmother a story about the orally narrated story of Pannari Amman, whose temple is situated in the northwest part of Erode District. The story goes as follows: Once upon a time, a washerman was washing the clothes by the river and he covered all the professional tools he needed with the big pot washermen use for laundry-bluing the clothes for post-wash whitening. After finishing his lunch in the afternoon, when he lifted the big pot the tools had disappeared and had turned into a statue. That statue was worshipped as Vannari Amman whose name has now changed to Pannari Amman. This oral story tradition is still a part of the Vannar community.

The Vannar caste, identified thus by the work they do, has been the caste that provides services to this day to specific castes like Velala Gounder, Vettuva Gounder, Mudaliar, and Nadar. Particularly, this community has not only been doing the washing for the dominant caste of Velala Gounder, but is also a very important part of their auspicious and inauspicious functions.

Even now the people of the Vannar community are very loyal to the Gounder community they depend on. One can even say that they see the Gounder as their masters to this day. There is a reason for this. The Vannar are not only given the payment for their work annually but, on happy occasions, they are given a part of the harvest; and on auspicious occasions new clothes and grains are given to them. Apart from this, their family problems would be judged fairly and resolved, and their children educated. Thus, in many ways, the Vannar are dependent on the Gounder. This dependence has been there for hundreds of years and it has become their way of life. It would not be an exaggeration to say that the truth is that they are happy to be grateful servants and slaves of Gounder, who have taken care of their needs.

More than being hurt by the dominant castes whom they serve, or other castes, what is irritating is the mental agony they are subjected to, from within the community, and their idiotic lifestyle. As far as I am concerned the identity of a Vannar creates great pain for me personally. The Vannar very strictly follow all the rituals, caste restrictions and customs of the Velala Gounder they depend on for a living. Even after revolutionary changes in professions and culture and despite the fact that the beliefs and customs of Velala Gounder have been somewhat watered down, the Vannar continue to blindly follow them.

For the temple festivals of family deities like Karuppannasamy, Angadi, Andichi and Muppattu Karuppan when relatives who are like uncles and brothers-in-law visit, even if there are 10 or 15 members in one family, all of them would be given new clothes. The same thing is done during weddings and auspicious functions.

There will be a truckload of such clothes in households. Rings, gold beads in thali, the sacred chain women wear after marriage, and loans taken on interest will come handy to keep up the expenses of such customs. I have been seeing this for the past 25 years.

There is a long list of things to be done during weddings. Exchange of horoscopes, matching the horoscopes, confirming the alliance, visiting the prospective groom's house, visiting the girl's house, paying advance money for the wedding hall and feast for the relatives, are the items on that list. Such problems may exist in all castes, but what is peculiar to the Vannar community is that for every function of the family, there would be at least 25 invited guests who would be relatives, and the maximum number of relatives attending a function could go up to 2,000 at a time. At least 50 to 100 relatives would go to shop with the family to purchase the bridal sari for the main event. The expenses for snacks and lunch for the entire group of relatives would be borne by the bride's family. The bitter truth is that the expenses for this would be even more than the cost of the bridal sari.

If a man or woman of this caste marries outside the caste, they would be excommunicated with no time limit set for the excommunication. After a few years, they would have to invite all the relatives to a mutton feast and fall at their feet and apologise. Only then would they be taken back into the caste. The mutton feast would cost at least ₹40,000. Apologising is called 'accepting blame' and the mutton feast is referred to as the 'hunting feast'. I had an inter-caste marriage and since I was not willing to organise such a feast, I remained excommunicated for an unlimited time. My parents were excommunicated for two years. After that my father organised a 'hunting feast' and was taken back into the caste fold. But he still does not have the right to participate in any ritual customs associated with the caste. Such punitive actions which even the dominant castes have forgotten, the Vannar community observes, showing no refinement in matters of caste.

It is not just marriage or after excommunication that relatives have to be invited to a grand feast. Relatives have to be invited to a feast even when a child is tonsured, for the ceremony of piercing the ears of the child, naming ceremonies and so on. Otherwise the family would have to face strong condemnation from relatives.

The identity of caste is something that gets attacked from outside and also has a lot of inner complications of the mind. The lifestyle and observations of customs of the caste I am born into are retrogressive. More than the oppression of the dominant castes, the mental anguish and vulnerability that one feels due to one's own caste is important. And it is this that has become an unendurable pain for me.

****

Snatched Freedom and Life

C. Chandiran

Vaigarai is a village where only those who belong to the Mutharayar caste live. This village is in Thuraiyur Circle, Tiruchirapalli District. It falls within the Kalingamudiyanpatti Panchayat. Muthusamy and Pachaiammal who lived in this village fell in love. This love was thwarted and Pachaiammal was married off to one Ramasamy who also belonged to the Vaigarai village. A couple of years after her marriage Pachaiyammal began to revive her old love relationship. Ramasamy admonished his wife when he got to know about it. Muthusamy took Pachaiammal to Valparai and stayed there for a few days. A distant relative who had gone there to work in the dam construction project gave them shelter.

The relative who gave them shelter thought that if the other relatives came to know about this there would be problems. So he gave Muthusamy some money and sent him off to Chennai. Muthusamy took up a job as a conductor in the city transport service. They had two children, Murugan and Nirmala. After a few years they got Ramasamy married to a distant relative who was also from the same village. Muthusamy and Pachaiammal began to visit Muthusamy's elder brother. Although initially the villagers were hesitant and afraid to renew their relationship with the two, over a period of time it became natural to talk to them as before. The main fear the villagers had about relating to them was because Muthusamy was living with someone else's wife.

Things became normal enough for relatives to stay with them when they were visiting Chennai. However, since Ramasamy lived in the same village, the relatives tried to make sure he would not find out about their renewed relations with Muthusamy and Pachaiammal. If he did come to know about it, they did their best not to make things obvious; they avoided attending occasions of marriage and death and related ceremonies and rituals. The agnates of Muthusamy's family did not allow them to take part in the pooja performed in the temples, nor were they allowed to offer worship in the temples. Muthusamy had three brothers but they could not go against the agnates. They were afraid that if they went against them they too would be shunned.

Sometime later, Muthusamy's father passed away. Muthusamy came with his family to take part in the funeral rituals. The agnates and relatives made it an issue before the caste panchayat for they felt that Muthusamy, who had taken away another man's wife and married her, had no right to take part in the funeral rituals of his father. Muthusamy's brothers were told in no uncertain terms that they had to choose between their brother and the relatives. If the brothers decided to maintain their relationship with Muthusamy they could not have anything to do with the temple of the agnates nor could they have the usual relationship with them. So they consoled Muthusamy and told him to just have a look at his father's dead body and leave, and not take part in any of the rituals.

Muthusamy and his young son Murugan and daughter Nirmala, who had hoped to unite with the relatives and agnates at this time, were deeply disappointed and felt shattered. Muthusamy's son Murugan joined the Indian Navy. As soon as he got the job they began looking for a bride for him. Even though they looked for a bride outside the village, the proposed girl's family would come to Vaigarai, the ancestral place of the proposed groom, find out the details and would not continue the talks regarding marriage. The incident of not being allowed to participate in the funeral rituals, being denied worship in the temple of the agnates coupled with the inability to find a girl to marry within the caste began to affect Murugan's mind. He refused to talk to his parents. He was given medical attention. But despite this, one day he hanged himself from a fan at home in Chennai.

Pachaiamma's brother's son worked as a lorry driver in Chennai. Although he had the customary claim to marry his cousin Nirmala, the proposal was never made by him even though he visited their home. Nirmala is a graduate who is now 42 years old but has had to remain unmarried.

Murugan hanging himself has remained the cause of an inconsolable sorrow in my mind and it is this that forces me to question caste and the way it functions, affecting the lives and emotions of individuals. The reason Murugan hanged himself was because of excommunication from his caste. The reason for excommunication was that his father had married another person's wife. When did marrying another person's wife become a crime to deserve excommunication? During British colonial rule until the time of Independence, various castes had made several restrictions within their caste in order to retain their influencing power. Those who did not submit to those restrictions were excommunicated. Until the law for reservations came into being, the differences among castes kept getting enhanced in a way that they soon became sharp divisions.

Where Thuraiyur Circle is concerned, those who are called Ambalakkarar and Muthurasa are the same now. We also have historical evidence of many castes in Tamil Nadu calling themselves Kshatriyas, and Brahmins looking upon them as Shudras, during the British rule. The Brahmins reasoned that those who called themselves Kshatriyas in Tamil Nadu were those who were soldiers in war and farmers otherwise and so they could not be termed Kshatriyas. The Mutharayar caste was no exception to this kind of argument of the Brahmins. In 1909, in a mortgage paper dated 10 August given by Nallakutti Muthiriyan, son of Thadha Muthiriyan of Meenakshipuram in Trichinapalli Taluk, his caste was not registered as Kshatriya. So he filed an appeal against the Sub Registrar V. R. Radhakrishna Iyer to District Registrar John Issac and Inspector General Smith. It is stated in the documents of this case that since the mortgage paper had already been registered in the government order, if the applicant so wished, in the mortgage paper and registration paper it could be added that the applicant wishes to state that he is a Kshatriya. This issue was blown up by the Kshatriya Muthurasa Association members who did propaganda that in the future on all official papers, stamps and handwritten statements, the Muthurasa caste should be recorded as the Kshatriya caste. We can infer from this that the Ambalakkarar were then seen as being inferior to the Muthurasa.

Clan meetings were conducted by various castes to sustain their influence in the colonial period and, as mentioned above, they wrote several restrictions into their lifestyle and functioning. These are clearly seen in the resolutions taken by the Mutharayar clan meeting where seven different clans met and took decisions. They disciplined themselves by making certain rules: no thieving, no stealthy marriages, no child marriage, no remarriage, no taking payment from other castes claiming to protect them or claiming money for the right to protect, and no consumption of liquor or other intoxicants. There is also a resolution that if someone cheated a married woman from among the relatives and took her away, they would be excommunicated from the caste, but there wouldn't be any enquiry ordered against these people. In order to retain their power and keep the distance among castes, many caste associations created strict restrictions and turned those who could not follow these restrictions into a caste inferior to them in the pecking order.

Among the Ambalakkarar caste is a branch that is known as 'Aruthukkattura Ambalakkara jathi', the caste that allows the remarriage of women. One does not know at what point of time and for what reason this caste was formed. In the Ambalakkarar caste that allows remarriage, a woman who does not like to live with a husband she dislikes, can cut or snap the sacred thread of marriage around her neck on her own, and marry any other man from within her community. A woman whose sacred thread has been cut after her husband's death could also remarry. This community accepts such customs. Widow remarriage and women who dislike their husbands getting a divorce and remarrying may seem revolutionary to dominant castes. But women who belong to the Ambalakkarar caste, which allows both the snapping of the sacred marital thread and remarriage, continue to practise this custom as an assertion of their traditional rights.

Today, the influential castes that want to retain their power and influence by turning the castes that continue to assert their traditional rights into inferior castes, have murdered innumerable people in their own community. The Muthurasa community today is split into the Ambalakkarar and the Ambalakkarar who remarry. There is no inter-marriage between the two groups. In the reservation for caste, Muthurasa is a backward class and Ambalakkarar is a most backward class. Those who fought for being registered as Ambalakkarar today register themselves as Ambalakkarar due to reservations. Even though in the caste certificate they are registered as Ambalakkarar, in wedding alliances they are particular about the sub-groups. Had they been born in the Ambalakkarar caste that allows remarriage, Muthusamy and Pachaiammal need not have suffered so much. Murugan need not have died and Nirmala need not have had to live as an aged spinster. There would have been no excommunication. They would have had all the rights and the family could have lived like everyone else. Where caste cultural habits are concerned, upward mobility means freedom being snatched away. Downward mobility is what is needed. That is life with freedom.

*****

Like Eating Faeces

A. Chinnadurai

Journeys by bus are not as comfortable as journeys by train. Every time one travels in a crowded bus, one feels like the cattle being taken to Kerala for slaughter; for one gets wounded in so many different ways that one's heart is filled with hurtful bruises. If you happen to lean on someone by mistake the person would snarl at you. Each one sits in the bus feeling like a lamb thrown amidst wolves. Even we become wolves at times! Sometimes the bus is not crowded. People known to you would be sitting in different seats all by themselves. When you stand by them as if begging for a seat, they would not oblige and would stretch out their legs in a wide 'V' or fold them in a broad 'W', looking like Hanuman in a new avatar.

It is in order to avoid such embarrassments that I prefer to travel by train when I have to travel for answer-paper correction jobs. One can have leisurely conversations with people one likes or read a book or sleep when one travels by train. Some even prefer to have their breakfasts in the morning train. There are many such comforts in train travel, but what I appreciate the most is that the ear-splitting loudspeakers that are part of a bus journey are absent in a train journey. More than 10 of us would travel together daily to Salem by the Virudhachalam-Salem train, for paper corrections. The rural folk travel mostly by this train. Even students and those who go to work use the train sometimes. Sometimes conversations would happen with total strangers. Some of them would find out that one is related to them and mention it with glee. The topics of conversations would mostly be family quarrels, family influence, personal sorrows and so on.

One particular day, I got the single window seat. An aged person was sitting opposite me. He wore spotless white clothes, had a small kumkum mark on his forehead and was fair in colour and seemed a handsome old man. He might have been a retired government servant. He had a new yellow shopping bag in his hand. There were some notebooks in the bag. They might have even been books. He gave enough indications to me that he wanted to strike up a conversation with me. Normally, during such journeys I prefer not to talk to strangers because it would finally lead to the question on caste or they would make efforts to somehow find out my caste. To my knowledge in such conversations, there has never been a time when the question, 'Which caste do you belong to?' has not been asked. If the other person also belonged to the same caste there would be immense happiness. But if the other person found out that the person he was trying to strike up a conversation with is a Shudra-Dalit, the conversation and the journey would turn as bitter as neem. The old man I met in that journey gave me one such bitter experience.

When the train halted at Ethappur station, I saw a bird fallen on the ground right outside my window. The old man also saw it. It did not look like the bird had been hit or wounded. The old man mumbled to himself: So much pollution everywhere. Gutter water. Plastic garbage. Fertile lands have been turned into empty plots. How can birds live? 'When crows and sparrows that live with nature meet this fate, what will be the story of our life?' he said aloud and looked at me. I told him I was interested in continuing the conversation on these comments of his.

He began to talk about birds and animals. I was thrilled that our conversation revolved around the life of birds, their mating, food gathering and nesting. But that joy did not last long. I somehow slipped into answering his questions which probed into details about me.

'Are you going up to Salem, Thambi?'

'Yes, Thatha.'

'What do you do?'

'I am a teacher.'

'Government or private?'

'Government.'

'What is your salary like?'

This is a question that embarrasses most men. But since there was no way he would take away my salary, I told him, 'Thirty thousand, Thatha.'

'I also have granddaughters, Thambi. They also have done teachers' training and have applied for jobs. My elder granddaughter said she would get a job in a couple of months....I have a granddaughter by my son and two granddaughters by my daughter. I am going to Salem for some work in connection with the granddaughters. Auspicious work, of course. How long can one keep girls at home when they have reached the marriageable age, Thambi?'

When the old man began to speak thus, I was sure he was going to ask about my caste. He seemed to have guessed my thoughts and came to that crucial question. He did not ask directly but was beating about the bush. How I tortured him and how he suffered for having asked that question was really amusing.

Whenever someone has spoken to me either highly or derogatorily about caste, I don't remember taking part in that conversation without using abusive language centred around genitals and fornication. I often regret not having used all the abuses which come so easily to me, but never felt guilty about having used them. A song of Sivavaakkiyar, a Siddhar or a Saivaite saint, says: Are carnal pleasures derived from a Paraya woman different from the pleasures derived from a rich or Brahmin women? And critic P. Velsamy has said that to be dressed in a suit like a gentleman and still observe caste customs, is like eating excrement. I think of these two statements often.

Since the old man wanted to be polite and go about the whole thing in a roundabout way, I answered him gently.

'What are you personally, Thambi?'

'I am a careful person Thatha, otherwise can we manage in this world?'

I knew what the old man wanted to know but he did not understand that I knew. So he asked again:

'Which clan do you normally hobnob with?' (Obviously he belonged to a caste that had different clan groups.)

I began punning on the word 'kulam' meaning clan which is pronounced with a light 'la' sound and used instead the word 'kuLam' pronounced with a stress on the 'la' sound, which meant a pond.

'You mean where we meet? Until we dug a bore well in our house we used to meet around the common pond of the village. Now these ponds have become gutters. So we don't meet there anymore, Thatha.'

He kept quiet for a while and then asked:

'Which is your clan god?'

'The clan god I worship is my paternal grandfather. He left behind some land and two pairs of red-hued bovine cattle for this grandson's education. So he is the clan god I worship.'

Now the old man used his Brahmastra, the most powerful weapon.

'Are you a… Harijan?' He pronounced it as 'Arjin'.

Anyone who is not a Dalit would be startled by such a question. Immediately, they would respond by saying, 'oh, no, no, not that at all' and reveal their caste. If it were a Dalit, they would say yes lackadaisically. Or else they would remain silent. I admired the old man's intelligent ways. But I could not let him off so easily. Here is what I told him:

'I don't like Arjun, Thatha. I like Rajnikanth. I love watching his films.'

'That is not it, Thambi. I was asking about your caste.'

'Oh, that?…'

(Thatha seemed happy I had understood at last).

'We belong to a caste that does not live off others. We belong to the caste that believes in its own labour.'

Now the old man lost his temper.

'Come on, Thambi. You say you are a teacher but you lack prudence. In which caste do people not work hard and remain lying around? In all castes there are thugs and honest people. Are you a Vanniyar, Adi Dravidar, Udayar or Gounder? Tell me that.'

I did not belong to the four castes he had mentioned, but I did not want to enrage him by saying that. Since my caste did fall within one of the castes he had mentioned I answered without running into explanations, 'Adi Dravidar, Thatha.'

'Thambi, are you saying this because I spoke a bit angrily?'

'No Thatha, I am really an Adi Dravidar.'

'Well, you don't look like that.'

'How do you say that?'

'Thambi, I have retired as a primary school teacher in Kadalur District. I have worked only in rural schools. I know how people look. I know how those Adi Dravidar folks look when they come to school. Just tell me the truth.'

When he spoke the last word, I lost all respect for him. In how many young minds would he have sown these poisonous seeds? Finally, I answered him thus:

'Thatha, there was a film called *Ranuva Veeran*. The hero's sister fell in love with a person from an extremist group and had a male child by him. The hero brought that child as a young man to his house. According to the story, the hero belonged to a Brahmin family. The hero's mother asked, "Who is this? Which caste does he belong to? Which gothra?" and then turned to the young man and asked, "Which caste do you belong to?" He immediately remove his trousers and showed her. Even if you open your trousers you can't make out the caste, Thatha. One can know the caste only if the person concerned mentions the caste.'

He looked at me as if bewildered. I wonder what he thought. He may have even thought it was a good thing I did not remove my trousers before him. After that, he did not once look at me. I also got up and went and stood near the exit door. In a couple of minutes the train arrived at the station. I got down and melted into the crowd of that big city.

*****

Born of a Father, Born into a Caste

P. Suresh

Our street is called Kamarajapuram. But in Senthamanagalam, the place I belong to, no one can direct you to this place. They would not know where it is. The entire village knows our street as Ward No. 1. More as just Ward actually. From my father's time, it has been known as Ward No. 1. A few years ago our street, Ward No.1, was divided into sixth and seventh wards in the Panchayat register. But what was in people's minds was still Ward No.1. If I go into details of this, it would mean elaborating on the empty pride of my street, rather my caste. In short, the entire village generally believed that it was the street of those who indulged in atrocities, ever willing to beat up someone or get into fisticuffs and that cobras and Pallar caste fellows were no different. Except for the Parayar in the village, my street was famous for getting into confrontations with all the other castes in the village.

When I was studying in the fifth or sixth class, there was a big clash with the Gounders of the next village. Four or five huts in our area got burnt to a cinder. I thought it was the first time that such a clash had taken place. But from the incidents I got to know about later, I realised how utterly wrong I had been to think that that clash was an isolated incident.

The incidents I got to know about began with a policeman being tied to a pole and skinned by old man Veerabhathran, because he had entered the village without his permission, and extended to many similar incidents. The youngsters in our street had the insolence to claim, 'Oh, we have been like this for a long, long time.' The Chettiyars who owned shops in the market street would panic if people from our street went and stood before any shop. Even if they had many other customers they would take care to ask customers from our street what they wanted and would try to quickly get rid of them. The other castes were also respectful towards us. How can lowered castes be given respect as such? This so-called respect was born of fear and nothing else.

Due to all this, many of us came to know that we belonged to a lowered caste only after seeing the caste certificate. But no one felt like a lowered caste person at heart; especially the young people. Even now some youngsters, who come to know about their lowered status after seeing the caste certificate, would come and ask me innocently, 'Anna, are we SCs?' So where my village is concerned I have no problem in saying that I belong to the Pallar caste. In fact, it protects me in a way. But this can't be so elsewhere, isn't it? I had to go through a lot of mental struggles, especially in educational institutions.

When I was doing my B.Ed, the teacher entered the class and announced, 'All SC students please come forward. The scholarship amount has arrived.' There were some hundred students in our class and about twenty to thirty of us rose. The others who were not SC, especially the girls, looked at us as if to say, 'So, you are SC, is it?' I felt humiliated and it was as if I was a criminal being arrested by the police. I felt crushed. I could make out from their expressions that the others with me also felt the same. That teacher could have said that those who have applied for scholarships must come forward. His mentioning the words SC hurt us a lot. Imparting education is one thing but educational institutions should first learn to approach students more gently.

When I was doing my postgraduate studies in Aathoor, Vijayalakshmi, a senior student, had chosen Chitheri Malai in Dharmapuri District as her field of study for her dissertation. She asked me to accompany her. My fellow student Kannan and I went with her. Through an acquaintance she had arranged our stay in a person's house there. After a long bus journey we reached there around five in the evening. This person was cutting firewood when we reached his house and we introduced ourselves. He sat down and began a relaxed conversation with us. He said he was a Siddha medicine practitioner and that he was of the Gounder caste which is also known as Malaiyala Gounder and that he had been once in charge of the village. He enquired about us, our villages, and our education. He detailed the various things he had done when he was in charge of the village for the benefit of the village. He was also a bit upset that after all that he had done, the village ignored him these days.

He spoke about many things but finally came to the question of caste. 'Nowadays all the benefits are for them. What is there for us?' he said and then stopped short. He looked at us. He said, 'Well, I hope no one is SC here.' We pretended that we had not heard his question and kept looking at his face blandly. He came to some conclusion on his own and said, 'I want to know because, see how many benefits the government has given them.' Since he spoke about SCs in the third person we could make out that he had concluded that none of us was SC.

During the bus journey Vijayalakshmi had told us that we would not be allowed inside anyone's house if our caste was known. We gathered information from the villagers till 11 in the night and then went to his house. Our friend went inside the house and she and the gentleman's wife slept in one room. We slept in the corridor outside. In the morning we were standing near the entrance and brushing our teeth. Our host came close to us and asked the girl, 'Which caste do you belong to?' We thought there was no end to this and that the old man was never going to give up but just then the girl said in a low voice, 'Parayar' and we were taken aback. His face became small. 'But when I asked yesterday, why did you not say anything?' he asked. The girl did not reply and kept brushing her teeth. I thought I would tell him who I was if he asked me directly. Kannan told him without being asked: I belong to the Thottiya Nayakkar caste. 'Oh, if you are Thottiya Nayakkar, do you practise black magic and so on?' the gentleman began to probe. Kannan kept repeating firmly that he did not practise any black magic, but that he did belong to that caste.

Kannan did this all the time. Although he belonged to the Sakkiliyar (Cobbler) caste, when asked anywhere he would insist he was a Thottiya Nayakkar. In Aathoor, where we lived, the house owner was a Thottiya Nayakkar. The old man and his wife lived on the ground floor and we lived on the first floor. Kannan became very close to them. Whatever snacks or vegetables were cooked there would be shared with Kannan. He too helped them. Helped in the sense that he would patiently listen to their non-stop chatter. What other help would one need in old age? If we needed anything from the house owners we would send Kannan to them for he was in their good books. They would never say no to him. He had become their pet child.

When I asked Kannan about this once he casually replied: 'We are all one. In the past both the castes were together. They separated later.' But I found out the distance between both the castes when I went with him to Manjanayakkanur village which is off Bommaikuttaimettu, for a function in the family of one of his relatives. One early morning I invited him to the tea shop opposite his relative's house. He was not enthusiastic and indicated with his eyes that we should not go there. I insisted and asked him why we could not go there. 'But I am telling you we should not', he said adamantly. I thought maybe the tea there was not good and he was refusing because of that. 'Look I must have tea in the morning. Even if it is like hot water I must have a gulp of tea in the morning. Come, let us go,' I insisted. 'You keep insisting even when I say no. Come, let us go,' he said and came along with me. He whispered in my ear as we walked, 'Anna, they are Thottiya Nayakkars. They will give us tea in a different glass. Don't mind it.' I was shocked. I wondered if such things happened even these days as I neared the shop. There was a 40-year-old lady in the shop and a little boy. Kannan said he did not want tea and stood outside. I asked the woman for a cup of tea and came and stood next to Kannan. I saw a small boy approaching the shop. At a distance of about 10 feet he took off his slippers and came barefoot inside the shop. He gave the money without touching the woman and took whatever he wanted to buy.

I sat on the wooden bench outside the shop and Kannan stood by me. Three persons stood in front of us drinking from steel glasses. The woman came out with tea in a plastic tumbler, gave it to me and went back in. I lifted the tumbler and saw that it was a crushed one which had fold marks all over. I kept a serious face and asked her, 'Why is the tumbler like this?' 'So, how is it?' she retorted. 'What do you mean? Will a new cup be like this?' I asked angrily. Kannan was literally shivering. He held my left hand and kept begging, 'Anna, be quiet, please be quiet.' I lost my temper. I pushed his hand away and shouted, 'What do you mean, be quiet? I am going to slap you now, why are you silent?' Now the woman changed her tone. 'No, Sir, the child was playing with it. That is why it looks crushed,' she said apologetically. But she must have known that I was not satisfied with that reply. She turned to her child and slapped him twice saying, 'This wretched child is so naughty.'

When I passed the exams to qualify as a teacher, I had chosen a school in the Dharmapuri district. I went there with the government order to join the school along with my younger brother who came to give me company. There was another person from the next village who had also qualified and his father also accompanied us and that made four of us. The other person's father had gone there a day before to arrange a place for us to stay and had come back to accompany us. While we were waiting at the Dharmapuri bus depot for a bus to that village, the other person's father asked me, 'What is your caste?' I was furious but I said, 'I am a Pallan.' 'SC, is it?' he asked. 'Yes', I said. 'You see the house owner asked me about it. He told me, "We are Vanniyars. What are you?" I said, "We are Udayars." "You said one more person is coming. What caste is he?" he asked. "He is also one of us," I told him. If he asks you, please tell him the same thing. Don't tell him you are SC,' he said. That was the time when the problem of Ilavarasan and Divya, the couple from Nayakkan Kottai, was a burning issue. (Ilavarasan was a Dalit and Divya was from the Vanniyar caste. They got married but it led to a series of disasters with her father committing suicide, Divya being taken away and Ilavarasan himself being found dead near the railway tracks; it was alleged to be a suicide but murder was suspected.) All kinds of thoughts came to my mind. I looked at my younger brother. He looked even more perturbed. I did not know what to say. I did not speak. He took my long silence as my consent to his idea.

Every morning we used to go for tea to a nearby tea shop. It was a small tea shop. No youngsters of my age came there. Mostly, I found old people and middle-aged people in that tea shop. As soon as they would see me they would give me a place to sit and also offer me a newspaper. All this because I was a school teacher. One day after drinking tea I was reading the newspaper. An old gentleman sitting opposite began a conversation with me. 'Which place are you from?' he asked.

'I am from Namakkal,' I said

'Where in Namakkal?' he asked.

'Senthamangalam, which is 10 kilometres away from Namakkal,' I said.

'Do you have land in the village?' he asked.

I knew that was the first attempt to know my caste. Namakkal was mostly populated by Gounders. And if you have land you would definitely be a Gounder.

'We had some land but have sold it now,' I said evasively.

This must have disappointed him. So instead of the usual ways of finding out someone's caste he began to use his own tricks. 'There is a teacher who comes to our village school. He is a Nadar, it seems,' he said generally to those sitting around. I understood that he was talking about my friend who had come from Virudhunagar. He assumed that after this I would mention my own caste. But I did not speak and remained silent. He understood that indirect conversation would not work and asked me, 'Are you a Velala Gounder?' I shook my head indicating that I was not. He raised a sound like 'Oh' which was an indication for me to come out with my caste. All eyes were on me eagerly waiting for a reply. I felt totally unarmed before them. There was silence for a while. Finally, the tea shop-owner broke the silence saying, 'Velala Gounder or Kulala Gounder, one thing or the other, let it be.'

Had they asked me directly what exactly my caste was I was ready to say with no hesitation that I was a Pallan. I was not bothered about how faces would change and how the way people looked at me would change. I feel that hiding my caste and identifying myself as someone from a different caste is as disgusting as pointing out to a stranger and saying he was my father. Not only that. If in this age of science, someone is shameless enough to ask me what my caste is, I would feel no shame to mention the caste I was born into.

******

Upper Caste Goddess

C. Sureshkumar

I am a wild mushroom that came out of the black soil of the Karisal area. The place from whose soil I pushed myself out was a small village called Siluvampatti. There are some 250 houses in this village. Reddiar Theru and Vellar Theru are two streets in which just three castes live. On the eastern side of the village is the Reddiar Street near which live some 100 Gounder families and some 30 Sakkiliyar (Cobbler) families. On the western side in the Vellar Street live another 100 Gounder families and 30 Boyar families. The Boyars are a subcaste among the Scheduled Castes. The Boyars were, to an extent, respected by the Gounders and were like their right-hand people. But the Sakkiliyars were oppressed. During the times of my grandparents, when Arunthathiyars, who were working in the Gounder farms, had to cross their streets, they had to remove their slippers and hold them under their arms. Even if they went in a cycle they had to get down and push the cycle till they crossed the street. Such restrictions have now eased out due to modernisation.

I did my primary school education in my village itself. The three teachers were Gounders. They made the Gounder students sit in a row and the Arunthathiyars had to sit in a separate row. Our class teacher was a Gounder from our village. So, after lunch, all the Arunthathiyar students had to go and graze their cows and pick up cow dung from the cow shed in their house.

It was by cleaning the cowsheds that we acquired education part-time. I was a good student when I was in the fifth standard. Karthi, who was the son of a Gounder, used to stand first. I used to study hard to get more marks than him. In the half-yearly exams I stood first. The teacher from Ernapuram remarked, 'The Sakkili dog stands first whereas the Gounder dog is fit only to eat' while handing out the report card. Someone who could not tolerate the remark wrote it in the attendance register and got me into trouble. I was beaten and abused and they were planning to expel me from the school with a TC. The wife of the schoolteacher from our village was the headmistress then. She reasoned that if I am thrown out of school there would be one person less for picking up cow dung, and so she allowed me to continue in the school. I studied well and stood first in the fifth standard. The Ernapuram teacher got really jealous. He called Karthi and told him, 'Dey, this Sakkili dog has stood first. You go pick cow dung instead of him.' He scolded him in front of me and gave us both a TC to continue our middle school education elsewhere.

After two or three years, there was a dawn of hope for our hut mired in the slush of Karisal. Half a kilometre away was the road from Namakkal to Thiruchengodu. Behind the S. M. R. Mills there, government quarters were built for us. Only Arunthathiyars lived there. This put an end to discrimination on the basis of caste. To a certain extent we could put some distance between us and the Gounders, and seek jobs elsewhere.

There was a custom that every year we could celebrate the festival for our goddess Mariamman only after the Gounder festival for their goddess Onkaliamman. When the festival for their goddess took place there was a custom which required the Sakkiliyars to go and cut the wood to provide wood for the pit of live coals, euphemistically called the flower pit, for the ritual fire-walking, done to fulfil a vow. Those who did not go to cut the wood were severely punished. When the temple chariot went in procession, the Arunthathiyars had to stand separately in a queue and offer puja. Onkaliamman who accepted the wood cut by us by shedding our sweat, for the 'flower pit' to accept vows made by others, made us stand on the other side of the pit to offer our worship. It was only after the celebrations of the goddess of these ignoramuses were complete that the festival of our goddess Mariamman would take place. This went on for two years.

The district collector's office was not far from our living quarters and we were called for construction work for the collector's office. Poverty forced everyone to take up this construction work. This came in the way of doing the farm work for the Gounders. We were beaten for not going to do the farm work. We lodged a police complaint about being beaten. After that the Gounders became a little scared of us. When I and friends like me became young men, we became brave enough to counter the Gounders in certain ways. Our street had also expanded to include some 80 houses. So caste fights became a regular feature, and they would ask for a Panchayat meeting for these quarrels. We refused to be bound by the Panchayat. My father and others began to support us and opposed them. After these spats they invited us to cut wood for the Onkaliamman festival the same year. None of us came forward. They cut the wood themselves and celebrated the festival.

This event split the Gounders into two. One group argued that without the Sakkiliyars their work wouldn't get done and that they need Sakkiliyars to survive; and another group took the stand that low-caste Sakkliyars cannot be this arrogant, and that they should not be allowed within the village. The village literally split into two. Due to this we got treated with a little bit of respect. That year we celebrated our Mariamman festival a month before the Onkaliamman festival. The Gounders did not protest. One or two Gounders passed away that year and they began to say that Onkaliamman was punishing them and the battle began once again. The elders of our caste accepted that this was Onkaliamman's punishment and surrendered to the Gounders. I began to wonder if this was going to be our destiny.

The very next year they renovated the Onkaliamman temple and decided to perform the consecration ceremony. Since the police quarters and the government offices were in our village the temple became a government temple. The government officer announced that anyone could go in and offer worship. The Gounders accepted this and came to our street and appealed to us saying now that the temple had become a government temple, Gounders and Sakkiliyars could be together and that for the sake of Aatha, the goddess, we should come and cut the wood during the festival. Our caste elders accepted this and decided that there was no harm in cutting wood for Aatha, and one person from each house went to cut the wood. The consecration ceremony went off well. However, people of our caste did not make an attempt to go inside the temple. They stood outside and offered their prayers.

Then there was the 48-day cycle puja. Groups of two or three Gounders got together every day to do *annadanam*, free distribution of food. Since they came to each of our houses and invited us a day before the puja, all of us attended it. Young people from our street got together and decided that since we were eating every day at the temple and since it was a government temple, we should also offer puja one day and offer food to everyone. We collected ₹600 from each family and gave ₹30,000 to the temple trustee. The elders told him to do the puja on our behalf and also arrange for the free distribution of food. The temple trustee accepted the money and told us that the 35th day puja would be ours. We were thrilled.

The very next day the temple trustee came to us with a few others and a primary schoolteacher of our village and returned the money to us. When we asked them for the reason, they said that the goddess had possessed a girl and converyed through her that she would not accept the puja of Sakkiliyars. The Sakkiliyars got really wild and said, 'Your goddess can accept the wood we cut and accept it when we clean the temple but it would say no to our puja, is it?' The teacher lost his temper and used abusive language, saying, 'Must the Gounders eat food cooked by Sakilliyars? Don't you know your status?' We decided we did not want Aatha who takes such decisions and took the money back and decided not to attend the puja anymore.

But our decision could not really be implemented as some people in our caste needed certain favours from the Gounders. So they began to attend the puja like a herd of goats. I also went on the day a Gounder I liked offered puja. We were, as usual, standing in a separate queue for food. The same teacher came to us and said, 'If all of you were Gaunders and we were Sakkiliyars, would you eat the food we have cooked? If you want to do something make a piece of jewellery for the goddess. Don't you have a conscience?' We thought it was strange that someone who had a warped mind was talking to us about conscience.

The youngsters of our street really want the people of our caste to enter that temple and, not only that, they should be able to go in and offer puja. I yearn for it to happen at least in my son's time.

****

Non-Existent

M. Senthamarai

During school days I did not know much about caste. My mother would get up in the morning and finish her household work and send me to school with the advice: 'Don't roam around with all and sundry. Sit with our people. Make them your friends. Don't mix with others.' I used to nod my head in agreement to whatever she said and leave for school. But I used to beat up someone or the other in school every day. That girl's father would come and complain to my father. My father would come home and scold me, 'Why do you beat others? You invite trouble unnecessarily.' I would not respond and would remain quiet with tears flowing. 'And now, all this drama and tears,' he would grumble.

When I was in fifth standard, there were only six girls in my class. All of us used to sit and eat together at lunch time. I always took curd rice with me for lunch. The others brought whatever was made in their homes. We used to share one another's food. One day I gave mine to a girl of another caste and ate hers.

At home my parents would normally ask me what lessons were taught at school and my father would ask me to show him my notebooks. He would then proceed to teach me. Whenever I lost interest I would make excuses, saying that my neck ached and that I was not able to sit long and study. Or I would say I was hungry. I always had some excuse handy and then I would go off to play. But I had the habit of telling them all about what happened in school every day. So on the day that I ate the other girl's food I told them that I had exchanged food with Valarmathi and eaten what she had brought.

'What! Valarmathi's food? She is a low caste girl. Why did you eat her food? Instead of eating what I gave you, why did you eat hers?' my mother said and hit me with a stick. I wondered why she was beating me for eating Valarmathi's food, considering she had never beaten me when I had told her on other occasions about eating food brought by other girls. Since I was small I could not understand anything. That day I decided not to tell them any more whose food I had eaten. Whenever they insisted on knowing I would tell them I had eaten the curd rice.

A lady from our neighbourhood, who worked in our school as a cook, prepared the mid-day meal. My mother had told her to keep an eye on me because I had the habit of eating food brought by others. The lady was of our caste. She caught me red-handed one day. She told me I could not eat food brought by others; I could share my food with them but not eat theirs. So, she also became my enemy. I looked at her defiantly, thinking how it mattered to her whose food I ate. 'Why are you giving me that defiant look? I will report to your parents,' she said and promptly came and told my parents.

That night my parents harangued me saying, 'What kind of a child are you? A good person needs only one scolding and a cow needs only one branding.' I was furious with the mid-day meal lady. I stopped talking to her from that day onwards.

Next day my father came with me to the school and told my teacher, 'Take care of this girl. She is disobedient. She is so small but still she has a temper. Give her a bit of advice.' My teacher Saroja Devi was also of my caste. She also advised me like my mother and father and the mid-day meal lady. I thought if I was with girls of our caste no one would scold me, so I decided not to mix with lower caste girls. But there was a great conflict in my mind. Girls of my caste came to school but girls of other caste also came to school. It was difficult to find out who belonged to my caste and who didn't.

I thought, instead of discriminating between my caste and another, it was best not to talk to anyone at all. Then there would be no problem. From that day onwards I stopped talking properly with my friends. When they asked, 'What is the matter? How come you are not talking like before?' I made excuses saying I had a cold or that I was unwell. I withdrew from their group. I did not speak to anyone and remained aloof and quiet. The mid-day meal lady came to my house one day and told my parents, 'Nowadays one can't make out where your daughter is in school.' My parents were ever so happy to hear that.

*****

Dealing with Inability

V. Dharmalingam

In the 30 years that I have known the word 'caste' it has not been of any great advantage to my family, my relatives or, for that matter, my friendships. But there certainly have been some losses due to caste. It has ruined some of my personal desires. It has brought some false moments of joy but, to a very large extent, has also earned me a bad name and created situations where I have lost friends. One could say these losses were not due to caste, per se, but because at one time, I held my caste identity high in my hands, like a banner. At the same time, I realise that caste has given me some advantages, to a certain extent, where education and employment are concerned.

My caste experiences have been at two levels. The first was my immediate family, my relatives and my general life. The second was at the level of education and my employment experiences. Where the former was concerned, when I first got to know my village, it was only as a village of our Vanniyar caste. What I mean is, whichever street I went to, up to a certain distance, our relatives were spread in all directions.

I began primary school education around 1983 or 1984. I remember that my elder sister, elder brother and I went to the same school. Due to the oversight of a relative or may be of a teacher, my brother's caste was registered wrongly. My sister came to know about it and she promptly told everyone at home and he was endlessly teased.

In the school, one knew the teachers only by their caste and the village they came from. The primary school near our house had only two teachers. The third person in the school was a mid-day meal official. He was also called a teacher, because whenever one of the teachers did not turn up he would take their class. But he was called the mid-day meal teacher. Among the three teachers, the headmaster belonged to a lowered caste. The one next to him in hierarchy, who worked in the school for a while, belonged to a so-called upper caste. The teacher who replaced him after he left, belonged to our caste. Similarly, initially, the mid-day meal teacher belonged to the Nayakkar caste and later the other mid-day meal teacher who came, belonged to our caste. The three teachers were referred to as Periya Vadhiyar (senior teacher), Chinna Vadhiyar (junior teacher) and Sathunavu Vadhiyar (mid-day meal teacher). The headmaster was very strict about instilling discipline in us. So, he was often referred to insultingly by the students. Generally, everyone in our village was identified by caste. Our Periya Vadhiyar was from the Pallar caste. So he was always referred to as a Pallan. If the headmaster asked the students to get a rupee each, those at home would grumble, 'Why is the Pallan asking for a rupee?' Even when they wanted to threaten us about something they would say, 'We will come and talk to that Pallan to straighten you out.' They did not use respectful suffixes to address him.

Unlike these days, we had to go to school at 8:30 in the morning to clean the school premises. The woman who came to cook the mid-day meal, normally swept the corridors and did the major cleaning. We used to pick up pieces of garbage, fallen leaves and broken stems from under the tree. We used to gather them and hold them like a broom and play. Sometimes when we heard the voice of the headmaster calling out to us we used to say, 'Pallan is scolding us.' Often, when we complained at home about a beating we got, we used to say, 'It was that Pallan who beat us up.' We, also, did not use a respectful suffix when we referred to him. Our parents also would respond saying, 'We will come to Kaattukottai and pull up that Pallan.' They had to go to that area to supply milk every day. They may not have really pulled him up but they used to console us by saying so. If the junior teacher of our caste or the mid-day meal teacher beat us to punish us, we never came home and complained. Even if we did they would say, 'Well, you must have done something wrong.'

When we were in middle school, we used to call a teacher who came from the village Sarvay as Sarvay teacher. Sarvay was like a mother village to our village. Our village was called Sarvay Pudur. The area we stayed in was called Samberi. For all administrative facilities like revenue and information and communication, it was Sarvay village that was the centre. And ever since I have known, the teacher's family was the only Iyer Brahmin family in our area. We depended on that family for all auspicious and inauspicious rituals. Naming all the children born (except for the first child) according to their birth star, setting an auspicious date for the nuptials and conducting funeral rites, everything was done by that one family. So everyone knew that family. It was the daughter-in-law of that family who had come as a teacher to our school. Nobody could question her about anything. She terrorised students while teaching them math. Many dropped out of school midway unable to bear her beatings. All those who studied in our school during 1985–86, both girls and boys, got a taste of her beatings and stopped going to school. No father would dare ask her why she had beaten his child because there was the general impression that if the Iyer teacher from Sarvay beat the children, it must be for their own good. Finally, when she got transferred to her own village, Gopal, a teacher from Aathoor, came to our school. He was also a Brahmin. Which meant again that nobody could tease him or stop him from beating the students.

If I understand now how brutally communities in my society deal with their inabilities, it is because my high school experiences provided the ground for this understanding. I did my high school studies in the Government High School near my house, in the Vadachennimalai area. Many teachers in that school belonged to the Gounder caste. There was one Brahmin teacher and five or six others were of other castes but definitely non-Dalit castes. As far as we knew, there was only one Dalit teacher who was a drawing teacher. His name was Kaliyamurthi.

The people of our village were capable of identifying the caste of a person just by his looks. But Kaliyamurthi Sir had a towering personality that could shatter all such notions. We, who did not even know our English alphabets, were the heroes of our school. There were eight of us from our area who went to the same school and were in the same class. But when we went to High School, from heroes we became zeroes. We were forced to learn English. When we could not even say the alphabets, how could we recite poems? We just could not learn, whatever efforts we put in, and the amount of humiliation we went through for this cannot ever be recounted. We were humiliated in the name of our village school and the middle school we went to. We had completed our quarterly exams and had failed in all the subjects. All our parents were called to the school. The parents of all eight students from our village normally came together to school. When our parents came, the teacher in charge was on leave. So we were forced to meet the drawing teacher. He saw our progress reports and asked our parents about their profession and income and chastised us before our parents. Our parents liked him very much. But we got furious with him. 'That Sakkili (Cobbler) is insulting us before all of you. And you approve of that. And we have to be witnesses to that. We don't want to go to school,' we said and refused to go to school.

The drawing teacher came to our class the next day and started by being very good to us. He asked us what our problems were and he taught us how to study. He made an indelible impression on our minds and he is the one teacher I cannot forget to this day. If I recall how he became somebody we admired, what I remember is how he explained to us how the dominant caste teachers in our village were partial to students of their own caste and how they coached them in the name of tuitions to answer questions that would appear in the exams. He gently explained to us where we stood in this kind of situation and taught us how to study to overcome it. He went beyond caste constraints to help us. To this day, my angrily referring to him as 'that Sakkili' when I spoke to my parents, has remained as a festering wound in my mind. Today, when I am strict with some of my students, I wonder if they would also refer to me in this manner. And again, that abusive word I used would bother me and my face would become small. No one's death has affected me as deeply as the news of his death in 2003, when I heard that he had passed away after a heart attack. He is the only educator who would always occupy a special place in my heart. Those who could not teach students shunned him because of his caste. Not to talk of students like us who were not capable of studying and who also insulted him. I am not excluding myself. He was not even given a chair in the staff room meant for teachers. He used to sit in the room meant for the office assistant and the clerk. Maybe he decided to stay away from the so called upper caste teachers even before they kept him away.

Another incident that happened while I was in High School confirmed that the Brahmin caste was much too dominant. In the primary school, and middle school as I have said before, we were used to referring to teachers as senior teacher, junior teacher or class teacher. An Iyer was our class teacher when I was in the ninth. Although other teachers were referred to by their names the Iyer teacher was always referred to as Iyaru by the entire school. Maybe because he belonged to what was considered a higher caste, his caste name was mentioned instead of his name. No one questioned him, even when he beat the students. Even the other teachers were a bit scared of him. It may be because he was efficient or because like those in our village who were dependent on that caste, the school also believed that an Iyer cannot go wrong. My urban education experiences were not like those of the village where caste was a dominant factor. When I studied in the Aathoor area I could know the caste of those from our village who came to study there but the caste of others was not so obvious. At the same time, there was also a group that did not hesitate to refer to the caste of a person when it wanted to find faults with a person or did not like the person.

While this was going on on one side with regard to education, my own family and relatives had bound me with the chains of caste. In the beginning of the eighties, I had no idea of the names of other castes and did not know who belonged to which caste. This was because I saw only people of my own caste all around me. An entire street in our village was that of our agnates. In the very next street lived those who had a relationship of customary claims with us. In the secluded areas, especially on the eastern side, lived the Dalits. The very end of our street was the beginning of theirs. They did not need to come to our streets. They had other routes to connect to the cities. In case they had to pass through our streets, they could not ride a cycle, smoke a bidi or fold up their dhotis. They could come to the general stores but had to form a separate queue. Ever since I have known, the Dalit living quarters in our village was not called a cheri or slum but was referred to by their caste as Pallar Street. There was no Dalit uprising, like those we read about in modern Tamil literature, in our village. Maybe because they were not Parayars. The Parayars stayed in the other village which was the main mother village. I could see them as visitors coming for marriages and deaths, for rice-winnowing work during harvest seasons and also as announcers of death.

There were no Parayars in our village who would fall into the present categorisation where Pallars, Parayars and Sakkiliyars are identified as Dalits. There were only Pallars. There were a few Arunthathiyar households. We did not have any close contacts with them. When I say 'we', I am referring to the Vanniyars of our village. The Gounders maintained contact with us but also functioned independently. They did not have any direct contact with our village though. They did not have houses in any of our streets nor did they own lands in our village. I could say for sure that 99 per cent of the lands were not owned by them. Like the rivers and mountains that act as boundary lines between districts and states, there were streams and roads that separated the Gounders and us. In fact, we came to know about castes only through some proverbs. The Gounders who came from the west were known as Kongars. A person from the west who was a Gounder would simply be referred to as a Kongan. The relationship with a Kongan would hurt like a bamboo splinter getting into the eyes; help given to a Pallan or Parayan is as wasteful as the decoration done to a funeral bier; being close to a dog, or a nai, would be harmful to the sari and being close to a Nayakkan would harm the job being done—these were the proverbs that introduced me to castes and their attributes.

In 1985, the only two other persons I knew from another caste were Valli Pallathi and Pazhaniyammal Pallathi. Both of them used to come to our farm to do the sowing work. We had very little land and worked on it ourselves. But for paddy sowing work it was always Pallar women who were called. I remember that they were paid a little extra for coming and doing the ululation and singing before starting the sowing work. It was the same situation until five or six years ago, because until then it was my father who took care of the entire agricultural work.

The other person of the Dalit caste I came to know was Kandhan. He was from the Sakkiliyar caste. He used to do farming work for the Gounders on a regular contractual basis. He was a good storyteller and our relationship with him was restricted to just that. He lived in a hut in the farm of the family for whom he worked. If we ever went to that side we would only get beaten by our family. I don't really know how our village and the Pallars had come to have a working relationship. I also don't know the reasons why there were no Parayars or Sakkiliyars in our village. It is possible that since the mother village had all the castes, people of our caste may have come out here as a group. Just as the Sakkiliyars were associated with the Gounders in farming, it is possible that the Pallars were associated with our caste.

The first page of our school textbook said that practising untouchability was a sin; it was a major crime; it was an inhuman act. But I was punished severely for not practising it. I was punished not by my parents but a relative of ours. As a small boy, I pulled, in jest, the cloth tied around the head of a Pallar caste woman. I knew only the Indian national flag and the yellow flag with a fire pot that belonged to the Vanniyar Association. The Vanniyars consider themselves as those born of fire, hence the fire pot in their flag. The big handkerchief tied around her head fascinated me as it looked like the American national flag. In primary school, our teacher had shown us the flags of many nations and the American one had attracted me the most. The one the Pallar woman had tied around the head looked similar to that. I took it from her head to look at it. My Periamma, elder aunt, viciously attacked me for that. I was only 10 years old then.

After that, I was only on speaking terms with Pallars. There was no opportunity to have physical contact of any kind which meant not touching anything they used, nor even accidentally touching them. Ever since I could understand things, our relationship with the Gounders, who were higher than us in the caste hierarchy and for whom we worked, was somewhat similar. We were not untouchables in the sense that we could touch what they touched and vice-versa, but we could not go inside their houses. But I see that things have changed now. The relationship between our caste and the Dalits has also undergone changes.

My days in college was when I began to harbour the same notions of caste that had shattered whatever I considered was joyful and the dreams I had cherished for many years. In 1996, when I joined college, my mother may have thought that girls would chase me as if I was some Manmadan, the god of love or something. The first thing she told me was, 'The dog who is going to college must stick to studies. There will be people of many castes there. If you come with some Pallathi or Parachi, you will not get a pie of the property; beware.' If I had in those college days the arrogance that I have today because I am earning, my life would have taken a totally different direction. I am not sure if my dreams and desires got charred because of my need for property, or if the fear of my mother killed my first love, although it was one-sided. I am unable to fully analyse it.

I have mentioned earlier what my mother's words were when I joined college. So whenever I came across a girl, my mother's words would also come to my mind. If I was attracted to a girl, especially in the Tamil Department, I would try to find out her caste. We had a very informal relationship with our teachers and so I would check the attendance register to find out the caste of that particular girl. The attendance register would have the details of name, date of birth, native place and caste of each student. If MBC (Most Backward Classes) or SC (Scheduled Caste) was marked against a name, details of specific castes like Vanniyar, Navidhar (Barbers), Vannar (Washermen) and Ottar would also be given. Perumal Murugan caught me checking the Attendance Register once and asked me without mincing words, 'What is it that you are checking? Are you trying to find out if girls of your caste are there? Is that part of their body different? Is it made of gold?' Such a direct attack affected me and I felt quite ashamed. During the student elections, I approached Perumal Murugan and told him that there should be a student representative from my caste. He berated me and made derogatory comments about my behaviour and totally ignored me. I cannot forget how ashamed I was made to feel for my caste prejudices, and my professor Perumal Murugan's words, although they were spoken as if in jest, still bother me and I bow my head in shame.

In the college, most of our teachers were intellectuals who looked beyond caste. Mostly, no one was asked about caste. A Brahmin teacher used to invite us home, share food with us and give us books to read, although he had rented the house from a Brahmin house owner from the village, to whose house if we ever went, we would be made to stand outside. Another person from the Gounder caste also behaved like the Brahmin teacher, without any prejudices. I enjoyed tasting Ven Pongal, wheat dosai, ragi dosai and rice with cooked lentils only in their homes, because they lived close to the college. I have even gone to theatres to see films with them. However, there were other teachers who gave more importance to caste. When we were evolving as persons with the other teachers, they got so jealous that they even sent anonymous letters to spoil the situation for us. These were also teachers who were not good at teaching their subjects. So, they don't deserve to be a part of our memories.

An experience I had when I stayed in a city for my education proved to me that good educators don't bother about caste. I did my postgraduation in a Brahmin college. Most of the teachers were Brahmins. The students were quite scared of them. It is possible that some non-Brahmin teachers may have said something against them to draw the students towards them. When we showed interest in studies they showered us with books. Ours was a department where only a few students showed interest in going to the departmental library and borrowing books. These teachers were very happy when we regularly borrowed books and returned them after reading them. The teachers would, normally never allow students to ride pillion with them. But now they were willing to even lend their bikes to us. They invited us home. Caste lost its capacity to harm in the face of genuine talent and intelligence. Those teachers who gave importance to caste had to stand aside with nothing to speak for them.

My experience when I began to work was similar. When I began to work in 2002, all that camaraderie based on caste slowly got erased and caste notions ended only in a slush of experiences. When I look back today and realise that those who showed me the road to progress were all those who rose above caste, I do feel a bit awkward about the kind of positions I myself have taken.

Even two years ago, when anyone mentioned caste, I always argued that caste was necessary. That was because it was caste that made education possible. I was the son of totally illiterate parents and the first-generation male of the family to attend school. In the open competition I could not have made it in the general 31 per cent reservation category. It was only in the 20 per cent reservation category for my caste that I could find a seat to do my graduation, postgraduation and MPhil. If there was no caste-based reservation, I might not have studied at all, because I could not have been able to afford education in private colleges. Likewise, after I completed my education, I struggled to get a government job, and then worked very hard to get through in the general reservation category. But in the department that I had chosen during counselling that was given to students, I could get a place only in the caste reservation category. So, although I think that caste is not all that bad, I am also able to understand that it was my low marks that pushed me to go for caste-based reservation. When I consider this aspect, I can see that caste is an intoxicating alcohol that fills the cup of inability or not being capable.

I feel that those who were of the service caste and served a higher caste person, were looked down upon. I have known the Gounders of our village scolding their sons in exasperation saying, 'Dey, you Sakkili dog.' I have heard my relatives admonishing saying, '*Poda*, go away, you Palla.' In the nineties, I had to go with my relatives to work in the fields. I used to do the work as if it was a game I was playing. I noticed that when someone was humiliated or scolded or when some relatives were abused or when they pretended to shun someone, they used abusive words based on lowered castes. For instance, I had a cousin; he was my uncle's son. He was not good at studies. He had failed in the ninth standard four times and only then gone to the tenth. Whenever he teased us he would say, 'There comes the Government Iyer.' For a long time, I did not understand what this meant. Then I understood that it was a reference to the lowered castes. It was only later when we discussed it that I understood the real meaning had to do with the lowered castes, as I had suspected. Around 1998 when I went to college, I saw my teachers reading a book entitled *Government Brahmanan* (by Kannada writer Aravinda Malagatti translated by Pavannan). I also read the book. There was a general image of the Brahmins as the most privileged of castes. There was also a general feeling among people that Dalits got a big chunk of the reservation quota and that once the Dalits were educated the government would allot the majority of the jobs to them. It was seen as a case of the government granting them major privileges. The Dalits were, therefore, compared to Brahmins who were privileged, but with the prefix that they were government Brahmins, which meant they were of the lowered castes. It was an expression used by people who bore a grudge against the lowered castes who were getting government privileges for education.

The reality was, of course, different. It took me some time to realise that 31 per cent was for the general category, 30 per cent was for the backward classes referred to as BCs, 20 per cent was for most backward classes known as MBCs, 18 per cent was for the lowered castes known as Scheduled Castes (SC) and 1 per cent was for tribal communities. One could not say that the Dalits alone got the privileges. So those who could not study addressed anyone who came under reservation as Dalits and Government Brahmins. Actually, by calling us by these names, they were trying to prove that they belonged to the upper castes. It took me a while to figure this out.

It took me a long, long time to understand that caste is something that is full of very deep grudges. But I could not get rid of it easily. I tried many times to be like people whom I considered my gurus and failed miserably. I remember, at one point, I had said of someone: 'That dog would remain that way; that is his caste mentality.' I don't know what to say about my inability to deal with caste.

When I tried my best to go beyond all kinds of notions finally, I was dubbed a person who had caste arrogance and was told I was not really worth anything. I was not even a member of any caste-based association. I always felt that in a government atmosphere it is capability that should bring dignity to a person, and hence I was always cautious and never took any hasty actions. I also wanted to treat everyone as a fellow human being and felt that I myself should be a good human being first. For the last one year I have been carefully and unhurriedly proceeding in my life. And then, I met a person who was five levels above me in seniority in the course of my work. I did not know his caste. Nor do I want to know. But he knew all about me and my background. It was what he said at the end of our conversation that made me delay this essay by 20 days. He told me, 'Thambi, you make a note of everyone who is of our caste in this office. We must form an association. Look at all those Dalits. They are always in a group. We should also be that way.' I feel I am under great pressure and helpless. Will my helplessness take me away from my current position on caste? Only time can tell.

******

Testimony

M. Natarajan

The Thottiya Nayakkars are one of the castes that have migrated from Andhra and settled in different districts of Tamil Nadu. During migration they did not want their group to be scattered and destroyed and for that reason, they created some restrictions so that other castes would not get mingled with theirs. They are economically backward but think that their caste has some unique characteristics and that they are superior to other castes. The other castes also respect them a great deal.

In the villages where they live, people of other castes don't normally come and settle. In many villages Arunthathiyars live close to the houses of Nayakkars. In the times when farming was yielding good results the Arunthathiyars were traditionally associated with the Nayakkars as farmhands. It was considered their right to work in the farms of Nayakkars. They considered farm-work, making basket-like traps with bamboo splints to catch fish falling from a cascading stream, and cobbling footwear as their privileges. During weddings, temple festivals in Nayakkar households or birth and death events, it was always the Arunthathiyars and not the Parayars who would play the drums. When those belonging to the Arunthathiyar caste entered the living area of the Nayakkars they were not supposed to keep the towel on their shoulders or wear slippers. The Arunthathiyars could not ride a cycle but had to push it till they went past the streets where the Nayakkars lived.

The Pallars and Parayars live in Puthoor which is about two miles away from my village. We have absolutely no contact with those castes. Among the lowered castes the Pallars are considered a little superior, so drinking water in their houses was allowed. But the Nayakkars won't eat in their houses. With other castes though, the Nayakkars would have no relationship. Women of the Nayakkar community will not eat food even in the houses of the Gounders whose households form the majority in Namakkal district. Only the men might eat sometimes in Gounder houses. Even in cities Nayakkar women will not go to a restaurant to have a cup of tea or even drink water. During the weekly fairs, they go to the fairs and buy goods and when they return home they sprinkle water on the purchased goods to purify them from caste pollution and only then take them inside the house. Since many mixed castes come to the fair and touching them may be inevitable, after returning from the fairs the women always bathe first and only then enter their houses.

The Nayakkars consider not mixing with other castes the unique quality of their caste. The women and men of this caste are not supposed to enter into a physical relationship with someone of another caste. If anyone enters into a relationship by choice or if someone is raped, that person is excommunicated. They would be considered 'those who have gone astray'. Such a person can openly declare the relationship and leave the village and live somewhere in a city but can no longer keep in touch with the village or the relatives. If the person who has 'gone astray' insists on staying with the family, she or he would be coerced to commit suicide. They would torture, beat and leave no other choice but suicide to the 'wayward' person or they might even forcefully feed pesticide and kill the person.

Even if a person thinks that one's activities could be kept a secret, they would put the fear of god into them saying that during temple festivals the person who gets possessed would reveal their name to the village or that they would go blind. Very often, at some point, out of the fear of being found out through divine intervention, such persons would come out in the open about their deeds and leave the village. A person might think that an entire life could be lived without revealing anything. But when a person is cremated people would go to the cremation ground the next morning to check. In case a dog has shat there the dead person would be seen as someone who has hidden a misdeed. No memorial stone for worship would be erected for such a person. Memorial stone worship is considered a very important ritual of this caste. Every year during Pongal in the month of Thai (January) memorial stone worship takes place. The heirs of the dead person and the relatives offer the worship. The person who had 'gone astray' would not be honoured with such worship.

With such severe restrictions, there were hardly any educated people in this caste. Boys may study up to twelfth and girls may, at the most, study up to eighth. Since there were primary and middle schools in the village, education up to the eighth standard was possible. Nowadays since private colleges send their buses to pick up the students and drop them back, college education has become possible for at least some.

From my area, I am the first one who has broken with this restriction to come and study in Chennai University. I did my graduation in Anna College, which was a boys' college. But in Chennai University the girls and boys sat together and not in different rows. Anyone could sit anywhere. This was new to me. I was told not to talk to girls when I left Namakkal. And I had resolved to follow that advice. So I kept away from my classmates who were girls.

I stayed at the hostel on Beach Road. But after dinner, if I felt like taking a walk on the road lit by lights from the beach, I never went alone. I used to take C. Chandran or Kumar along with me. I was always afraid that if I went alone the girls walking in a group on the beach road may sexually assault me and that I would not be able to go back to the village for I would be excommunicated. The same fear rose whenever I travelled by local trains and transgender women would come sometimes and ask for money and caress my cheeks. When I first got into the university, I stayed with a friend as his guest before I got accommodation in the hostel. We ate at restaurants three times a day. We had to come to Triplicane to eat. It was very close but I would still be afraid when we crossed the ground opposite the Kannagi statue. Not for reasons of poisonous insects or thieves but because I was afraid my chastity would be harmed.

Until recently this fear ruled my life. Two years ago I had gone to Mumbai and a friend of mine took me to a bar. For me Mumbai meant a city with a lot of sexual freedom. I had decided not to go out in the night. But I went because my friend insisted. From outside it did not look like a bar at all. It was such a quiet place. But as soon as we opened the door, we heard loud music blasting in the room. A group was singing songs and there were five or six beautiful women around. People were sipping their drinks sitting at round tables. My friend and I also sat at a table. It did not seem like a decent place to me. I told my friend we should leave. I felt I was in a predicament. My heart began to beat fast. I saw a client pointing out to one of the beauties and calling her to him signalling with his finger. The beauty gracefully walked up to him. The man held in his hands a sheaf of notes like one would hold playing cards. The lady took the money from him and left. And many others followed suit inviting women of their choice and giving them money. As they got more and more inebriated they had no idea how much money they were giving. My friend told me that it was usual for people to lose even ₹10,000 or ₹20,000 a day this way.

My friend got a call on his mobile and thinking he would not be able to talk in all that noise, he went out to take it. Just then, a person sitting at our table opposite me invited one of the beauties. When she came and stood near me, I began to sweat. I started feeling agitated and began looking for my friend. I spoke to him on my mobile and called him inside. He came after a while. I insisted on leaving the place and finally we came out. I felt relieved.

During my time in Chennai University, when I was asked why I did not mix properly with others I had told them innocently about my caste and the restrictions. That made me the butt of many jokes. Even if I spoke to some girl casually they would tell me, 'Beware! A dog would shit on your ashes!' Professor V. Arasu who was head of the department of Tamil still identifies me as the boy from a peculiar caste. In later years even Professor Perumal Murugan used to tease me saying he would report to my village people that I had misbehaved when I was studying in Chennai.

After getting to know about my caste, my classmates who were girls began to move freely with me. They may have felt that it was safe to be friendly with me. This kind of feeling among women, I know, continues to this day. In cities, if one is looking for a place to rent in the suburbs they would definitely want to know your caste. If one says that one is a Nayakkar there is normally no problem in getting a house on rent. They feel that is a kind of protection for the other women around. Whenever a woman has to go out somewhere they trust you to take them in your vehicle. They have faith in you. But it is people of our caste who are constantly afraid that something wrong may happen.

It is this fear that leads to early marriage in this community. I also got married after my MA. In the initial days after getting married, a new fear took hold of me. I was scared that someone might harm my wife when I took her to see a film or when I travelled with her to other places. In 2000, I had to come to Chennai on some work and I wanted to bring my wife along to show her the university where I had studied, the beach and nearby places. She too was keen to come along. But my in-laws did not give us permission. 'Both of you cannot go alone to the city,' they argued. But since I was very adamant about taking her along they reluctantly agreed.

In this kind of situation where they don't even allow you to leave the village to go out elsewhere, we lived in Thiruchengodu Kootappalli Colony on rent during 1999–2000. The house owners were an old couple. Their son was a divorcee and he lived with another woman. He was about my age. My in-laws worried about how my wife could remain alone in the house after I left for the college. The way others had described that person who was a divorcee made me apprehensive as well. So once I left for the college my wife would close the door and spend the entire day watching TV. She would rarely come out. When I visited the village after that, I wanted to leave my wife behind at her parental place because there were going to be some government holidays within a couple of days. But they insisted on sending her with me saying her job was to take care of her man while he was alone in a town. They felt that I would go astray if left alone.

The land next to ours belonged to people from the Boyar caste. They could touch things in our houses. They were allowed inside our houses. But we did not have food in theirs. They had a daughter, Parvathi, who was my age. Another daughter was Papathi who was my elder brother's age. It was an age when we were mostly together while herding goats, digging out peanuts that had fallen from the plants with the weeding hook, gathering castor seeds that had burst open and got scattered around, and collecting castor and lentil plant sticks as firewood. According to our ages, Parvathi was my friend and Papathi was my brother's friend. Whenever my brother and I quarrelled, he would call me Parvathi and I would call him Papathi. That was a way of calling each other names. My grandmother did not appreciate our being casually friendly with these two girls. She did not tell us anything directly but would always monitor our activities. I could make out from her behaviour that she was afraid that we may go astray.

Normally those from the Vannar caste were known as those who washed the clothes of other castes. But our relationship with the Vannars was different. The women of our household were not allowed inside the house during their monthly periods. Only on the fourth day after a bath were they allowed inside the house. It was the job of the Vannars to wash the clothes of the women during the monthly seclusion. They were not given any other clothes to wash. Among other things in my caste, the monthly periods and the accompanying restrictions were something I abhorred. The women would stay out for three days and early morning on the fourth day they would have their bath. There was a secluded place in the village for women to bathe after three days of their periods. They would hang their period clothes on the branches of the tree there and have their bath with no clothes on. After bathing they would wear fresh clothes and come home.

When I was in my third standard, my elder sister got married. Until then when my mother had her periods my sister would pour water on her on the fourth day. After my sister got married, it became my job to cook for three days when my mother had her periods. I had two elder brothers but one of them had joined, at the age of 10 itself, an agricultural farm as a labourer on annual wages. The other one had taken up the job of a cleaner for a lorry service. I could cook a meal with sorghum rice and pearl millet rice easily. On the fourth day, I would get up early in the morning tottering in my sleep to make hot water for my mother's bath and pour the water when she bathed. Amma used to bathe naked. Sometimes the milkman would arrive on his cycle. When she saw the cycle lights she would go and hide in the dark away from the light. She would do this even if someone came walking on the road with a torch on. She would finish her bath with all these difficulties and then come into the house. A son pouring water for his mother's bath was something that was taken casually in our caste. But I felt very bad about it. Bathing one's mother when she is very old and changing her clothes is like doing it to a child. But it was not the same when my mother was still a young person. I felt very uncomfortable about this. Once I went to high school I started requesting the women next door, who were like my sisters, to pour the water for her.

After my marriage whenever my wife had her periods she would go to her mother's place. Otherwise even if my mother poured the water for her she would still have to bathe in the secluded area of the village completely naked and then change and return home. In the early years after marriage one cannot bear it if another person so much as looks at one's wife. And I used to feel agitated worrying if someone would see her all naked. It was a common thing in my community but I could not accept it when it came to my wife. My wife also did not accept it when I told her she need not go out of the house when she had her periods. She was afraid of what others would say. So, for a few years this situation continued.

Even after we came to the city my wife would go to her mother's house when she had her periods. Or she would remain secluded in one room of the house. I would cook and do the other jobs. After much persuasion and telling her that we should be like other castes, she accepted to stay in the house during her periods.

After my son's birth my in-laws moved in with us to help us look after the child. My mother-in-law is still very orthodox. She would make my wife remain in the portico during her periods.

But on the fourth day it would again be a naked bath in the open. When we stayed at Kondichetti Patti, she would make my wife have her bath on the terrace very early in the morning. Since that house was taller than other houses no one could see her bathing on the terrace. But after we came to Nallipalayam she had to bathe in the backyard in the dark. The house was close to the road and vehicles would pass on the road every now and then. I lost my temper and told them, 'I am a teacher. Don't insult me this way. People here will wonder how a teacher can behave this way.' My yelling at them worked and from the next month my mother-in-law went away when my wife had her periods. She would go to her village and return only after we had ritually cleaned the house on the fourth day. At least my problem was solved.

When I was in high school I had many friends and one of them was Kanakaraj. I am still in touch with him. He was from Kondampatti and belonged to the Arunthathiyar caste. I used to go to his house often. I would not even go to the front portion of the house. We would remain on the street or near a kiosk close by or sit by the lake and have long chats. He knew about my caste and so he would avoid offering me tea or food. He would buy me bananas and colour soda at the kiosk every time I went there. These days when I go to his house I go and sit on the chair placed outside. Even when I was young I was critical of the ways of my caste. I used to feel sometimes that good friends were being separated by caste restrictions. But I was not bold enough to break the rules either. Whenever he came home I made him sit outside but, unlike the way in which Arunthathiyars are normally treated, I would offer him food on a banana leaf and sit near him and see to it that he enjoyed his food. I can invite Arunthathiyar friends only on normal days. On special festival days, I don't like to invite them and discriminate against them.

When I was working in K.S.R. College in Thiruchengodu, Che. Kodiyarasi was one of my students. She was one of my favourite students. She was from the Arunthathiyar caste and I considered her my sister and helped her out when needed. At present, she is a senior Tamil teacher in the Pallipalayam Government High

School. After I joined Arignyar Anna Government College, she did her MPhil under me. When she wanted to come and meet me at home regarding the research she was doing, I met her at the bus stop and spoke to her and then sent her back. My heart was heavy after that. After my son was born, every time she called, she would always ask first, 'Is Thambi doing okay, Ayya?' My wife and I were childless for many years and she was one of the well-wishers who wished that I should have a child soon. Such a student has not seen my son who is now two and a half years old. Nor have I invited her to come and see him. I cannot invite someone who respects me so much to come home and be treated with disrespect.

A classmate of Kodiyarasi was Pa. Jayapal who was also someone I liked very much. Once when he visited us we gave him nice food with fish curry but served it in a porcelain plate. After he left, my wife, guessing from his appearance, asked me if he was from a lowered caste. When I said yes, she stopped using that porcelain plate. After that incident, when friends of the lowered castes visit me, I don't mention their caste at home.

Once we had gone to Athoor for the wedding of one of Perumal Murugan's students. I had gone along with Ayya and his wife Ezhilarasi Amma in the evening itself. We were supposed to stay the night and then leave after the wedding the next morning. The student belonged to a lowered caste. I had decided not to eat at the wedding even as I was leaving for the wedding. But there were no hotels in that small village. It was also raining at night. I could not do anything. If it was food in the wedding hall it would normally be cooked by people of other castes. But there was no wedding feast in the wedding hall. This was home cooked food served for those who had come the previous evening. I tried to avoid eating when they insisted that I should eat. Murugan Ayya admonished me and insisted that I should eat. So, I ate that night but I did not enjoy it. I was filled with guilt and found it difficult to swallow the food. I spent a sleepless night.

A friend of mine who works in a government college is Dalit but not of the Arunthathiyar caste. He is my well-wisher. So, I try not to be so strict about my restrictions and eat at his place whenever I go there. We are very close friends so far. There are not many educated people in my caste so my friends are mostly those who studied with me, those who work with me, and those who are part of the Koodu association we have formed. Many of them are Dalits. I try, therefore, to do away with some of the restrictions deeply embedded in my mind. Professor Perumal Murugan is one of the reasons for this change.

There was a time when the mere touch of Sakkiliyars was considered polluting. This was a very deep-rooted prejudice. If the vessels had been licked by a dog, they would be broken if they were mud pots. If they were brass or vessels coated with lead, live charcoal would be put in them and they would be washed after that and used. Maybe the villagers thought that fire is supposed to purify everything. Nayakkars who do this to vessels licked by a dog, however, would not use vessels touched by Sakkiliyars. They would tell them to keep the vessels. In my teenage years, I rode my cycle with an Arunthathiyar friend riding pillion with me. After he got down when I rode further I saw an old gentleman from my village and asked him if he wanted a pillion ride. He refused. 'You want me to sit where a Sakkilyan has sat earlier?' he said. He was a strict follower of the practices of untouchability.

When I was four or five, Muthan was responsible for doing farmwork on our lands. Muthammal was his wife. Their daughter was Dhanalakshmi. Muthammal never wore a blouse and had sagging breasts. My mother also did not wear a blouse. I am supposed to have drunk from my mother's breast till I was five. One night Muthammal was sitting on the big stone outside our house. There was no electricity then. I could not make out in the dim light who was sitting on the stone. I thought it was my mother and ran to drink from her breast. She also may have allowed it because I was just a little kid. In later years Muthammal used to tease me narrating this incident and I used to feel ashamed.

In villages like Kondamanayakkanur that are close to the village Puthan Santhai, where on Wednesdays there were fairs, it is the Sakkiliyar women who bathe newborns for a few months. If a speck of dust falls into the eye and one rubs the eye it would go further into the eye and irritate the eye. No one would go to an eye doctor those days. There was a Sakkiliyar woman who knew how to remove the speck of dust from the eyes. She would put her tongue in the eye and grope and find the speck of dust and remove it. Even those who had very strong notions of untouchability would not hesitate to undergo this medical treatment. Sakkiliyar women could also bathe their children. Evidently, when there was no other alternative, they would compromise and become lenient with regard to their restrictions.

A friend of mine is in the business of selling gunny bags. All those who work in his shop are Arunthathiyars. He would treat them in the usual orthodox way when he was at home but in the shop he would ask them to bring him tea or lunch from restaurants. During Ayudha puja day when all the instruments of business are worshipped, the Arunthathiyar friends in his shop would do everything including cleaning the shop, wiping the framed images of gods and smearing kumkum and doing the puja. This is accepted.

In our village, there would be at least one lorry driver in each house. They are all very professional and experienced. In a caste that stuck to its lands and never went out, if there was anything that brought about some leniency more than education it was this profession that did it. When they went to other places and other states they had to eat at restaurants and they would not know who had cooked the food. It would not be considered important under those circumstances. Even today, when we ask those who argue strongly in favour of untouchability, if they knew who cooked in hotels and who served the food and tell them it is the lowered castes who do it, they would retort saying so long as they did not know who the person was there was no problem.

There are many oral stories which say that Sakkiliyars and Nayakkars are like brothers and that it was because Sakkiliyars ate beef that they were ostracised. They say that Nayakkars worshipped the cow. As far as I know until 10 or 20 years ago people of our caste did not eat beef. But they do now. When you ask them if the person who cooked it was not from a lowered caste and if it was proper to eat what that person had cooked, they would make excuses saying it was a good medicine for TB and other diseases.

When they went in lorries to Kashmir and Punjab and other such places, two drivers would go in a lorry. Even if one of them happens to be a Sakkiliyar from the village the other person cannot refuse to go. Normally when they go to other states they would cook inside the lorry itself. They would not go to eat in hotels. They would stop the lorry somewhere and cook and eat. During those times, they would have to eat what the Sakkiliyar friend had cooked. That cannot be avoided. They would return to the village and discriminate against the Sakkiliyars, knowing that they had to work together professionally. That is why the young Sakkiliyars who used to address the Nayakkars as 'Sami' and 'Devara' as if they were gods don't do so anymore. They address them as Anna, elder brother, taking the liberty to place them in a fraternal relationship. I consider this a great change. Once agriculture was given up and people came out for education, and to take up professions like lorry driving and other service jobs, the tight hold of caste loosened somewhat. When such factors increase, caste may not be so impenetrable.

In our area, even 40 or 50 years ago there were rare instances of one or two people who had studied to be doctors. One of them is a famous doctor now practising in Coimbatore. He never comes to the village. They say that he has got his children married into other castes. Another doctor who is in the Namakkal area has also done the same, they say. But no one from the Nayakkar caste would dare to ask them about it. Rules and restrictions are only for the poor. Not that I want them questioned. What they have done is something to be welcomed.

In 2004, a friend and I wanted to set up a rural library in our village. We managed to set up a library and when we wanted to inaugurate the library, the Councillor in our village said that he would like to invite an MLA from his party for the inauguration. This created more obstacles than even setting up the library. The Councillor was very caste-conscious and hated the Sakkiliyars. We did not want to create any problems. So, my friend and I went along with the Councillor to Salem. The MLA from our constituency was Pa Dhanapal, the speaker of the legislature. He belonged to the Arunthathiyar caste. He lived in Gugai area, a dense residential area in Salem. We had to wait outside before going in. Once we got permission and went in we had to stand like Arunthathiyars normally would outside our households. I had no problems with that. I felt like laughing. I remembered the proverb which says if elephants have the upper hand one day a time would come when cats also would gain the upper hand, and many similar proverbs. The Councillor was not bothered about any of this and thought he was doing the MLA a favour by inviting him. I was happy thinking how much change can be brought about in the society when the lowered castes acquired economic strength and political power.

When I became a professor in the government college they asked me to write about the glories of my caste in the caste journal *Thottiya Nayakkar Murasu* published by our caste association. I refused. Educated young people of our caste who are in the software field contacted me and told me that since I was doing research on the Thottiya Nayakkars I should write something about the caste on Facebook. This is what I told them: If you get rid of all the restrictions of this caste and if you are willing to start a struggle against this caste, I would certainly write.

****

Keeping Friends

P. Nallusamy

My village is Olappaalayam, which is near Puduchathiram in Cuddalore District. It is a small village. Twenty years ago, it had no conveniences like buses or even two-wheeler vehicles. To go to college from my house I had to cycle up to Agaram and park the cycle there, and then take a bus.

It was fun to take the bus to college. Girl students and boys would be sitting in the bus. I would hand over my notebooks and tiffin box to them and walk from the entrance to the exit at least four times. Even though I was not on familiar terms with the students, both girls and boys, I used to behave as if most of them were familiar with my face. Every year we celebrated a Bus Day. We would collect money from the students and decorate the bus with a banana tree and other festoons, like one does during festivals, put on loud music and dance in the bus. No student would buy a ticket that day. We would take advance permission from the bus depot supervisor to do this. We would also compensate the driver and the conductor. We would distribute sweets to all the passengers and burst crackers at all the stops where students got in, stop the bus for a minute and get down and dance and then get back into the bus.

I would go for odd labour jobs on Saturdays and Sundays and save that money for the bus fare and other expenses. My father was a handloom weaver. He did not go for agricultural jobs as he was not skilled in those jobs. But I did not mind doing the job of an agricultural labourer. What I earned on Saturdays and Sundays helped me not to be dependent on my parents for my education. Since I was a good worker, many began to call me for working in the fields. They would book me in advance for the next weekend job. There were also times when there was no work. Then I would have to struggle for small expenses. I would worry about whom to ask for a loan and how.

A girl from a Gounder family in the village was also studying with me in the village. Even in those days her mother had studied up to Pre-University and the father was a degree holder. She also used to travel by the same bus as I. One day when I did not have money to renew my pass for the week, she asked her father for the money and gave it to me. I was very happy with her gesture. I worked in their fields on Saturdays and Sundays and repaid that loan. The family had a lot of respect for me. They referred to me only by name and did not add any caste suffixes. They spoke to me a lot about my studies. So, I began to go to their fields to work on the following weekends also. They gave me whatever they cooked in their house to eat. I also did not stick to accounting when it came to their work. I worked in their field as if it was my own. I would go early in the morning and have my breakfast and lunch there. I could eat a bellyful in their house. They had given me a separate plate and a tumbler for my use. I would keep these tucked in the eaves of the thatched roof. Whenever I had food or tea, I would remove them from there, use them and put them back after washing them.

Once the festival of the goddess Mariamman took place in their area. They came home to invite me with due respect. I had also promised to attend the festival. But I was very sure in my mind that I would not go to their house during the festival, no matter what. I knew that their daughter would invite her college friends and if I had to go there for food, I would have to sit outside the house and eat from the plate and tumbler especially kept aside for me. Her friends would look askance at me. I did not want to be seen thus by them. They sent word for me. But I had decided not to go and thought I would go the following day and make some excuse.

If I had to go to the shop or to get the bus, I had to go past their house. That day it so happened that I had to go to the shop to make some urgent purchases. I rode my bike fast so as not to be seen by them. But their young son, who was in class IX, stopped me. I tried my best to go past him. But I couldn't. I told him I would go to the shop and come back but he would not let me go. He held the cycle handlebar and dragged me home. The parents knew why I had not come and why I was hesitant to come in. But they were still happy to feed me.

Their relatives and their daughter's friends were staring at me. Some of the friends were known to me. Everyone began to say that I should be served food. The mother told me to wait and began to attend to other relatives. The grandmother brought a leaf and I was happy it was not going to be the plate and tumbler set aside for me. She placed the leaf in the cattle shed where the cows were tied. But the girl's mother arrived then and scolded her for putting the leaf outside and told her she should have placed the leaf inside. I washed my hands in the cement tank tap and sat down to eat. They properly served food, sweets and snacks and filled the leaf. But they had a problem serving water to drink. I had also forgotten to bring the tumbler. To bring the tumbler I would have to go to the backyard and take it out of the eaves in the thatched roof. If I did that, the dog that was standing nearby may put its mouth into the food. It was the dog of a Gounder household and I could not have chased it off either. I was baffled about what to do. Unexpectedly, the grandmother brought water in the moss-filled mug of the water tank and placed it next to my leaf. The relatives and college friends kept watching me. By that time the mother who had gone in had found my tumbler and had washed it and brought water in it. She began to argue with the grandmother for giving me water in a tin mug. A big argument ensued between the mother and the grandmother. At the height of the argument, the grandmother began to shout, saying 'Go, serve him food right inside the house….' All the sweets and snacks served on my leaf became tasteless to me. I ate hurriedly, folded my leaf and threw it in the garbage bin and left after placing the tin mug on the water tank. I did not go to their house after that. I took a roundabout seven-mile route to go to college. They invited me many times to their house. But I never went. After that, whenever they happened to meet me they avoided inviting me. I went to many other fields after that to work but never went back to their house. I have not gone back to this day.

I had another friend Sakthivel who was a Gounder and we studied together till the twelfth. If any fees had to be paid, my father would not trust me. He would check with him and then give me the fees. We used to go together to the cinema without telling anyone at home as well as to village festivals and other places together. My mother used to work in their fields. During holidays, I would accompany my mother. I would go in the mornings for the two-hour work of plucking brinjals, ladiesfingers, chillies and tomatoes. They would pay me ₹10 to ₹15. They would also give me some rotten vegetables to take home.

When the buffalo was taken to the bull for breeding I would go along with my friend's father, helping him to herd the buffalo. During my schooldays I liked to wear nicely ironed white clothes. Once when I had to go with his father I went wearing my usual white clothes. When we took the buffalo to the Gounder in the next village who normally hired out his stud bull, he asked, 'Is this your son?' My friend's father said, 'No, he is the son of the family who own the fields next to mine.' Since I was with him, he did not mention my caste. After a while coffee was brought for us. They thought I was also a Gounder and brought the coffee in a regular tumbler of theirs. I was hesitant to take it and drink it. I stood there confused about what I should do. The Gounder who had taken me along also did not tell me to drink the coffee. I did not have the presence of mind to say that I did not drink coffee. I kept refusing and they kept insisting. I just walked away from there. I did not know what he told them in my absence. They did not seem to mind my not drinking the coffee. We herded the buffalo back home.

Four years ago, Sakthivel got married. I had started working by then and was living elsewhere on my own. They came home and invited me formally for the occasion. They requested me to come for dinner the day before the wedding. I accepted the invitation and reached there. All their relatives were sitting down in the front yard and eating. The family told me to have my dinner. I said I would, of course, have it. They were serving food for people of my caste in the backyard in a temporarily erected thatched roof shelter. I too went in to eat. It was a small shelter and many people were sitting in it. And a part of the ground had become slushy because of the food flowing out of the leaf plates. I had worn white pants and could not sit down there to eat. I came out.

They asked me if I had eaten. Others were around. I told them it was a bit crowded and that I would eat later. I told them to carry on with their relatives. It did not look as if it would become less crowded in the shelter soon. My son at home was unwell. Since I had set up an independent household after my marriage and did not live with my parents, I had to hurry back home. I was aware that they would mind if I left without having food. I kept thinking of how I could handle the situation and then arrived at a decision. I pretended I had had my food and told them I had eaten and wanted to take their leave. But they found out that I had not eaten and kept asking me why. Even when I assured them that I had eaten they kept insisting. The next day that Gounder came home and told my parents, 'Your son attended the marriage in our family but left without eating. Did we not respect him enough? I thought here was a Sakkilian boy who had worked in our fields and had been close to us and came all the way home to invite him for the wedding. And he has insulted us.' The Gounder also said, 'Since he is educated and has a job, is he thinking of honour now? Did he leave in anger because we did not offer him a chair to be seated to have his food in front of our relatives?' Since I heard all this, I have not been to his house.

From the sixth to the twelfth standard I studied at the Ezhur Government Higher Secondary School. It was a village which did not have much of a bus service. Once they had passed the tenth standard, most students preferred to take a TC to start their eleventh standard elsewhere; the school became a Higher Secondary School just two years ago. Not many students continued there after their tenth. In fact, in the year it became a Higher Secondary School there were only two boys and a girl studying there. And the only option they had was the First Group which included mathematics. There were no teachers for mathematics and chemistry and they were appointed only at the end of the academic year. And they too, normally, would take a transfer and leave. So, the final results looked very bad. All the parents therefore preferred to send their children to schools in Gurusamypalayam, Kalangani or Karaikurichipudhur.

When I was in in my tenth, Uma Shankar, one of the teachers, used to give tuitions. He was very good to everyone. I was very weak in math so he would give me special individual lessons to make me do important sums. If I did not do them, that would be the end of me. He would thrash me severely. The tenth exam results were normally published in the eveninger *Malai Murasu*. We went with the tuition teacher to Namakkal in the morning itself. When my number appeared in the paper I was thrilled. Then I had to join the 11th. So, like other students, I told my father that I would like to join a new school and not continue here. It was mostly because I was weak in math. All my friends began to join other schools too. When we went to the school and asked for the TC the teachers began to plead with me to continue in the same school. When parents boldly told the teachers the drawbacks of the school, their children were given TCs. But those parents, who hesitated to speak openly, were not given TCs. They would be somehow persuaded to keep their children in the same school. My father was a person who, by nature, always spoke in a tentative manner. So, I was forced to continue in the same school. There were seven boys and four girls in my class. I did not look my age and looked much younger. I was always a front bencher and whichever teacher came to the class, their questions would be directed at me. And when my reply was wrong, I would be slapped a few times till the teacher got over his anger. The students in the rows behind me got beaten less, and the students in the last row would only be advised. Those friends who did not get beaten up would come up to me and make solicitous enquiries.

I could manage all the subjects, but math was my bugbear. When I had done my tenth examinations, I had passed math with great difficulty and with the help of tuitions. There were those never-ending puzzles of theorems like delta functions, gamma functions, integrals and matrices. We had to know many formulae to work out a sum. Aruchamy had been newly appointed as our math teacher then. He came to our class. He had the habit of looking at his notes while teaching the class. If we raised any doubts he would consult his notes and only then reply, and would not answer us immediately. When some students sought clarifications, he would say, 'Idiot, you don't even know this?' and then consult his notes and answer. I would never be able to understand his explanations. Scared of being scolded, no one would ask him a second time. So, nine of us went back to the tenth standard teacher for eleventh standard math tuitions. Since his tuition premises were now taken over by someone else, he began to take classes in a Gounder's house. I felt a bit hesitant to go there for my tuitions, for if they found out my caste they would not let me into the house. There was also another person of my caste who was in that group. Since he was also there I felt bold enough to join the tuition group. But I would literally hide myself in the group and attend the tuitions.

The owner of that house had got his daughter married into a family in our village. His daughter's father-in-law visited him once. He knew me well, so he recognised me. He kept staring at me. The next day when all of us arrived for tuitions, we found the owner sitting outside looking rather angry. The other student of my caste belonged to his village. When he came in, he shouted saying, 'You Sakkili dog, don't go in. What guts you have, you Sakkili mother-fucker, to come and sit inside my house?' Shouting this he slapped him hard across his face. That boy went home crying. I stood there not knowing what to do. My other friends also stood there looking at me. I thought that it would be my turn next to be beaten. The entire class was silent. The teacher who normally spoke in a resounding voice spoke softly that day. I did not go the next day. The teacher also did not ask me why I had not come.

I wanted to study but there was no one to teach me. The friends who went for tuitions did well. I did not understand a word of what the math teacher in the school taught us. The others did not have that problem. They could learn what they did not understand in the tuition class. The prospect of failing loomed large only for me and two other boys. In the unit tests, quarterly exams and half yearly exams, I failed with poor marks. But I wanted to pass somehow. The three of us who could not go for tuitions, got together and started sitting by the Ezhur lake to do group studies. I was the weakest of the three. Nothing really registered in my addled brains. I learnt some important sums by heart. Whenever those sums appeared in the test given in the class by the teacher, I would do well. The teacher would be surprised. 'How did you do it? Come and do it on the board,' he would say. I was so scared of the teacher that I would say I couldn't do it. 'So you have copied from someone else,' he would say and hit me. When the final results came I had scored 40 per cent marks and had failed. I knew I would fail and so had taken up a job in a paint shop in Namakkal. But my father was adamant that I should not give up. He brought me back and admitted me in a tutorial college in Rasipuram. Later, I passed my 11th and completed my college studies also. But the thought still remains with me that had I gone for those tuition classes, I need not have wasted a year. My lifestyle also may have been different.

I did my postgraduation in National College at Trichi. I stayed in the main hostel. There were five friends from Aathoor who were my class fellows. I was the only one in our group who belonged to a lowered caste. Some may have known my caste, but they did not discriminate. The way I dressed and my manner of speaking did not reveal my caste. Normally, those who function within the caste system would address one another in terms of relationships like Maman (uncle) or Macchan (brother-in-law). When we went to see a film, I did not hesitate to spend money and was in no way unlike the others. Students from other departments would call me Mappillai (son-in-law), a familiar term of address. We were together when we went out to see a film or when we went to the hostel mess to eat. At one point, I wanted to give up studies and take up a job and it was my friends who stopped me from doing that. It made me so happy to know that they cared.

Before the semester exams we would have 20 days of holidays. No food was served in the hostel mess till the exams got over but we could continue to stay in the hostel. We used to eat outside then at some restaurants. In Trichi, all the hotels served very pungent food. They would serve tomato chutney that looked deadly red and was pungent as hell. If we ate two mouthfuls we had to drink half a glass of water to be able to eat the next mouthful. It was so pungent. I ate that for five days and got an upset stomach. The food expenses also increased. I thought I could handle this easily. I was not adept at cooking but could manage it. I bought a kerosene stove and some vessels and began to cook for myself. One of my friends joined me and gradually all seven of them began to eat what I cooked. Even though my cooking was not all that great, they would praise me sky high. But they did not come forward to wash the dishes, cut the vegetables or even to do other small errands. All of them were busy studying for the exams.

It was really difficult for me. I had to cook three times a day for seven people and study only after that. It made things really tough for me. The moment I finished cooking one meal, I had to think of the next. I could not get out of the task of cooking nor could I entirely stop cooking. I cooked many different dishes. One day it would be salty and another day it would be watery. But they would not complain; their unanimous comment was that the food was excellent. I would feel terribly irritated. They would each go in different directions to study and come together only when it was time to eat. In a way, it made me happy that they did not mind however I cooked. One morning I added a lot of Dalda when I made uppuma, the roasted semolina porridge. It made them drowsy and a few of them went to sleep. I felt the cheap thrill of revenge on seeing those who had not raised a finger to help me in cooking, asleep and not studying.

I explained the whole thing to them the next day. I told them none of you helped me when I cooked, so I added a generous amount of Dalda and made you sleepy. They had a hearty laugh. After that they began to help me cook. But I did not overwork them. I cooked for them during that entire period. A student from a different department in this group got the first rank and he wrote in my autograph book that the first rank had been possible only because of my cooking. I felt quite rewarded.

The students of the lowered caste in the hostel did not receive their scholarship for a while. All of them got together to protest. I, too, joined them. Some students asked me if I was also from the Scheduled Castes. It was only then that everyone came to know that I belonged to the Scheduled Castes.

Among my six friends I was the oldest. So, they always called me by my name and not in any relational terms. They were respectful to me. Once my friends came to know my caste, I saw a change in the attitude of the youngest among us towards me. And over a period of time, he began to call me with the familiar but disrespectful suffix 'da'. Initially, I took it lightly because I belonged to a caste where even those much younger would address me in that manner. All the same, I could not bear to be addressed in this manner by him. However, I did not object. I did not have the heart to address him in a similar manner. Gradually, he began to call me thus just to tease me, in the class, canteen, hostel mess and even when we were with other friends. I could not sleep at night. I would keep brooding over this.

One day he arrived earlier than me to eat in the hostel mess. When I came in he began his usual teasing by addressing me disrespectfully. I tried to be patient but lost my temper at some point and threw the plate he was eating from and slapped him hard on his face. He could not bear being humiliated before others. He did not eat that day. He remained in his room and closed the door to others. He didn't come out even once. I slept well that night. I stopped talking to him from then onwards. Even if he came forward to speak, I avoided him. We would sit at the same place. I would even give him a pillion ride on my cycle when all of us went to see films. But I never spoke to him till the end. At the end of the second year after the completion of our studies, everyone exchanged autograph books and my friends asked me to write in theirs. But I did not ask him to write in mine. He did write his name in mine although I had not asked him.

On the last day, at the farewell function I said that I was not angry with anyone and that all were my friends. I mentioned that friend by his name and spoke highly of him. After completing college, I began to speak with that friend again. Now we are on talking terms. In fact, I am closer to him than to my other friends. I share everything, including my family matters, with him. He remains one of my best friends. Even now he takes the liberty to address me as 'da' but I don't mind it one bit. But when I talk to him I use only his name and I don't address him in any other way.

Everyone knows what hostel life is. It is full of fun. I used to keep making fun of people. But I never hurt anybody. That is why many people liked me. No one went to see a film without me. I had my own comedy track, a better one than the film we would have gone to watch. From going to the playground in the morning to jog until we went to sleep at night, we would all be together. At meal times, along with other department friends, there were at least 10 of us who would be together. We were good eaters and never told the server that we had had enough; we always told him that for the time being it was enough and that we would take more later. Once a week in the night we were given vegetable biriyani along with idli. The biriyani used to be very tasty. We would do full justice to it. There were those who were jealous of our friendship. Some from the other departments used to call me Mappillai. One of them was from Thiruchengodu, the village next to my village. He found out my caste name somehow and began calling me Yoh, Lollu and so on, which is not a very nice way to address someone. I too did not spare him. I would also give him quick, witty retorts. He became one of my good friends-from Aathoor.

During holidays, people would take their close friends home. I never took anyone home. Even if they happened to have some work near my village, I would not make that an opportunity to invite them home. I never accepted anyone's invitation either. One morning, no one woke me up to go jogging. I wondered why no one had woken me up for so long and went to their rooms to check. No one was there. Where could they have gone? Why did they not inform me? I could not understand. When I asked their roommates they said they did not know either. The next day the roommate of my friend from the English Department asked me why I had not gone to his house. I said I had no work in his house. But all your friends have gone to his house, he explained.

I knew then that that friend had invited everyone and that he did not want them to even inform me about it. I was deeply hurt. I would not have gone even if he had invited me. But the fact that they had all gone without even informing me upset me so much that I could not sleep the whole night.

Since I knew where they had gone, when they came the next day I did not ask them where they had been without telling me. They did not tell me either. They seemed a little withdrawn compared to the days when they indulged in their usual happy banter. I wanted them to forget it and diverted their minds to other things. We are friends to this day.

****

Black Coffee in a Coconut Shell

P. Balasubramanian

Among the many incidents that my mother has narrated to me about my life, there is one that I still can't forget. It seems I was born in a private hospital and that I was so fair and good looking when I was born that the lady doctor who did the delivery for my mother asked her, 'How many children have you had before this child? What kind of work do you do?' My mother told her, 'This is our second child, Madam. We work as hired labourers.' The doctor told her, 'This boy is very cute and fair like the child of an Iyer Brahmin. Please give this child to me. I will bring him up well.' My mother told her, 'Whatever you say. I cannot give my son to you. We will bring him up ourselves,' and she hastily left the hospital within two days and came home.

I don't know if the doctor had said that seriously or was just joking, but whenever she narrated her memories of me, my mother would relate this incident and say regretfully, 'Had you been with that doctor you would have been someone important by now and doing well. Here you are struggling along with us.' And I would console her, 'Amma, don't say that. I lack nothing because you have educated me to this extent.' To this day, because I am fair and good looking my birth in a lowered caste gets temporarily hidden, creating the illusion that I was born in an upper caste household. Very often in the past, and even now, this has made it possible for me to escape caste atrocities. But possibilities of this kind of escape are very little in my own village. A majority of the people in our village are Gounders. We are dependent on them for our living. In this life that we have lived together as two castes, I have had some very bitter experiences.

Our village is Kavettippatti which is at a two-mile distance from Namakkal town on the Paramathi-Karur highway. I studied in the Panchayat Union Primary School in this village. During that time I stayed with my Periya Appuchi (father's elder brother) in Chithappa's house (father's younger cousin and Periya Appuchi's son). He lived with his wife and two-year-old child and worked as a daily wage labourer in a nearby dry fish factory owned by a Gounder. He used to leave early in the morning at six and return at eight in the night. Occasionally, to get over his fatigue, he would have a few drinks on his way back home. He worked at the factory and also ran other errands for the owner without any complaints, which kept the owner happy. The factory owner began to trust my uncle a lot and gave him loans, and even his salary in advance, once in a while. If the job was done properly the owner would be kind, but if something went wrong his anger knew no bounds.

Chithappa fell ill one day and could not go to the factory for a couple of days and stayed back at home. He had borrowed ₹2000 from the owner at the time. He could barely move and remained indoors. Unexpectedly one morning, we heard the sound of a car in our street. Appuchi and I heard the sound and came out from the corridor to check. Chithi was doing the morning chores of sprinkling water mixed with cow dung at the threshold to later draw the usual threshold designs which were drawn every morning. Chithappa was fast asleep on a rope cot lying in the corner at the entrance. The owner got down from the car and headed straight to the entrance of our house. He never spoke a word to any of us. He kicked my Chithappa lying in the cot a few times. My Chithappa began to shout 'aiyyo, aiyyo' in pain but the owner would not let go of him. Watching this, Appuchi and Chithi began to plead, 'Sami, please don't beat him; please spare him, Sami.' I began to cry. The owner kept kicking him till his anger subsided a bit all the while shouting, 'Dey, Sakkili dog, you Sakkili motherfucker, have you become so impudent? You think you can swallow someone's money and cheat?' He had no control over the words he uttered. While he was threatening Chithappa saying, 'Wait till you see what would happen if you don't turn up for work today,' the entire village had gathered there.

We were being humiliated before the entire village, and nobody spoke a word and watched quietly. This made me cry even more. The owner gave a general warning to everyone gathered there and hurried to his car and drove away. Appuchi began to console me saying, 'Don't cry Kannu, we are after all, Sakkilis. They are like gods. We can survive only if we please them. We have no other choice but to be their slaves.' I was a child and not old enough to grasp the situation fully, but the appearance of the factory owner and his abusive words still pierce my heart like a javelin.

Elections were held for the Panchayat in our village. The factory owner I mentioned also fought the elections for the President's post. The one who had been President before was also standing for elections again. There was a strong competition between the two. The reason was that although they were from the same caste, one was known for his good work and the other for his money. Gounders were in a majority here, as I have mentioned before. The Sakkiliyars were the next in terms of numbers. There were also some Boyars and Uppiliyars in small numbers. Most of the Sakkiliyars had moved to the new colony that the government had allotted them. Only some 30 families still lived near the place meant for them, next to the living quarters of the Gounders. All of them were dependent on the Gounders for their daily wages but, without taking either the elections into consideration or their own dependent status, they decided to build a wall around the goddess Mariamman they were devoted to, who was housed under the tree, and put a tiled roof above her head. They collected 'temple tax' from everyone. But they did not get enough funds. So, the elders held a meeting and decided to ask the factory owner, thinking he would not refuse if they said it was for the temple. They were keen to build the small temple and worship there. They went to see the factory owner. He listened to their demand and said, 'The loan that I am giving you, keep it as my donation for the temple. But all the Sakkiliyar votes must come to me to make me win the Panchayat elections.' It was more of an order. Those who had approached him thought they would be getting a lump sum, and if they gave up this opportunity, they may never be able to build the temple; and so they agreed to his condition.

They got the money, built the temple and also had a grand festival. Then Election Day neared. Just a few days before the Election, the Gounders got together, and with great effort elected the earlier President unopposed. The factory owner was shocked and livid. He had spent a lot of money but could not get elected; instead of getting angry with the Gounders, he pounced on the Sakkiliyars. He sent word to the Sakkiliyar living area and asked the elders to come and meet him. The anxious elders hurried to his place. He showed no consideration for their age and though he was much younger, he began to shout at them saying, 'You Sakkili dogs who are dependent on me, all of you have betrayed me!' Finally, he said, 'I don't know how you will do it, but you have to return the ₹5000 I gave you to build the temple,' and threatened them with dire consequences if they did not return the money. The Sakkiliyars got so scared that they again collected money as temple tax from each one and, within a month, returned his money. It was because we were Sakkiliyars that he could threaten us and get us to meet his demand. Would he have asked the Gounders to return the money had he given it to them?

My father worked in many farms around the area that belonged to the Gounders. Sometimes, he was also offered food in places where he worked. They would also give money. On one of my holidays, I accompanied my father. During the day, I jumped around and played in the fields and orchards of the owner. Towards the evening, I began to feel very hungry. I ran to my father and shouted that I was very hungry. He consoled me saying, 'Just bear with it Kannu, let me ask Gounder madam, she will definitely give you something to eat, Kannu.' He took me along with him. He stood outside the entrance and called out, '*Aenga,Aenga*!' in the way agricultural labourers address their masters and even wives address their husbands in many households without using their names. The Gounder madam came out and asked, 'So Kuppa, your work is over, is it?' My father told her, 'My son is hungry. Please give some food, if you don't mind.' The Gounder madam said, 'Okay, please sit in that corner. Let me see if there is anything left over,' and went inside the house.

Meanwhile, my father took out a crushed lead plate shoved in the corner of the cowshed, washed it with the water in the cement tank, and brought it. We sat down. The Gounder madam brought leftover rice mixed with water in a lead bowl. My father placed the lead plate two feet away and stood aside. She put the rice mixed with water on to the plate holding her bowl high so that it did not touch the plate. In the process, rice and water got spilt around the plate. Gounder madam was not bothered about all that and told my father, 'Dey Kuppa, ask your son to eat this. I will make some coffee. Drink it and then you can leave.' Saying this she went back inside.

Watching all this I began to think of how we ate at home. While I mixed the water and rice and hurriedly began to drink it, I asked my father, 'Appa, Appa… in our house Amma does not serve us food in this manner, isn't it Appa? She keeps the plate near the clay rice pot and serves food; why does this lady throw it from above the plate?' My father said, 'Aiyo Kannu, don't speak aloud. If they hear it they would beat us up.' He then lowered his voice further and said, 'We are low caste and they are upper caste. We have to obey them. Or else we cannot survive. Just eat your food.' Even while he was talking to me, the Gounder madam brought black coffee in a vessel. I quickly drank the rice-water and walked towards the cement tank. By the time I washed my hands and returned, my father had cleaned and brought two coconut shells from which we had removed the coconuts that morning. He placed the shells before the Gounder madam and stood at a little distance. The lady poured coffee to the brim in the shells and went in.

It was piping hot so we drank it slowly, blowing into it. I asked my father, 'Appa, these people own many buffaloes. And they get a lot of milk from them every day. The coffee their children drink looks different. Why is our coffee black?' My father said, 'Kannu, we can't ask such questions because, they may have a lot of milk at home, but they will not give it to Sakkiliyars like us. They are afraid that if they give us milk, we will cast an evil eye and the milk of their milch animals will dry up; that is why even if they have a lot of milk they will give us black coffee only.' I could not understand then what exactly he was trying to say.

My mother was an expert in massaging the bowels into place when the intestines moved out of place due to adhesions, causing pain. If she used water or oil and just massaged once, no one needed to come again for the same ailment. Her home medicine worked so well that people did not have to go to doctors. People not only from our village but from other villages, too, who had heard about her, would come to her. From kids to grownups, many would come to be massaged by her. More than Sakkiliyars, there were Gounders and other caste people who came to be massaged. In our village, when Gounders entered the area where Sakkiliyars lived, looking for labourers, the Sakkiliyars could not remain sitting on a chair or cot; they had to stand while talking with the Gounders. Such restrictions are almost gone now, though not entirely. Even I am not able to give up this habit. I would keep thinking that when someone from another caste arrived, I would not stand up and would continue to be seated while talking to them; but due to the behaviour of my parents and their insistence, I am not able to prevent myself from rising when someone of another caste comes to the house.

Two years ago, when I was working in Chennai, I had gone to my village for a holiday visit. One morning a Gounder came to our house to get the bowel massage done for his grandson. He stood at the street and called out to my mother. My mother left whatever she was doing and hurried outside when she heard his voice. Seeing him, she welcomed him and asked, 'Sami, what is wrong with our little master?' And he said, 'His bowels have moved out of place. He needs a massage.' My mother acknowledged what he was saying and asked me to draw a chair for him. I brought a plastic chair from inside and told him, 'Appa, please be seated.' He refused the chair and kept standing and I also remained standing there.

By that time my mother had gone to fetch the castor oil bottle. When the Gounder saw the castor oil bottle in her hand he said, 'Kuppan's wife, don't use that oil. Please use the oil I have brought' and took out the oil kept in the car. 'Sami, why should you bother to bring the oil?' my mother started saying but before she could finish saying it, he quickly interjected saying, 'Don't use your oil. Use the one I have brought for the massage.' My mother did not object and finished the massage and sent them back.

I could not bear what he had said and asked my mother after he left, 'What is this Amma? When people from outside come, you have always used the oil at home. Nobody has objected to that so far. The one who came today did not even want to sit on the chair and he refused our oil and wanted the massage done with the oil he brought with him. We also buy oil in the shop. So, what objectionable thing is stuck on our oil?' My mother calmly replied, 'Kannu, they are only bothered about what they want and would go to anyone for that. Once the job is done they ignore us; they couldn't care less for us. Those who come from outside, come only to get cured. But those in the village have problems about coming to this area. Even if they come, in their hearts they would nurse a grouse about coming to a Sakkiliyar's house. Whatever one may say, they are from a Gounder household and this is a Sakkiliyar household. No one can change that.' I felt totally shattered.

Anyone can talk, write or opine about caste. However, it does not lose its character and keeps appearing at some level or the other in our life. It is deeply rooted, changing according to the time and environment and spreading its malevolence in many different forms. We survive. So does caste, surviving along with us, doing its work with much greater force.

****

Acceptance or Rejection?

R. Prabhakar

I am not able to give a firm reply to the question whether I accept or reject caste. I used to be a staunch believer once. In the temple of goddess Namagiri in Namakkal, on the way to the sanctum sanctorum of the deity Narasimhan, there is a chamber of another deity. Devotees do not offer camphor to be burnt for the god in that chamber. I was at an age when I knew nothing about these matters. When the Brahmin priest extended the plate of flowers and kumkum and ashes for the devotees to take, I placed a piece of camphor on the plate as is normally done by devotees who want to make various offerings. The priest gave me such a chiding that I lost all faith in god. I became a god-hater and also someone who totally disliked Brahmins. To this day, I am not interested in either going to a temple or maintaining a good relationship with Brahmins. When I was doing my graduate studies, whenever any discussion started about god, Professor Su. Durai would say, 'The poojari knows the strength of the god.' I used to immediately think of that priest from my childhood. However, I often wondered if I was totally against caste even though I hated god and Brahmins.

As far as I know, caste has wound itself around me all through my life, whether it was during my student days, when I worked in colleges, my medical treatment or my marriage. Now I am in a government job but I still have to confront caste. Many who work with me are Gounders, the caste to which I belong, and it makes moving with them seem naturally easier. I am not sure how their behaviour would have been towards me had I been of another caste; particularly, had I been from a lowered caste.

In my student days, I got to know a few things about hierarchy in caste and the context in which caste took root. After reading many different books, I could understand the oppression of caste.

During my graduation since I still had some papers in arrears, I could not continue my studies and was forced to look for a job. I thought I could work in a shop somewhere and went to many shops asking for a job. But my Gounder caste came in the way of getting a job in a shop. I came to know later that the shopkeepers had argued, 'Gounders don't come for such jobs. Even if they do, we make a person who is of our caste work. We won't be able to force him into doing more.' So, I gave up looking for a job in Namakkal and decided to go elsewhere and finally got a job in a Xerox shop in Salem. I managed to get jobs for two of my friends in the same shop. We were all from different castes but all of us belonged to dominant castes. One of those friends got a job in the same shop for a person from a lowered caste from his village.

The shop did photocopying at a very low rate so there was a lot of work to do day and night. All of us stayed in a room given by the company and handled the management responsibilities of different Xerox shops of the company. Two months went by. When the owner came to know that our friend belonged to a lowered caste he said, 'How can you bring Sakkilis and Parayans to live in the room?… Have I made rooms available for them? You don't have to bring such persons all the way from Namakkal; I can get enough of them here itself. I just have to say I can offer a room and I can get so many like you. I said you can bring someone to stay with you and you do this.' That day I experienced the height of caste hatred. I gave up the job, annoyed that even for this lowly job the Reddiar owner wanted an upper caste person. That day was the first time I abused someone using his caste name.

For six months after leaving the photocopying job, I grazed cattle. I feel that period was a wonderful one. I would let the cattle graze in the large field and sit and read novels and short stories. I was not someone who spoke much with others but I learnt about the experiences of others through these books. That is when I understood life. Even now I feel that what gives me great joy is to go and graze cattle when I am free and read during that time.

My economic circumstances forced me to take up a job once again. I thought I should finish the paper in arrears and also obtain a master's degree. Thinking that a job that was not strenuous would allow me to study, I took up the administrative job at the Kongu Youth Association. There was not much work but the Association was full of the absurdities of caste. Dheeran Chinnamalai was the hero and leader of these so-called youthful lions of the Kongu region. The birth anniversary of Chinnamalai and conferences were celebrated as caste celebrations. I began to wonder how a freedom fighter like Dheeran Chinnamalai had become a caste leader. I realised only then that every freedom fighter was being celebrated as a leader of his particular caste. After getting through my arrears paper, I left that place, saying I wanted to study further.

Studying Periyar's concepts in my master's studies had added to my already existing notions of atheism and Brahmin hatred. I had decided that I would go against caste and have an inter-caste marriage. I thought that in my marriage, there should be no thali, the yellow wedding thread considered sacred and auspicious, thread tied around the bride's neck in traditional marriages, no relatives, and only friends surrounding me in a Registrar's office. I had emphasised this to my many girl friends later in life. I had decided to marry only a person who would agree to this. I had not visited or partaken food in the house of a lowered caste person until then. I had had no opportunity to do that. I thought an inter-caste marriage would provide an opportunity for that experience also.

From the second semester onwards, I had taken a room on rent in the Housing Board colony opposite the University. With me was one of the employees of the University. When one of my professors came to know about my living arrangements he asked me, 'How do you manage? You can't get along with people like him.' I could not figure out why he said that after I completed my postgraduate studies and vacated the room. Later, I came to know about the professor's normal stance that made him seem above caste, as well as his real feelings about caste.

At home, caste was observed strongly. If anyone was mentioned in a conversation they would always want to know which caste he belonged to and if he was one of us. But they became lenient when it came to my marriage. I was slightly hearing-impaired and they thought no one from the Gounder caste would offer me a girl and so they said, 'Let him marry whom he wants but the girl must be from a caste we can associate with.' 'This is like vainly trying to filter out the shit that has fallen into the curry one eats. What will you do if I marry into a caste we don't associate with?' I would ask. 'But still....' they would prevaricate. 'What do you mean?' I would say to prod them on to speak. Their reply was always, 'Don't do anything like that.'

When I went to do my course in Education, I fell ill. I had to undergo a kidney transplant. The expenses ran up to an unbelievable amount in lakhs. I must say I had a rebirth with the help of many people. I was in the hospital for three months and was under continuous treatment. During this time, I became friendly with a nurse there. Once while we were chatting I asked her to marry me. She agreed. I got so excited. I thought this girl was the right person and best suited for not only my ideology of a casteless society and my health status then but also to blunt the prejudices of my family. The thought thrilled me no end. But it did not last for long. Within a few months she made caste the main factor saying we were all people from a higher caste and left me.

As I was recovering, I got the opportunity to work in an Institute for Education being run by a fellow Gounder. Some girls who had completed their degree courses and had come to do a further degree in Education were interested in marrying me. They were all Gounder girls. But when they came to know about my health they quietly moved away. A girl from the Udaiyar community, however, firmly stood by me. I consoled myself thinking she was not from a lowered caste as I had desired but she was at least willing to marry me despite my health complications. But without giving any reasons, she also rejected me finally and married someone else she loved. I just could not understand why she did that and it is a mystery until now. It took me a long time to get over that rejection.

I had decided not to marry. But my family continued to talk about my marriage and also continued to emphasise the caste factor linked to it. Whenever the subject came up I would shout, 'When I was struggling for life, did your caste people come up with those wads of currency?' Whenever I was confronted with questions I did not want to face, it became my nature to shout to stop others from talking any further. Due to my health I could not even drink water outside. I could not eat food at the weddings of my friends who belonged to the lowered castes.

It was at this time that I began to work at an arts and science college being run by a Gounder. There were people from many castes in the department but I was the only one from the Gounder caste and I was viewed from that perspective. My colleagues would tell me, 'Your people would take care of everything for you. You won't be harmed or asked to leave.' Before all those people could leave the college, I became the first person to leave the college.

My Gounder caste became the reason for my leaving the college. I have not yet understood how belonging to the same caste ever helps in working in a college for there were people there who would kill you with kindness; like not killing you with poison but with sweet jaggery. I could not soak in their jaggery syrup and taste sweet.

After giving up the college job I began to prepare for competitive exams and that is when the question of my marriage became a big issue in my family. I gave up my rigid stand on inter-caste marriage and thought that I should agree to marry anyone who understood my health complications. My wife is someone who accepted me in that manner. My family was really happy because she was someone whom I had a customary claim over and hence from my own caste. But my wife's family did not accept the proposal because of my health and so we had a secret registered marriage and continued to live separately with our own parents. There were a lot of problems and struggles even after that, after which we went through a traditional marriage. I had rejected god because that Brahmin priest had admonished me and had thought that I would have a marriage without a Brahmin priest, without looking for an auspicious day, without the traditional thali, without my relatives and with friends around me, in a Registrar's office. But due to circumstances, I had to marry in a Siva temple on an auspicious day and tie the thali around my wife's neck, with the Brahmin priest chanting sacred *mantras*. I could invite only a few of my friends. Only my mentor, my teacher, whom all of us called Ayya, could come. I had wanted to have my marriage with him conducting it and with a non-vegetarian feast. But he could not come with his family and it turned out to be a hurried affair. So, I still do not know if I accept or reject caste.

****

Distancing

K. Poonkothai

When I was a little girl I stayed with my Aachi (my maternal grandmother) and went to school. My mother's younger sister, my Chithi, used to take care of me. She was not married then. People from many different castes lived in that town. If Chithi ever saw me playing in any street other than ours, she would beat me. I got beaten many times. I was scared of getting beaten, so I would hide from her and play wherever I wanted.

Agriculture was the main livelihood of that area and it needed the cooperation of many castes. Without them agriculture would not be possible. But if I entered their streets Chithi would beat me up. I asked her one day, 'Why do you allow them to enter our fields then?' In reply, I got beaten as usual. That was the way Chithi treated me.

Chithi now lives in Erode. Her daughter was studying in ninth standard in a school in Dindigul. She brought her friend home one day. That girl belonged to a different caste. Chithi did not seem to have any objections to that. Her not objecting and the friend's visit did make me happy but I felt like asking, Chithi why was I beaten as a child for doing the same thing. I did not ask her, however.

I came back to our place when I was in the ninth. There was only one caste in our town. It was difficult for other castes to enter our town. There were too many restrictions. I had to walk four miles to go to school. I never took shortcuts. If I ever did, my mother would give me a good beating with the broomstick. The reason was that other castes lived in one of the roads on the way. My mother's beating would hurt much more than my Chithi's.

When I was in the twelfth standard, my maternal uncle's daughter brought her friends home. They were of a different caste. Athai, my paternal aunt made them stand outside the house. I invited them into our house. My mother did not say anything until they left. After that, I had to deal with Amma's wrath and I nearly died doing it.

My father was not as caste-conscious as my mother, Chithi or Athai. In his business hours if someone brought something to eat after a festive celebration in their house, my father would receive it with no qualms and eat it. Till today he has been without any caste feelings. But my mother is just the opposite.

In the Nadar caste there were mainly joint families. They usually did business in groceries, iron products and plastic things and ran shops associated with these. They did not educate their children much but taught them business. In their community, there was no respect for women. The parents showed great reluctance to fulfil even the smallest desires of their daughters. The daughters did not have even the right to express themselves. If ever they spoke out of turn they would be severely scolded. It was the same in their parental homes as well as in their marital homes. They were considered a great burden. The men were highly respected. Whatever the sons asked for, they paid heed to their request.

The dowry system among the Nadars is made up of a cash and gold combination: 31 sovereigns of gold and ₹31,000, 51 sovereigns of gold with ₹51,000, 101 sovereigns of gold with ₹1,01,000, and so on. But they would say they would not even drink a cup of tea in the homes of their in-laws. Even my father would say this time and again. I would feel so proud when he would say that. But when I think of it now, I find it very demeaning.

If anyone else asked for the hand of an uncle's daughter or a paternal aunt's daughter over whom the male cousins had customary claims, it could lead to murder. Most girls were married into the families of relatives. It was normally a marriage with one's maternal uncle, maternal uncle's son or with the sons of paternal aunts.

I have heard of a proverb that a Nadar boy's customary claims lie within a pot and a trunk, which meant that marriage took place among close relatives. Rarely would there be a marriage that fell outside the customary claims. Athai, my paternal aunt, had one such marriage that fell outside customary claims. Her husband was a distant relative who in a convoluted family line would be her paternal uncle. Yet, he had married her. I never addressed him according to the familial address. If anyone asked for him I would go near him and tell him someone was asking for him and come away. I would not speak to him.

I had a marriage of my choice and came to Namakkal and began to live in the street where the Arunthathiyars lived. When we moved there we did not know it was a colony of Arunthathiyars. Even after we came to know, we continued to stay there for it was a very secure and comfortable atmosphere. After coming there I made up my mind that I was not going to indulge in any caste discrimination. But I would not say that I changed entirely. There was that hold that caste had within me. For a week after we started living there I did not know that those in the street were Arunthathiyars. I never asked them about their caste. But they did ask me. 'Why do you want to know?' I asked them. They told me, 'We don't allow Pallars and Parayars inside our houses. You look like you belong to a Pallar or Parayar family. Your man looks like he is of our community. That is why we want to know.' Then I told them that I was a Nadar. But this question was asked by someone or the other at least once in six months and when I told them about my caste they would quietly move away. I don't think about my caste but those around me keep reminding me of my caste.

Once a couple came and asked for ten rupees and some old clothes from each house. I did not know them. When I asked them, they said they made these visits to the street once a year. When I asked the owner of our house about them and the others around, I was told that they belonged to a caste lower than that of those who lived in that particular street. I did not pay any more attention to that. The next day the couple came again and asked for a plate, a *chombu*, a metal rounded mug to carry water, and a tumbler. I gave them what they asked for. They said they wanted to keep them. I told them they could use them and return them. The neighbours, even those I was friendly with, spoke to me rudely after this. I just ignored them. The couple stayed there for three days. They would ask for rice and kozhambu from everyone and sit on the street and eat the food. They slept on the street too.

On the first day, they slept on the street. In the morning, they came and asked me for some tea. I gave them tea in the tumbler. After they finished drinking I took the tumbler from them and took it inside. I thought no one had seen me taking the tumbler back from them. But my friend Vanitha had seen it. She merely told me not to do this in front of others.

The next day it was raining and it was around seven in the evening. I asked the couple to come in and sit down. My husband was not at home then. After the rain stopped they went to the temple and slept there. Fortunately, the owner of the house did not come out of his house till the rain stopped. He had seen them once in the corridor of my house and chased them away. I had got angry then. Normally, when women talk about upper caste women they would say, 'As if a Gounder woman is someone great.' But they were unwilling to accept someone who belonged to a sub-group of their own caste.

Although I do many things with them I stand apart when I act differently in certain matters. Once, one of them said that they would like my elder daughter Sangamitra to marry their son. I was burning with anger but did not show it. I felt bad that my situation had been reduced to this. I always felt annoyed when anyone gave my children mutton to eat. And my anger knew no bounds if it was beef. Beef was taboo in my caste. So, although I allowed my children free movement on other days, on Sundays I kept a watch on them and did not allow them to go anywhere. I did not let them go out even to play.

My grandmother always used to say that each caste had something special about it. I cannot deny that there are many advantages I enjoy because I live in a street where the Arunthathiyars live. They have helped me to attain maturity. But I cannot get rid of thoughts about caste even when it relates to insignificant matters. When such thoughts rise in my mind I keep others away or distance myself from them a little. Although I live with them in my heart, I do stand apart from them, too.

****

Everyday Moments

Perumal Murugan

There is a lot one can write about caste. Caste is as omnipresent as god in our society. There is not a day when one can forget about caste. Some moment or the other in everyday life makes you realise the existence of caste, makes you think about caste. We also meet every day the stances being taken about there being no god. Some say there is caste in the rural areas and not in the urban cities. In the villages, one can feel the force of the wind. Even though the wind loses its force when it hits the buildings in the cities, it is not non-existent in the city streets. Caste is something similar.

A math teacher from Velur District got transferred to the college where I was working. Namakkal District is, after all, known as the Oxford of Tamil Nadu in education. So, with the intention of making his son a doctor, he had admitted him into Vidya Vikas School known for its reputation for the highest scores. Since he was a math teacher he felt he could help his son in math, and he wanted to bring his entire family and settle down in Thiruchengodu. My house was close to Vidya Vikas School. The Housing Board Colony was in that area. It was a large area with more than a thousand houses. He asked me if I could find him a place to rent in that colony. I enthusiastically began to look for a house for him.

Many of my relatives and acquaintances lived in that colony. Through one of them we settled on a house and went to pay the advance. They were sure that there won't be any problem in the payment of rent as he was a professor. But the house owner did take me aside and ask, 'What caste does the gentleman belong to? If he is an SC it won't work out.' I had no idea of his caste until then. It had not even occurred to me to ask him. What could I do under the circumstances? I told him, 'We work in a college. We never ask about caste nor do we observe caste.' That was, of course, a lie. There were caste groups even within the college. There were those who knew the exact caste of everyone there. In order to confront the house owner, I answered him that way. But he wasn't one to give up. He told me to ask the professor and let him know. I approached the professor hesitantly and asked him. But he seemed to have anticipated such a question. 'I am an SC, Murugan,' he told me. If this was conveyed to the house owner he may have refused to give the house and that would be an insult. So, we thought of telling him that the professor was a Mudaliar. And that is what we told him. He stayed in that house for two years and there were no problems.

It is not as if such problems exist only in small towns. Big cities are in no way less conscious of caste. I lived in Chennai for eight years. I was actively involved with a Marxist-Leninist student organisation at that time. I used to go around Chennai distributing pamphlets, pasting posters on the wall and doing similar activities. I never had enough money to meet my expenses then. So, I had to exercise a lot of self-control over matters of food; not self-control exactly, but there was a dearth of food. I used to cook just rice and eat it with some chilli powder mixed in it. There were just a few days when I made a khichdi of rice and dal. If I ever prepared rasam that meant it was a feast!

Once in a way I would visit some comrades. During such visits, even if I was asked for courtesy's sake to eat I would immediately accept the invitation and be ready to eat. Those were times when I understood that hunger had no dignity and felt no humiliation. Once I had gone to a comrade's house. He himself visited his house only rarely. I always looked upon the mothers of all the comrades as if they were like the mother of Pavel, the hero of Maxim Gorky's novel *Mother*. In their own way, they helped the revolution indirectly. Yes, isn't offering food to people an act of indirectly helping the revolution? But no one ever wanted to go to that particular comrade's house. One could go only if one had the resilience to listen to the complaints and abuses of his parents.

I was going there for the first time. The comrade's mother looked at his face and, perhaps she realised he was hungry. So, she asked us to eat. One could sense from her different expressions in the conversation that she was disappointed with her son giving up his studies to become a full-timer in the Party. She was preparing the food as she spoke. Her conversation fell on my ears like a strange unfamiliar song. I was only thinking of the food. She came and set four or five utensils. I assumed it was going to be a good meal that day. I thought I would put up with her talk. All that one had to do was make a sound of agreement during such conversations; one's mind could wander about anywhere. I was used to that.

The lady placed just one plate before us. I was shocked thinking she was going to serve food only for her son. She called the comrade and asked him to remove the leaf plate from the alcove above. The comrade made a face and told her to serve in the plate but the lady insisted. The comrade took out one leaf from a bundle of leaves. It was not a banana leaf but one of those leaf plates made with dry broad leaves of mountain ebony joined together with thin palm ribs. She placed it on the floor and invited me to sit down for a meal. I thought this was a special leaf plate meant for guests and happily washed my hands and sat down to eat. I sprinkled water on the leaf and wiped it clean. My comrade friend had gone to the washroom.

The mother, like Pavel's mother, was going to offer me food. I wondered how many comrades these very same hands would have fed. I felt overwhelmed and was almost in tears. The mother sat before me and asked me, 'Which *varna* do you belong to?' This was the first time I was facing such a question in my time in Chennai. First, I could not quite get the word *varna* but then I could guess its motive. I immediately understood why the leaf plate was being used. Even revolutionary mothers observed caste restrictions. In front of me was the leaf plate washed and clean. There was the cooked food before me. I understood at that moment what the proverb 'there is many a slip between the cup and the lip' really meant. Even in hunger my mind was sharp. I told her, 'I belong to BC, Backward Community.' By then the comrade came out of the washroom. His mother removed the leaf plate. What was the problem even after I had said I belonged to a backward community, I wondered. The comrade asked his mother smiling, 'So, have you made the enquiries?' 'Go on, leaf plate is not convenient to pour rasam,' she said and went in and brought a steel plate and placed it before me. I drank a lot of rasam poured into my plate and had a satisfying meal.

When she found out that I was a university student she asked me to advise her son. I told her that I was also asking him to remain a student while working for the Party. After that she served me with more care. After the meal, I thanked her and when I came out I told my friend, 'Comrade, even though mothers observe caste restrictions, they also help the revolution. After the revolution, even mothers will not talk about caste, isn't it?' I also made sure to know what caste he belonged to. When I went to his house on another occasion, his mother asked me which group I belonged to among the BCs. Since I knew my comrade's caste, I mentioned that as my caste. She would not talk about caste when the comrade was around. But when he was not around she happily spoke about caste-related issues. After that whenever I went there I was given special attention. She would enquire about people of her caste from our village. I would also tell her half-truths I knew. I would be served good food. The comrade himself would invite me to go with him saying that his mother did not scold him whenever I was around. That is the caste role I donned in the city.

Sometimes without intending to, one is forced to use caste in certain situations. I found out from a research student that on the way between Namakkal and Mohanur, in the village Melappatti near Vazhavanthi, there was a rock inscription. I was curious to know what it contained. The thought that, if it was an important one I too would get recognition for contributing to history, kept pushing me to explore it further. I did not know how to read the rock inscription nor did I know how to copy it. I asked Vellakkalpatti Duraisamy, generally addressed as Ayya, who was known as a rock inscription expert in Namakkal, if he would come someday to that village. He was always eager to go to any place that had a rock inscription. There is not a place he has not visited in Namakkal and Salem districts. He said it is possible he may have seen this rock inscription and already copied it. Yet he agreed to come along.

Before that, he checked a few details with me. He wanted to know the name of the village and the dominant caste of the village. I told him that in that village there were mostly those of the Nayakkar caste who were known as Kollavaru and Erra Kolla. There was a temple near the spot where normally memorial stones were laid for ancestral worship and this rock inscription was near that temple. I also told him about this detail.

'The Nayakkars are fools. We won't be able to deal with them. Find a boy of their caste and ask him to join us,' Ayya said. It was a boy of that community who had given us the information. So, we took him along with two others who knew Telugu and went on our way. It was a village where just one bus went only twice a day. We reached there on two-wheelers. The site was a cremation ground situated a little distance before the actual village began. The temple stood next to it. The rock inscription was in front of the temple at the corner of the street. One could vaguely make out the inscriptions on it. When they had celebrated the temple festival, the locals had whitewashed this rock with lime along with the temple walls. Not knowing what the rock was, they had almost turned it into a god. Ayya plucked green leaves and crushed them and smeared the rock with it. By then many men and women had gathered around us. They seemed agitated that someone was doing something to their god and that all this was being done without any proper permission. The student who had come with us immediately switched to Telugu and spoke to them. They calmed down. The student explained to them in Telugu that this was a rock inscription and that the government itself had sent these professors.

We allowed the students to talk to them and Ayya and I became busy with copying the inscriptions on the rock. Ayya was reading it out line by line and we noted it down on a piece of paper. The rock inscription was about a Nayakkar's gift to the temple and the deeds he had done for the temple. Some of the lines had gone under the soil. The inscription did not seem so important that we should take the trouble to remove all the soil around it and read it. So, we left it at that. The student who spoke in Telugu and the other students meanwhile had become friendly with the villagers. So, we returned without any trouble.

There was something else I noted during my journey that day. It was in a village that had all the facilities of a city but was far away from the city. There wasn't even a tea shop nearby. We had tea in the Vazhavandhi village which was five or six miles away. I had heard that in many Tamil Nadu villages they had the two-glass system and in some they had the three-glass system where the so-called upper castes and lowered castes are served tea in different glasses. In my own village, I had seen the two-glass system. I had not seen the three-glass system until then. One glass was for the dominant castes, another was for Dalits who were not Arunthathiyars and the third one was for Arunthathiyars. The three-glass system I saw in Vazhavandhi was a bit unusual. The dominant castes were given steel tumblers, Dalits glass mugs, and those who were outsiders were served tea in paper cups. It is difficult to easily identify the caste of outsiders. So, they were not served in the first two cups. They are served in paper cups which can be thrown away. In cities it is considered convenient and fashionable to serve in paper cups. In the village, this is utilised for other purposes and the three-glass system is observed.

Once when I was working in a college I was forced to use my caste for security reasons. I was the Head of the Department of Tamil in that college. It was impossible for me to get along with the Principal. He was a physics teacher and a landowner. He had many agricultural fields that had river irrigation. Domination, power, greed for good positions and money craze were part of his personality. Normally, only those who were promoted as Principals sat in the Principal's chair. Those who were acting Principals normally sat in a chair on one side of the Principal's table. He had not been promoted as a Principal but despite that he always sat in the chair meant for the Principal. His entire demeanour would change when he occupied the chair. The way he shook his head and gestured with his hands and remained glued to the chair became unbearable. He would begin to talk about humanism every five minutes.

When he became Principal I got to know about an incident. A Dalit student from his village had joined the college and was doing physics. In the holidays, the student had to go and work in the Principal's fields. He was not given any payment for his labour. If he did not go to work on some days, the Principal would call him and threaten him saying that he would fail him in the practical exams. The student, who was eager to study, got intimidated enough to work in his fields without any payment. During practical classes, even though he was not in charge, the Principal would come and give the student a threatening look. The student was dead scared of him. Another teacher found out why the student was so scared of him and reassured him that the Principal had no power to do anything in the practical exams and he stopped the boy from going and working in his fields. Until then, the student had worked in his fields and the suffering he went through, fearing the Principal, was even worse.

When a person of this nature becomes the Principal, how would things be? He got into many corrupt practices such as taking money for the admission of students. One could not get along with him even in small matters. There were always arguments and quarrels. It was also said that he was related to the legislative assembly member of the area and that is why he had the guts to do anything he wanted. He belonged to a group in the Gounder caste. My friends and I were a bit worried that we may receive some political threats. I began to think of ways to deal with the situation. I decided that the best way was to create an impression that I also had influential friends in politics. At that time, C. Ponnaiyan had been elected as the legislative assembly member of the Thiruchengodu constituency and he was also a minister. He had re-entered politics after the MGR period. He occupied an important position in the Party too. I spread the news that he was related to me and that he was, in a way, my uncle and that I could meet him anytime I wanted.

My Appan knew Ponnaiyan. Appan had worked in the soda shop run by a relative of Ponnaiyan. Ponnaiyan was a school boy then and used to come to the soda shop often. When Ponnaiyan joined the MGR ministry in 1977, Appan used to talk about the soda shop days quite proudly. But he had not met Ponnaiyan even once after the latter became the minister. Nor was C. Ponnaiyan related to me. He was of the same Kongu Velalar caste in which I was born. It was a normal custom that people born in the same caste could always claim each other to be relatives if they met. And Kongu Velalars could always work out a way in which they were related. One of my colleagues, when he introduced me to a new teacher who had come on transfer, introduced him as my agnate. There were different groups among Kongu Velalars. Two persons belonging to the same group were agnates. Those from different groups would be related as cognates. That is how I claimed that Ponnaiyan was my uncle in terms of relationship. It had the desired effect. There was not much trouble from the Principal after that.

However much one says that there is no caste and that one does not believe in caste, one is forced to accept its existence. We had gone to the house of a student who lived near Kollimalai and stayed with him for a few days. I like such experiences. I had thought that only tribals stayed in the mountain areas. But during that particular stay, I found out that there was an equal number of Dalits who lived in the mountains. In the birth certificate of the tribals they would be mentioned as Malayalis. But they call themselves Malayali Gounder or Malayala Gounder. The Malayalis were not considered untouchables. In fact, they were like the dominant castes that lived in the plains.

In the village, where we stayed during that trip, I noticed that the Malayala Gounders and the Dalits had separate living quarters. It was the month of Aadi which falls between mid-July and mid-August. But it was still cold. We covered ourselves with blankets and fell into deep sleep. The houses had no windows. There were no fans. But we still slept well. We warmed ourselves with the heat of the kitchen stove and hot tea and came out just when the sunlight was spreading. The student said that there was a river outside the village and that we could go for our morning ablutions there and he took us there. We enjoyed the folds of the mountains we saw far away and walked through a grove of jackfruit trees. The wide mountain river was flowing between the rocks like a channel flowing in one path. When we saw the river, we began running towards it, shouting in excitement. The student from the mountains stopped us and took us to the lower level of the river.

The spot from where the river entered the village to where it ended was the area for the use of the Malayala Gounders. They bathe there, bathe their cattle, wash their clothes, and wash after ablutions and so on. The water that flowed down after their use was the river water that the Dalits used. That is where we went. There is a huge waterfall in the Kollimalai area called Agayagangai. I asked the student if the river was above the waterfall or below the waterfall. He said that it was the waterfall that turned into a river and flowed down there. I told him that many would have bathed in the waterfall and they would have belonged to so many different castes. The river that flowed down would have touched all their bodies; I asked him whether that was not a problem. For the first time, I saw in that village the unique custom of dividing a river for two communities.

In my experience, I feel caste is like god. There is no difference in villages, cities, mountains or among the educated or uneducated—god is everywhere; so is caste. Is there a day when god is not remembered? Similarly, caste is also remembered every day. There is only one difference. They say that those who have seen god cannot explain what god is and that those who explain have not seen god. But the everyday moments constantly produce before us visuals of caste.

****

Excommunication

R. Mahendiran

An old man had passed away in a nearby village. My mother had gone for the first day condolences. She asked me to go for the third day condolences, which was called the 'touching hands' day. This day was normally observed on the third or fifth day to share the grief of death. Those who offer condolences would extend both their hands and the others from the house of death would touch their hands in a gesture of shared grief. ! agreed to go. My mother reminded me that everyone from my village had already gone there and that from 8 am itself, the formal offering of condolences would begin.

On a vehicle, the village could be reached within 15 minutes. But it would take about three quarters of an hour if one went walking. Ten years ago, everyone used to walk to that village. A few would cycle down. But it was different now. The motorbike was the chosen vehicle now for such journeys. It took only 15 minutes to reach there on a motorbike, as I mentioned earlier.

I did not change. I went in the lungi and T-shirt I had worn the previous day. The reason I did not get into fresh clothes was that when you go to offer condolences, you normally do not wear bright clothes. Also, one has to come back and bathe after visiting a house of death. So, neither Amma nor I bothered about what I was wearing.

I had gone only half the way when I saw a girl walking ahead of me. I did not quite recognise her. Normally, that was the road taken by people to reach that particular village. She was not carrying a bag or anything else. She was walking fast, swinging her hands. I assumed she was also going to offer her condolences. I thought, if she was going to walk the whole way she would be late, she should have started earlier.

When I went close to her, on hearing the sound of the bike, she turned towards me. She told me she would like to ride with me. I was right in my assumption. She had set out as soon as she was done with the early morning chores without even washing her face or combing her hair. She had worn a very ordinary sari. I realised I knew her. She was, in fact, distantly related. So, I was sure she was going for the formal offering of condolences. She must have got late trying to finish the morning chores at home. I asked her to get onto the bike.

While we were riding, she asked, 'What is the occasion? How come you are going to that village?' I could not quite get her. I thought she must be joking. 'You think going to offer condolences is an occasion?' I told her. 'Offering condolences, is it? Who passed away?' she asked. I was surprised. The person had passed away three days ago. Didn't she know? She was married with a 10-year-old son, old enough to know when such events occurred. The person who had passed away was not well-known. But the news of death, in whichever corner it struck, normally reached all the villages around. I kept wondering and did not give her an answer immediately. After a while I told her, 'I don't know who exactly it is; but he has been gone for three days. My mother went on the day he passed away. She asked me to go today.' 'Aren't you going to offer condolences?' I asked her. 'We don't go to offer condolences,' she said. 'Then what are you going there for?' I asked her. 'Oh, I am just going to my mother's house,' she answered casually.

When she said she was going to her mother's house, I suddenly remembered the caste connections regarding her. I got perturbed. And I became more agitated because we had already reached the village. Memories of excommunications done before began to crowd my mind.

I remembered the story someone had told me once:

A husband and wife had had a huge quarrel. The arguments would not stop. Finally, the husband began to suspect her pregnancy. The wife pleaded with him that the child was his but he would not accept it. 'If you suspect that this child, that you have given me, is not your own, I don't need this tender thing in me,' she said and went away to get it aborted. Once she went to the hospital, the husband went to the elders of the village and said his wife had run away with someone and that he did not need her anymore and that she should be excommunicated from the caste. The village elders said that they would wait for three days.

The woman got the abortion done and came home after a few days. The moment she came home the husband told her, 'Either you die, or you get lost.' The wife did not know what was happening. When she asked around, she found out about his interest in having her excommunicated. If a husband and his agnates appeal to the village elders to excommunicate such and such person, a meeting would be called and they would ask those who appealed belonging to a specific temple. Nobody would argue but say that everything must be done according to the wishes of the agnates. Nobody really wanted to get into arguments over this. So, the wife knew that she would definitely be excommunicated. The husband kept pestering the wife to leave. She bore with it for two or three days. Then she hanged herself. The village elders also muttered, 'What a woman! She thought she would be excommunicated and so she died. She is a self-respecting woman,' and buried her.

I remembered many more such happenings.

One of them was the life of the woman who had taken a ride with me; she had been excommunicated. Her husband had run away from home. So, she lived with her parents. Her brother had gone away from the village to marry a girl from the Ottar caste and everyone always said he had 'run away' with her. Normally, when a family chooses a girl from another caste, they must fib that she was from their caste and that she was well off with a lot of landed property, and also that their relatives and elders had checked about the family and approved. Immediately after this cooked up story, they would fix the marriage and, before those in the village tried to check the story, they would have the marriage done and the thali would be tied around the girl's neck. Once that is done no one can do anything about it. No one can stop going to their house or inviting them home. They may grumble but they cannot excommunicate either openly or indirectly. This was the loophole in the Kavara Naidu caste. And it worked as a boon for those who looked for girls to marry from outside their castes. The woman's brother had not done it this way and had instead, gone away with the girl he wanted to marry. When people got to know this a few days later, he was excommunicated.

After a while, he returned. He told his parents that the girl who had eloped with him had gone away with someone else and that despite searching for her, he could not trace her. His parents did not object. He stayed on with his parents and continued to eat and sleep there as usual. He secretly maintained his relationship with his family. But the villagers carefully watched everything. There was no way a secret could be maintained where the villagers were concerned. Everyone came to know about him continuing to stay with his parents. Referring to his mother, they said: 'What guts this woman has! She can't take him in just because he is a son. These women have come to spoil the name of our caste. Such strumpets!' And they planned to excommunicate the whole family. Those who spoke to those who were excommunicated or took part in their family functions were also excommunicated. That was the caste rule.

Before they could be excommunicated another problem arose. It was a problem that had no precedence. Normally, within two years of a girl coming of age, parents would start looking for a groom for her. And normally the marriage would be arranged within those two years. If a girl remains unmarried even after she is 20 it would be assumed that something is wrong with her. So, a girl is normally married off by the time she is eighteen. For a man, it is different and there is more leniency for him in terms of marriageable age. If a man is 28 and unmarried it is not a big problem. But the moment a girl crosses her 18th year, people would start eyeing her differently. So, where girls were concerned, there were marriages of minor girls, which our laws mention. The big problem was with regard to this.

The month of Thai (mid-January to mid-February) is always full of marriage celebrations. Sometimes seven or eight weddings take place on a single day. Even 10 at times. When you are in a joint family, attending so many marriages in a day is not a problem. Five or six family members would divide the marriages among themselves and attend two or three each. That would make it easier. But for those in nuclear families, this is a big problem. They would grumble about fixing so many marriages on the same day and not looking for other auspicious days. How they were going to manage to attend all of them would be their problem. They would go and give the traditional gift of money called *moy* and leave, or send the moy money through someone else.

On such wedding days food wouldn't be cooked in the morning or afternoon in many houses in the village. The whole village would look festive. There would be songs playing on each street. Festoons would be hanging from all corners. Sometimes marriages would be fixed within a matter of two weeks. Close relatives would be invited first. Only after that would they buy the cooking pots called *arasanipaanai* and new clothes. The marriage expenses would not be very high. In a non-wedding season, one may have to cook one and half bundles of rice. But during the season, it would be only half a bundle because so many weddings would be taking place. Sometimes, even that much of cooked rice would get left over. The neighbours would be invited for dinner. But even if they didn't come, rice and kozhambu would reach their homes. Caste weddings took place in this manner. No one bothered about the legal age of marriage and other things. It was all a matter of working and earning one's food and no one thought that there was a place for law in such matters of existence.

One person pelted a stone on such happenings. That stone shook up the whole village. He brought this kind of caste marriage into the legal framework, and turned them into arrangements that broke the law regarding child marriage. He did not stop with that. He made excommunication also a matter to be broken. The fire he lit caught the whole village. The whole village wondered which whore's son had brought about this calamity. His name was kept secret. He complained in the nearby police station and the police came and threatened the village, and the villagers were enraged. Everyone thought that their particular caste had been dishonoured and there was much agony over it. The villagers united to ask the police which shameless fellow had complained. The police got a bit flustered. When the villagers surrounded the police jeep, the latter were scared that they would not be able to drive away. The villagers stood around the jeep saying they would not allow the police to leave unless they revealed the name of the person. The police were overwhelmed and began negotiations.

The police, somehow, managed to get out of the situation. The next day the Deputy Tasildar, the revenue official of the district, arrived. The only matter that remained prominent in the discussion even with him was who had complained about excommunication and child marriages. The revenue official could not do the work he had come for.

Many senior district officials came and tried their best. But the villagers did not yield. All of them had to return without achieving much. Finally, the District Collector came. 'How will the government help you if all of you behave in this manner? If you don't follow rules, your village will have no schools, no transport, no electricity, no water….' he kept listing what they would be denied. The only reply the village gave was what did it matter if they got all this, if they couldn't get the name of that shameless fellow who had complained. They pestered the Collector no end. Finally, the Collector and the police official could hold out no more and revealed the name of the complainant. The rage of the villagers was controlled and they merely said, 'Oh it is that man, is it? We guessed as much. Okay, we will deal with him.'

Other official actions followed. It was lack of education that was at the base of the practice of excommunication, the officials surmised, and began to do a survey of the status of education in the village. The villagers sent their children only to the local school. They were hesitant to send their children to other schools nearby. So, the level of education was, indeed, low according to the survey. The villagers complained that the girls who went to study in the schools outside the village had many problems to face. 'Is the school close enough to send them there? It is nine or 10 miles away. They are not boys that we can just let them go that distance. We can't send girls in the manner we send boys. Will you do that? You are well off and the bus may even come and stop at your house wall. Will it be the same for us? There is only the government bus. If we decide to go by that, it comes in its own sweet time at 10 or 10.30. So how can we go? The school here is up to the tenth standard. One has to just take four steps after you go past the Pidarisami temple in the corner of the village to reach the school. In the other school, they talk about this class and that class. By the time you finish all that, it would be dark when you return. You can't talk about law with a young girl at home. Our girls are important for us,' the villagers argued. At least they were not trying to do one-upmanship and were trying to tackle the situation.

The people played to the tunes of the District Collector and he, to theirs. They made a list of things that could be done. The Collector chose just one or two things from the list and hurriedly executed them. The middle school became a high school. An assurance was given that it would be upgraded to a junior college. A bus was to ply at 8.30 in the morning. The villagers agreed to not get their daughters married before 18 and not to excommunicate anyone after a meeting of their own or have any meetings related to caste. But they could not forget the man who had thrown the first stone to disrupt things.

Whether the monsoons happened or not, the village never failed to have the village temple festival. But after one particular incident, the village temple festival was stopped altogether.

After a conference with the Collector, the village temple festival had been organised. On the second day of the festival, all those who had been excommunicated came to the festival to be a part of the village. They were planning to cook the traditional Pongal before the temple and also do puja. The villagers got to know of this. They completed the temple chariot procession earlier than usual and brought the chariot before the temple. When those who were excommunicated entered the temple, others did not enter it; they moved away. Once they had finished their puja, the other villagers began their own. The puja of the villagers became much grander than normal and that of the excommunicated remained just a piece of exhibition of their assertion. The

Pidari goddess would have been overwhelmed to receive two separate pujas in one festival.

Those who were excommunicated filed a complaint at the police station that the villagers did not treat them with respect. The police came for an enquiry. The village elders evasively replied that they can't do anything about how those who were excommunicated offered puja. The rest of the villagers were not present. Those who were, told the police that, if they so wanted, even they could stand around and offer worship, and walked away smiling.

Finally, they set an auspicious date for the Kavadi festival, since the temple festival had not gone well. Every group had what is called a temple house, a temple they are attached to, and sometimes one temple house would have several groups attached to it. The kavadi pot is brought from the temple houses and first placed at a water source which would be a private well that is used only for such occasions, worshipped and then carried on the heads. The Kavadi festival is a preparation for the worship of the god Murugan throughout the year. When those who were excommunicated got to know about the auspicious date being set for the Kavadi festival, they arrived early in the morning with the police. The villagers gave up this festival also, thinking that if they did not hold the festival, there would be no interference from the excommunicated.

They kept blaming the person who had complained. 'He is responsible for this humiliation. He bought a third person to interfere in our affairs when we could have settled it ourselves. As if he is bringing about a big revolution.... When there was no rain and the children suffered, where was his revolution? Where was this law then? When we were dying for food where was he, was he sucking someone's dick? He should be excommunicated first....' Such angry words were in everyone's mind. There was no meeting and no one's permission was sought to actually excommunicate him. But no one participated in any function of that person's family.

Under the Mahatma Gandhi National Rural Employment Guarantee Act which was passed in 2005 (MGNREGA), 100 days of employment in a financial year was guaranteed to any rural household whose adult members are willing to do unskilled manual work. The Village Panchayat issued job cards to every registered individual. The mother of the person who had complained also worked under this scheme. She underwent incalculable suffering quietly. Whenever she came to get the job card, she would come alone. No one would even stand next to her. No one would touch the pan in which she carried mud or cement on her head. No one would take her card from the concerned manager and bring it to her. The manager was familiar with her name. If the officials sent any official news at short notice, she never got it. Their house was in the forest area so they never came to know even regular village news. They would move away from the son as if it was a sin to be near him. The temple and Kavadi festival, which were regular annual festivals, had now been entirely abandoned.

It was because of this problem that the meeting to excommunicate the parents of the woman I gave a ride to got stalled. But there were quiet murmurs that they had been excommunicated and yet some people were friendly with them; that there was no need to talk to this woman. They were also not friendly with their caste folks. They lived in the corner of the village. The agricultural land they had taken on lease was also of people from another caste. They never went to work in the fields of people of their own caste nor had I seen them take part in any family functions of their own caste. That is why I had assumed that they had been excommunicated. But I had also seen one or two persons talk to them. I had also spoken to them once in a way. I vaguely remember this woman going past our field while we were at work, and exchanging a few words with my father.

All this was in my mind as I was giving her a ride on my motorbike. I was also not very clear about the act of excommunication. So, at that point, I merely wanted to escape a problematic situation. I was afraid that if anyone saw me giving her a ride I, too, may be excommunicated. I thought, somehow I must get her off my bike. But how should I do it, I wondered. Should I tell her the truth that since she was going to be excommunicated, if I am seen with her I will meet a similar fate, and she should immediately get off my bike? Or should I think of a convenient lie? What should I lie about? Should I tell her that I needed to answer the call of nature and that she should go on her way as I will take a while, or should I tell her I felt nauseous and that she should go on her way for I needed to vomit, or should I just tell her I had some job to attend to and ask her to get down? But I had already told her I was on my way to offer condolences and it would be difficult to tell her I had some other job to attend to. She may get offended. What should I do? I had to do something fast within the next few seconds. Before I was seen with her, I had to let her off and then go on my own to offer my condolences. Once I crossed the Pidari Amman temple there was a likelihood of many people seeing me with her. I had to think of a good idea before that.

Right then my cell phone rang. I checked it. It was a text message from my company. Immediately, I had an idea. She was not going to know that it was a text message. I could tell her it was a missed call notification. So, I pretended to call someone even while riding. She believed me. I did not increase the speed of the bike; it slowed down and stopped. And I pretended to continue the call. I kept the cell phone at my ear for some time as if allowing the call to go on. If I spoke she would come to know the truth. So I did not speak. She was also quiet. Then I pretended to speak and after the pretence, I told her she should go ahead and that I would take a while; she went on her way.

What I spoke over the cell phone was this:

Where are you? At Ammai Thottam? What are you doing there? You said you were coming and then you never contacted. Okay...okay... what do you want me to do? Should I come there or go ahead and pay the condolence visit? I am standing beside the Pidari Amman temple... it will take me a while to go to his fields... hmm... hmm... Okay, shall I come to the fields then? Okay... okay... hang up then.

I pretended to talk with pauses and hung up. No... I pretended to hang up.

******

Penalty

P. Muthusami

The period before and after 2000 was the time when I was struggling to make correct choices in my life. That was the time when I worked as a labourer cutting tapioca tubers, making foundation pits for building constructions and hybrid cotton seed production, to make a living. I had to go to Ezhumathur near Modakurichi in Erode District for a tapioca tuber-cutting job. The sago factory in our area received the amount of tapioca tubers it needed from that area every year. The mill owner had many groups of labourers to do the work for him. He had come from that area to ours and bought pieces of land and started business here. He thus had more influence than other brokers. Those who owned the fields and the labourers had the faith that he would not delay payments. Vanniyars and Parayars worked together in groups and also as separate groups to cut the tapioca tubers.

When I took up this work in 1999 there were no Vanniyars in our group. Whenever the mill owner went to the area where the tapioca tuber-cutting had to be done, he would give instructions regarding what caste the labourers belonged to and how they should be treated. Likewise, he gave instructions to the labourers on how they should go about their work. This is what I had heard. It was in the same year that I had also joined the group. Around 11 in the night, the mill owner Kumaravel came and told us one day, 'I have told them that you are all Vanniyars. So behave accordingly.' After that we got into the lorry that was to take us.

Mayavilakku Ganesan, another labourer, was narrating the many incidents that had happened in that area earlier. Labourers from the Madari caste, a caste which came under the umbrella of the Arunthathiyar, a sub-group among the Scheduled Castes, were not even allowed into the fields. Once one Periyannan did not pay heed to the instructions of the mill owner and jocularly remarked to the owner of the fields, 'I am the only Parayan among these peasants.' After a few days, he went to the water tank and opened the pipe and drank some water. The owner of the fields rushed towards him yelling, 'You Madari dog, how dare you!' and tied him to a coconut tree after beating him up. The others did not know what to do and pleaded with the owner. But he would not relent. Then they rang up the mill owner and Periyannan was let off after his intervention. Periyannan caught a bus and came back to the village and after that he has avoided going to that area for tapioca tuber-cutting work. But he was with us that particular year. Ganesan wondered what he would do. Periyannan was fast asleep as Ganesan was narrating all this.

We reached Modakurichi by seven in the morning. We didn't do any work that particular day. We went to many fields but got no work. Finally, we reached Ezhumathur and went to a field that lay to the east of the village. It was four in the evening. One could not cut the tapioca tubers in the evening. So, we decided to do it the next day and stayed on there. We divided the work among ourselves: some of us would procure the necessary ingredients, and the others would cook dinner for everyone. The owner of the field showed us a large hall where he was staying which was normally used for sitting down and eating and told us we could stay there; and that there would be tapioca tuber-cutting work in his own field for a week; he told us we could also work elsewhere, and that we could continue using this hall to stay in. He was around 65 and seemed like a very nice person. He was staying alone there in the hall. His two sons were living with their families in Erode for professional reasons. He was staying on his own in his fields and cooking for himself.

Shakthivel was adept at conversations. He would narrate old stories and earn the favour of old people. He spoke to the landlord and got us many facilities. For more than a week we worked on his fields. We became so close to him that he began to say that there was a good harvest that year because of the luck we had brought. He ate what we cooked. And at nights we would go to watch a film. We had told the others who did not come for the film to eat early and go to sleep and not to indulge in too much conversation with him. Periyannan behaved in a very subdued manner this time. Ganesan's anxieties in this regard were assuaged. Everyone thought it was a good turn of events.

Things continued this way till we finished the work on his land. On the last day at around 11:00 in the morning, the tapioca tubers were loaded and the lorry was covered with a tarpaulin cover. The landlord opened the water connection for bathing. Everyone was bathing except for those who were tying up the load in the lorry. Since it was afternoon, we bathed for a long time. The old man also came to have his bath. While the others were bathing in the water that was overflowing on to a channel from the cement water tank; the old man got into the tank to bathe. He asked Shakthivel to rub his back. Shakthivel also got into the tank in the pretext of rubbing his back and bathed there. Periyannan was watching this. The old man told everyone to get into the tank and bathe properly as the channel water would not be enough to rub off all the dirt on the body. We had fun bathing in the large water tank. The old man left after a while. The others were bathing as if there was going to be no end to it.

Sakthivel asked Periyannan, 'You are thinking of what happened in the past, is it? Those were different times. Don't be afraid; bathe without any fear.'

'Well, you can talk what you want. You are lucky now to talk to me thus,' said Periyannan.

'If the truth that you are all Parayars comes out, then you would know what would happen.'

'We will deal with it when it happens. Why are you so scared?'

Periyannan left saying, 'Do whatever you want. I am leaving.'

We were so happy bathing that we had forgotten where the old man was. He appeared from nowhere and shouted, 'Enough of bathing. Come out, all of you.'

Everyone including Shakthivel was startled.

He had used very polite terms of address for all of us till then, but now he was using very impolite language. We wondered if he had overheard us talking. Fear began to show on our faces. My condition was worse than the others. I had been against telling a lie about our caste and saying that we were Vanniyars. There was not much difference between the Vanniyars and Parayars anyway. They are also like Parayars in terms of economic status, culture and lifestyle. They even worshipped the same clan god. But Vanniyars were considered upper caste and these lies had to be told and we had to do the role-play we did. And for this we had to live in fear. All these confused and scared thoughts crowded my mind. The situation became a volatile one filled with anxiety. The root cause of the fear was that the area belonged to them. Otherwise, we were 20 and he was alone. He couldn't have done anything to us.

He seemed to understand what we were thinking. 'You said you were all Vanniyars. Which group of Vanniyars do you belong to?' he asked us. No one knew about groups among Vanniyars. 'You Parayar fellows!" he yelled. 'Just see what I am going to do to all of you,' he shouted and went towards the hall. Hearing all this noise those around the area gathered there. They also shouted at us. The old man slapped Shakthivel. 'You dog, you have the temerity to come and rub my back. I was doubtful when I saw your faces. I trusted that young man. Let him come. Call him over the phone,' he said. Someone rang up the mill owner. No one knows what the mill owner said to him; he also spoke to the group leader Gundu Periyannan, another Periyannan. Gundu Periyannan apologised saying, 'What we did was wrong. We will agree to whatever you say.' Others around also spoke in a conciliatory manner: 'Speaking such lies about caste does happen when you go to work. One should clarify everything beforehand.' They also asked us to leave quickly and not linger on.

The old man, however, was still fuming. He said, 'I can't let them off so easily. I must do something so that they remember not to do this somewhere else.' By then the lorry driver had got a call from the mill owner. He said he was told to just leave and bring the lorry of tapioca tubers and he started the lorry. The lorry was moving without us. Ten of us went and stopped the lorry and began to shout and told him that we were not doing any work and that we were ready to go our village and should be taken along. The driver said he couldn't do that because if people travelled in a load-carrying lorry, the police would catch him. 'The mill owner has told me to leave you behind. So I am leaving,' he said and drove away.

All of us began to walk towards the Ezhumathur main road. Everyone was quarrelling among themselves. The leader Gundu Periyannan told us to let things be; no point fighting about it. Shakthivel doubted the other Periyannan. He thought Periyannan had left before others. Maybe he couldn't tolerate our being happy; he must have squealed to the old man. A few pounced on Periyannan. He kept on pleading he was innocent but they kept yelling at him. Gundu Periyannan intervened and said, 'Cool down all of you. It will be more worthwhile to think about what the mill owner told me.' No one let him finish what he wanted to say. 'What did he say? Even when they sell cattle they take them in the vehicle. We are lesser than cattle. We don't even have the dignity the cattle have. Leave alone dignity. Shouldn't we be treated as human beings? Are we so lowly that even that is not possible?' All of them began to complain and grumble.

Gundu Periyannan began his own lament: 'What are you all lamenting about? Do you know what the mill owner told me? "I have lost my honour, dignity and trust because of all of you. How am I going to do business now? Even if I say the workers are Vanniyars no one is going to believe me anymore." The land-owner has refused to give the payment for the work. The mill owner is saying, "How can I pay, when he doesn't?" What are we going to do now? We don't even have money for the bus fare.' Quarreling thus, by the time we reached the Ezhumathur main road it was 7 pm. Our group leader Periyannan had been given money for the food expenses. He had ₹500 left from that amount. How could 20 people reach the village with that? We also had to eat. There was no way we could travel or eat. When we collected money from everyone it came to some ₹200. That was definitely not going to be enough. We thought of other ways to reach the village. We thought we may stop some other lorry carrying a load of tapioca tubers and tell the driver about our problem. If only we could reach Athoor we were confident we could walk the rest of the way to the village.

All of us looked at lorries going on the road. All kinds of things were going on in my mind. I am here only for some time. If this is what I am going through in this short time, how do these others who live here bear all this? They must have got used to it.

Many years later what a friend told me shocked me. One of the things he told me was that when Gounders entered the street where Arunthathiyars lived, the Arunthathiyars had to stand up whether they were sitting on a cot, in a chair, bench or whatever. Even if they were sitting on the floor they had to stand up. That shocked me even more maybe because this was not so in our area. It is 60 years since we got our independence. Human life has changed in so many ways. There are some things that have disappeared without a trace. But the imprints of caste have remained like some rock edicts, I thought, and felt depressed.

I found the determination that day not to hide my caste even if I was going to die of starvation. One should first get rid of the notion from one's mind that mentioning one's caste is demeaning. I decided that revealing one's caste is not demeaning or humiliating as much as lying and deceiving others about one's caste.

Even after 10 pm we could not find a lorry going our way. So, we decided to for go food and caught a bus to Athoor. Throughout the night hunger was gnawing at our stomachs. We had eaten early in the morning and had not eaten lunch or dinner. We were also physically tired after the work. We were all dead, but there was nothing we could do about it and we came back to the village feeling terribly hungry. The fact that caste and lying had made 20 people for go two meals and starve is still a deep scar on my heart. The mill owner finally refused to pay us for the tapioca tuber-cutting work. That made us angrier. Later, mill owners, brokers and others negotiated and it was decided that our wages would be given by the mill owner after deducting just one day's wages. But the mill owner said that he would not be able to pay us right away. So we stopped doing his work. As for me, I stopped going for the job of cutting tapioca tubers altogether.

That was the last time I went for that job and till today I have not been paid wages for it.

The wages for 20 men for eight days' work would be about ₹15,000. We were cheated of the entire amount. Caste and lies swallowed our labour completely. We thought it was the penalty we paid for lying about our caste because the mill owner asked us to, and let it go. But they did not relent about not paying our wages for this lie and did not come forward to pay us for our honest labour. Cheating us and humiliating us did not seem to bother them in the least.

Many changes are certainly taking place when we discuss caste. These are not changes that can happen instantly, it will take time for them to happen. Some feel that we have to wait until then. That may be true as well.

****

Family of Snake Charmers

R. Venkatachalam

From the time of our forefathers, our agnates had followed the system of living closely with other castes. People of many different castes live next to one another in our village. There are more than 10 villages under our Panchayat. In seven among those villages live the Kolrus who speak Telugu and who are a sub-group of the Naidu caste. The Telugu-speaking Jenappa Chettiar caste people live in another village. In the other two villages, live the Pallik Kudiyanavars, who are basically Vanniyars. With all these castes is located my village of Dalits. We belong to the Kannada-speaking group known as Murasu Parayar. With us was also a family belonging to the Katti Parayar group. South east to the Panchayat were the Telugu-speaking Sakkiliyars. There were also a few Muslims scattered here and there. The Nadars, who are called Marameris because they were traditional toddy tappers, also lived in another village.

This area is backward in terms of education. For the Palli Kudiyanavars, who are Vanniyars as mentioned above, it is the people of our village who have been offering the service of scavengers and they are called Thottus. At present, this scavenging service is not there only in one village, because here the major livelihood is agriculture. The agricultural lands in this village are rain-dependent. There are also many mango orchards, coconut farms and palmyra trees. Cattle grazing, climbing the coconut and palmyra trees and doing other daily wage labour are jobs common to all the castes.

Our family was a family of seven agnate families. The scavenging service for seven agricultural villages had been divided among these seven families even in the past. This kind of functioning belonged to our ancestors. My great grandfather also practised the Siddha system of medicine along with his service as a scavenger. He could cure ailments of both humans and cattle and had earned a good name. He was much respected in all the villages around, even those from different Panchayats. Since he was particularly adept at treating snakebites, scorpion, centipede and other poisonous insect bites, our family came to be known in time as the 'family of snake charmers'.

In return for this service the farmers whom they served, known as Andai or masters, would keep aside bundles of Little millet, Sorghum, Kodo millet, Foxtail millet, Pearl millet and Finger millet, and give them once a year as payment called 'merai' to the scavengers who worked for them. This was also a custom that had existed for a long time. When goats were cut for functions connected with the agricultural land, temple festivals and for events of exorcism, a portion of that would be set aside as the scavenger's share. If the cow, bull or buffalo had a fracture in the leg or fell sick, it would be sold at half the price to the scavengers doing service for that family. If these animals died, the Andaimar, the masters, would take just their skin. At times, if they did not want the skin, they would set a price at which the scavengers could buy the skin. This was the normal custom.

To carry the dead animals they would use a thick bamboo pole which would be 10 feet long and six inches thick. This bamboo pole, used to carry dead animals, was known as *'paadai'* or *'vaarai'*, a bier or a wooden beam. Dead goats would be skinned and the skin would be salted and dried in the sun. Its hair would be removed with an arrow-like instrument and cleaned and used. The skin of the cow or bull would be used in the making of musical instruments like *thudi* and molam, also known as parai or *kottu*, two of which were also generally known as *molam*. The buffalo skin was used in the making of the bigger musical instrument known as *dhol*. The job of making these instruments would be done in the summer.

When I was a child I had to go to a nearby village where Chanars lived, to go to school. That was the nearest primary school. While hobnobbing with the villagers or the students from there, we would be referred to as 'Parayar boys'. During the lunch break, when we went to the village well, they would make us stand far away and ask us to bend down, and they would pour water into our cupped hands or into a bowl that we may be carrying. They would hold their pot very high while pouring the water. They would be careful not to let anything they were carrying be touched by us.

We had to walk through the fields of the farmers to go to school. If anyone came from the other side, we had to move aside and make way for them. Or they would abuse us using our caste name. We were not supposed to wear any footwear when we went inside the villages of the Andaimar, the masters. Our elders always addressed their Andais as 'Sami'. Even if on some occasions we had to be with them, we had to stand away and not sit down at an equal level with them. And definitely not sit at a higher level. We had to keep standing and sit down only when told to.

Just as my great grandfather was popular among the other castes, his younger brother, my other grandfather whom we called Chinna Thatha, was also popular. People called him and my grandfather's elder brother, whom we called Periya Thatha, by the same name. He was a folk artiste. He was also a carpenter but could even do masonry work. He would take cattle and poultry to villages and sell them. My father was like him. My father was also a broker for selling coconut farms, tamarind farms and cattle. He had expertise in many matters. Hence our family was very popular in the area for nearly a century. My father was fluent in Tamil, Telugu, Kannada, Urdu, Marathi and Hindi. By the time he was 13, he had learnt to be a broker and a folk artiste. He was thorough with the customs, habits and family traditions of many farmers' families in the area. My father and my grandfather had not really gone to school; they were just about literate.

Chinna Thatha was very affectionate towards me. So he used to take me along, whether it was day or night, whenever he went to his Andaimar's villages. And he would introduce me to them saying, 'Sami, he is my grandson; he is studying.' He would say that with such pride and his face would shine with happiness.

They would bring out whatever was in their house for me. They would ask if he had any vessel. If he had any plate or vessel in his hand, he would take whatever they offered. Or they would ask him to pluck a pumpkin leaf and bring it. Or else ask him to cut a serrated palmyra leaf and fold it like a deep plate. After that they would serve the food on that plate.

For water, they would take out the measure kept under the eaves especially for us. The iron measure was called '*manam*'. If that was not there they would take out a coconut shell and pour water in it. If it was a snack they would ask Chinna Thatha to spread the towel on his shoulder and put it in that. He would accept it. Some who had real concern for our family would ask us to eat the snack right there. Chinna Thatha would sit under the eaves near the pyol, and feed me. All this seemed very strange to me. I didn't understand any of it. If I asked about it he would say, 'They are our Andais, our masters. They are upper caste people; we are lower caste.'

During festival times my grandfather would be gifted with money. He would happily accept it. The money gifts would be given according to their financial position. If anyone was generous, he would wish them well saying, 'Have a good life, Sami.' They would also be happy. I would observe all this with curiosity standing next to him. He would buy sweetmeats and fill my hands with them. In the afternoons, Thatha would be served country liquor free of charge. He would take that local brew in a coconut shell and drink it as if it was heavenly nectar. If someone gave him toddy, he would take some for me too and give me. I would happily drink it. I would immediately feel sleepy. He would lay me under the eaves of someone's house and he would also go to sleep.

In the village nearby the Chanars had to be called Moopar. The Moopar were also Chanars who were toddy tappers also called Kiraminis, Nadars or Chanars. But in this area being called Chanars was considered degrading and Moopar was preferred. Whenever there were festivals in their village, they would invite Thatha and Appa. They had many admirers, friends and professional friends there. When they went there, they would carry a cane basket and an aluminium vessel. They would spread a cloth in the cane basket. People would fill the basket with pearl millet rice, foxtail millet rice, kodo millet rice, millet pap balls, idli and dosai. Pork curry and chicken curry would be poured into the aluminium vessel. A few would pour dry fish curry and lamb curry. The curry with mixed flavours would have a special taste of its own.

The farmers would invite us for their family weddings. If we attended the wedding at night they would make us sit in a corner in front of the house and serve food in the vessels we would take with us. They would be careful not to touch our vessels while serving. If it is the Mariamman temple festival, millet porridge would be served. To receive the porridge the people of our village would take mud pots and place them at the corner of the temple boundary walls. Once the puja was over, they would bring pots of millet porridge and pour it into our pots. If some overeager person so much as touched their pots, that person would be admonished and not given the porridge. They would say the touch was polluting. For village festivals or private pujas, they would keep aside food for scavengers working for them and those who played the molam drums and gave it to them.

On occasions of death, our caste people would be called for beating the molam drums. The payment for that would be mostly country liquor and they would buy it themselves and give it. Towards the end, they would divide the money that was left over among those who were called. When they handed over the money they would appreciate it if we bent to take it. If we accepted it casually they, would refer to us by our caste and abuse us before others saying, 'Getting big, are you?' Some would accept the money by turning over the molam and deferentially holding it out to receive the money. If someone did that, he would be called a good Thoti. The farmers had no qualms about abusing and they outdid one another in that aspect.

Under such circumstances a general meeting was held in connection with the Panchayat in the common grounds, chaired by the Panchayat President. All the villagers took part in that. A strong difference of opinion arose between our caste people and the Andais with regard to the division of things according to needs, rights, necessity and government concessions. When they were opposed and our people refused to give in, the problem took a different turn. The Panchayat President was a Naidu who had remained President permanently. He had done nothing for our village. Those who had never questioned anything so far were now speaking disrespectfully and in a disobedient manner and demanding things. The upper caste people got together and took a decision. They decided to issue a village dictum that no one must invite the Thotis, and those associated with them, for any work. This prevented the Thotis who were doing service from even taking up daily wage jobs.

Following this the Panchayat leader started disliking us. He had no concern for us. Although our village was near the road he would not allow buses to stop there. He saw to it that the buses stopped near his village. He refused to give space to build a housing colony with no cost, which was meant for us. These colonies were built in wasteland owned by the government or if there was no wasteland, land would be bought from other communities at government rates, and a free housing colony built for our community. He filed a case and went on to appeal right up to the High Court to stop the colony from being built. But our people did not give up and kept sending appeals to the government and the government officials, and succeeded in getting a space allotted for the housing colony and also had the colony constructed. He lost badly in this fight with us. Our people also managed to get a bus stop for the village. He was further humiliated when this happened. The Panchayat leader's nephew managed to grab the wasteland near the lake and he also built a house there. Not only that, he also set up an idol of Ganesh there and began farming work there.

That spot had been set aside by the government for our cremation ground. When the government banned burials near the lake, this wasteland was given as an alternative place for this purpose. Despite knowing about this, he did not allow us to use it and forcibly occupied it. To retrieve the land from him, all of us, including me, gave a petition to the District Collector in the meeting held for the welfare of the Adi Dravidars. We struggled to get the land back. In retaliation, the relatives of the said Panchayat leader filed court cases against me and more than 10 people of my village.

Our family god was the clan god Thimmarayaswami. This temple was on the coconut farm owned by the Naidus. Our gothra is Vishnu gothra. Our ancestors were ardent devotees of Tirupathi Ezhumalaiyan, generally referred to as Tirupathi Balaji, or Tirupathi Venkatachalapathi or Venkateswara. We have been doing the puja and worship of our clan god in this temple from time immemorial. But I have no memory of our ever being allowed to enter the sanctum sanctorum of the temple in all these years. We were expected to stand outside in the temple hall and offer worship. Even when they were on good terms with us, this one thing was never allowed.

We may be a family clan well known in the village, good professionals with a good name, but the Andais still consider us low caste. More than the Chanars, Nadars and Pallimars, the Naidus are caste-obsessed to this day. When it comes to abusing by using caste names and practising untouchability, they are the ones who take the lead. The only reason for all this is because they are the so-called upper caste and dominant caste and we are supposed to be lower caste. That we don't have lands, comforts and economic stability or education or work act as added factors for this situation to continue. That is the reality we are faced with today.

****

Stale Food

M. Venkatesan

It was a Sunday. I was in an animated conversation with my friend at the spot where I was building a new house. Electric wiring work was going on in the house. The contractor in charge of the wiring also joined our conversation. The conversation began with world politics and touched upon many different topics like the slow pace of Indian economy, rising prices and increase in onion prices. Finally, we ended up discussing Tamil Nadu politics and later the issue of marriage. The contractor told me, 'Looks like you are determined to think of marriage only after the house is done.' He did not leave it at that. He began to say rather sarcastically, 'You are getting old, Sir. Crops must be grown in the right season.' My friend also agreed with his advice. The contractor, as if premising his argument to come, asked me if I was a Mudaliar or a Gounder. He seemed very interested in knowing my caste. I confronted him quietly with a smile. But he would not give up. He said I looked like I belonged to his Mudaliar caste and that he was going to look for a Mudaliar girl for me. I did not pay much heed to what he was saying. He was grumbling to my friend about it.

I went in for some work. When I came back, my friend took leave of me. But the contractor thought that I was avoiding the conversation on marriage. He lost interest in the conversation. Maybe he had tried to ask my friend about my caste.... But when nothing came out of it, he got very upset. Later, whenever he spoke to me, it was only about the work on hand. I thought then of the black-shirted Marappan Sir who was the district in-charge of the Dravida Kazhagam, who always used to recall Periyar's words that the human brain was chained by caste.

I was born in the early seventies, in a village in the north of Tamil Nadu, into an utterly poor peasant family living on the fringes with very little land, doing rain-dependent paddy cultivation for a living. If the skies were kind we planted the seeds of little millet, horse gram, finger millet and red gram in our headland. If the rains flooded the streets, we planted peanuts meant for headland cultivation. My early days were extremely severe; filled with hunger and starvation. It was a time when poverty kept chasing us. My ancestors were Tholan, Muthu, Karukkappallan and Pachaiappan. They got a five-acre headland during the time of the British. One acre of that was sold for a few hundred rupees to an upper caste person who owned the land adjacent to ours, when my father married my mother Chinnakkannu from Arur.

My father still talks about that acre that had to be sold and feels bad about it. A piece of land once gone is gone forever. It is the land in the corner of the village. It has been turned into a mango orchard now. In the remaining land, we used to plant little millet, horse gram and pearl millet. So, when I was small, I mostly ate little millet rice, pearl millet porridge, horse gram soup and commonly grown greens which tasted like nectar from heaven to me. Only during Diwali or Pongal would we get rice, idli, dosai or the sweet *adhirasam* made with jaggery and rice flour. But that was only on rare occasions. To get four annas out of my father for firecrackers was a great struggle. I still remember how when I, along with some friends of mine, was collecting some firecrackers that had not burst from the compound of a Brahmin gentleman, one of the firecrackers suddenly burst and my hand started bleeding.

I was very fond of my paternal grandmother Chinnapillai, my paatti. No one could have a paatti like her and my dear paatti loved me as if I was all that she had in life. And she was my experience of heaven in my childhood. I had two older sisters and an older brother. And I had three younger sisters. I was the fourth child. It was a big family, so my parents were always out even before dawn, to do various jobs like planting, weeding, tilling the fields, plucking out peanuts, cutting sprigs of sugarcane, reaping paddy or threshing work, or running a pair of oxen on an already harvested field of little millet to coax out the remaining grains, or cutting grass. My childhood was thus spent mostly with my paatti. Paatti would make me lie down on her stretched legs and tell me stories of King Vikramaditya, *Mahabharatham*, tell me proverbs and riddles, sing lullabies and put me to sleep. Not only that. I had a favourite stone mortar in which grains were pounded. She would pound pearl millet in it and make fresh porridge for me with it. Then she would make rotis from finger millet flour ground in a grinding stone. And she would grind tamarind in the mortar with a pestle and make tamarind pickle for me. All this she would make with so much love. Her food tasted better than my mother's. She would light firewood in a makeshift stove of broken pieces of a mud pot, pluck leaves and flowers from the drumstick tree in the backyard, mix them in the pearl millet flour and make rotis. I can still smell the fragrance of those freshly made hot roti.

My father was my paatti's only son. She got her two daughters married into families related to us. At one time Appa worked as a postman with the central government. My sisters therefore grew up in comfort. After my elder brother was born my father's health was affected and he resigned from his job. It was very difficult to manage a big family. Paatti used to lament saying, 'Those days when my son did not work in the fields and the family lived in comfort are gone. Now he has to work so hard in the fields. Mariamma, please show us the way.'

Kamarajar, that blessed leader, who was chief minister then, had introduced the mid-day meals scheme for schools. My primary education went on unhindered in my village Nayakkanur. Paatti never sat quietly for even a moment. She would do all the work connected with the house and with the backyard. She would take care of the cow, clean the pearl millet or keep herself busy with one thing or the other. In the mornings, very often, there was no food for me to eat. Paatti would go to Kannapa Nayakkar's house. Alaththamman was our clan god and his too. She would go to that village elder's house and get porridge and she would keep it in our big house in the rope net vessel holder meant for keeping buttermilk, butter, etc. Our house was roofed with grass from the Javvadu hills. There was a small house and a big house both of them in the north-south direction. The big house was the god's house. I would sit and study there. I would drink the porridge made of finger millet bran kept in a vessel on the rope net holder and go to school. Sometimes even that wouldn't be there to eat and I would have to remain hungry. Then I would have to wait till lunch time for meals.

One particular year, there was drought. The entire village of different castes was struggling for food. Some well-to-do people of the village had bags of seed grains meant for sowing. They divided that among the people and distributed it. During those days whenever I cried of hunger, my paatti would take me to Nayakkar's house. As soon as she saw us, the elder Nayakkachi would spread a gunny bag on the pyol. My paatti would pluck a leaf of a castor plant from the backyard and bring it and Nayakkar's wife would place rounded balls of cooked millet and thick horse gram soup to go with it. She would be careful not to touch the leaf. There was no embarrassment or problem about that. Then she would bring a measure full of water. I was an innocent child then. I would gobble up the millet balls in hunger and it would taste heavenly. Then the whole day would be spent climbing the tree in the temple yard and swinging on its branches and it would be a lot of fun.

Sometimes while returning from school I would be thirsty. There was a well near the school where women from other castes would be drawing water. I would hesitate to ask them for water. If I was really thirsty, I would ask them. They would hold the pot at least the length of a hand above my cupped hands so that the pot did not touch my hands, and pour the water. It is difficult to forget that scene of my bending with cupped hands and eagerly drinking water that was thus poured, and quenching my thirst.

A street that stretched for about two furlongs was the main street of our village. The main street began where the tarred road of the Panchayat Union ended. First on the road was the school followed by the houses of Nayakkars, Vanniyars, Kurumbars and then the houses of Boyars who spoke Telugu. Then there was the house of the only Chettiar who ran a shop in the village. At the end were the living quarters of Adi Dravidars with one or two tiled houses. There were also some houses of Navidhars, the barbers, and Vannars, the community that washed clothes of the people of the village among other things. The Nayakkars and the Vanniyars (known as Pallis) owned most of the lands in the village.

The Adi Dravida people could not enter the houses of the farmers who were known as caste Hindus at any time. The Vannars, Navidhars and Kurumbars were more lenient in this matter. Once I was playing hide and seek in school with a student. I got so totally involved in the game that I went and hid behind the open door of a house nearby. My playmate could not find me but a farmer spotted me there and the result was a meeting of the village Panchayat where my father apologised on my behalf and also paid a fine.

The Muthumariamman temple in our locality was very famous. It was the deity guarding the village. From the time of our ancestors, when the goddess was taken on procession, the first puja would be at our house of god called *nadu veedu*, the house in the centre. To this day that is the custom. My father was a priest at the temple at one time. When my grandfather Pachaiappan was customarily the priest at the temple, the next village was afflicted with small pox. He went to that village despite the divine order he had received not to go. As a result, he also got afflicted with small pox and died the very next day. My father was a babe in arms then. Later, after being a temple priest for a while, my father did many rituals of atonement to assuage the goddess and got himself out of the job of being a priest at the temple. The goddess was considered very powerful. Even to this day, if the goddess is being taken in procession my father would be present there even if he was travelling. If he could not make it he would slap himself on the cheeks saying he had wronged the goddess. Appa also used to get possessed. He also used to utter predictions when he was in that state.

Summer was the time of the temple festival, when porridge was given to the villagers, and many other festivals. There would be exorcisms where possessed women from many different villages and castes would get whipped by the main priest of the occasion, who was also an exorcist. People from other castes from nearby villages and our own villagers would worship the goddess with a lot of faith. They would also make vows for the fulfilment of many different wishes. All that they wished for would normally be fulfilled. Earlier vows like giving the goddess a gold thali, gold jewellery, sacrificing a goat and making Pongal would be fulfilled without fail. People of all castes would enter the temple and worship. But our caste people did not normally enter the temple in the farmers' street. Those were days when caste restrictions were very strict. There was also a buffalo festival after Pongal and each caste competed with the other in celebrating it. At the end of all these festivals would be drunken fights, and even fisticuffs, where castes would disappear.

If a wedding took place in a dominant caste household the entire village would be fed for a week. No one would light the oven in their houses. Those days meant a lot of fun. One would get rice to eat. And in the wedding feast at the venue of the wedding there would be rice, kozhambu made with red gram, rasam, vadai, payasam and appalam and such varieties of food. Once a wedding took place in the house of the leader of the village, who is normally called 'Ooor Gounder'. Both sides of the streets were lit with tube lights, serial colour bulbs, and there were welcome boards lit with bulbs everywhere. The electricity was stolen from the electric pole for all this. The entire village was flooded with light. In the green pandal built in front of the groom's place there were leaves of banyan, peepul and the Indian beechnut tree cut along with the branches. The wedding pandal was really huge. There was music and auspicious musical instruments playing. The welcome offered to the bride's family went on beyond midnight. No food was offered until then. Then the first round of food was for the bride's family and relatives. Next came the groom's family and relatives. Only the last round of food was for us. And only rice and rasam remained for us to eat.... I had fallen asleep by then. My father tried to wake me up. In weddings like the ones among dominant castes, I have always eaten rice while being half asleep.

When I joined the government school in the small town of Singarapettai, I had to walk three kilometres to the school every day. Some incidents happened in that school. It was normal in that school to tease someone using that person's caste name. From our village, four of us used to go walking to the school and come back walking. We had no slippers. Since we carried the school bags on our shoulders, our shirts were always torn at the shoulders. We wore khaki pants which always looked worn out or were torn in the seat. Those holes were always referred to as the post box. These tears would be stitched with needle and thread and not properly darned. There was a group of boys who made fun of this. The small-town school had a different environment from our village school. A boy who belonged to the town, who was my class fellow and happened to be the son of teacher Rajapandian, encouraged me to fight back. We learnt to abuse those who teased us, calling them motherfuckers aloud… but it is true that we felt a sense of fear.

During lunch breaks we used to go to a barber's shop called Tirupathi Saloon. We used to comb our hair for free there. We also learnt to read papers there. At noon, hunger would gnaw at our stomachs. We would drink the water kept in a pot there and manage. If we had 10 paise we would buy tapioca fruit sticks to eat. When Deenadayalan, my class fellow whose father owned the Venkateswara hotel, guessed that we did not carry our mid-day meals, he started bringing pieces of bread from the hotel, stuffing them in his trouser pockets that really jutted out of his fat body. He would offer them to me saying, 'Venkatesa, eat this.' I would grab it and all of us would hurriedly gobble up the bread. This happened many times in a week. That great person who assuaged our hunger is no more.

The local boys from upper castes brought rice and similar food considered decent for lunch. But in our homes in the morning we had only porridge or cooked grain balls from the previous day. We had an inferiority complex about carrying this kind of food for lunch. So, water became the only medicine to treat our hunger. But even this medicine was not always available. Finally, hunger won. So, we decided to carry for lunch whatever was available at home (which was mostly porridge) and eat it secretly. We used to sit near the well which was a little further away and eat what we had brought without letting others know.

It was Gunasekaran who succeeded in his efforts to find out the secret behind our sitting away from others and eating our food. Our secret was out. We brought no tiffin boxes, so what were we doing near the well during lunch hours? He decided to find out and came to the spot where we were eating. His sudden appearance there, since it was unexpected, made us a little nervous. We had just started eating. He looked triumphant. He said he had come to attend to the call of nature and quickly disappeared.

There was a reason why we got nervous. We carried either porridge or cooked grain balls in brass or aluminium tiffin boxes and used to keep it at Tirupathi saloon on the way to the school. At one in the afternoon, we would go and fetch our tiffin boxes from the saloon and sit near the well to eat. We would get down into the well and scoop out water and add it along with rock salt to the porridge and loosen the thick porridge and drink it. During festival days, we got idli and dosai at home. We used to keep it for two or three days and bring it as lunch to school and enjoy eating it. Sometimes this food would get spoilt. This secret of ours slowly spread among other students. Some naughty boys used to call out to me saying, 'Little millet porridge' and 'Stale dosai'. I used to feel most humiliated.

I have lived in Pondicherry for nearly 10 years. During my college days, I have walked around with friends in the mango orchard near Laspet, which figures in Bharathi's Song of the Koel. I have also gone to Bharathi's memorial house many times. At that time it was Bharathi's opposition to caste that inspired me the most. When I did my graduate studies in Tamil in Tagore College, many incidents took place there. Slowly, I began to give up lying about my caste. Moving towards the city has brought about many changes in me. Particularly, it gave me the courage and strength to leave behind my inferiority complex regarding caste.

In Pondicherry, I lived in the Kuyavarpalayam area in a rented place with my elder brother. He was working in a private company.

In order to study in the college, I needed a caste certificate given by the government. In order to get Form 11 (which was for permission for education), which was part of the caste certificate which the Tamil Nadu government issued, I had applied to the Village Administrative Officer in the Nelli Thopu commune.

The officer from the commune came while I was not there and checked details regarding our caste and about how long we had been living there with our neighbours. I did not know about this. After continuous visits to the commune office for four days, at last I got the caste certificate. I joined the Kanchi Mamunivar Centre for Postgraduate Studies. A week went by. One evening at around four, I came home after college. Our neighbour Ganesh's mother began the conversation with me premising it with the question, 'Tell me Venkittu, can someone do something like this?' They were Saiva Pillais. They observed traditional customs and rules very strictly. She was fair skinned. I could not make out what she was getting at. 'They came from the commune and enquired about you. For the sake of government concession, will anyone change the real caste?' she asked in a tone of accusation. I understood what the problem was.

It was all about the caste certificate. I told her what my caste was but she would not believe it. Maybe my elder brother had mentioned some other caste. Or it is possible that since we generally behaved well and with dignity, not bothering anyone, she could not believe the truth. It is also possible she had caste prejudices. But when she kept asking why I was lying for the sake of government concession, it bothered me. But she began to behave differently towards us in a few days. She began to complain against us to the house owner. She stopped all dealings with us. A distance developed between us. I also began to avoid talking to her.

In the mid-nineties, I went to Delhi in connection with my research. Delhi University is divided into two campuses that are in the north and south of Delhi. The north campus was in Old Delhi and the south campus was in New Delhi. I was doing my research in the Department of Modern Indian Languages and Literary Studies. This was in the north campus and a very old department. I had just joined as a research student there. Before

I got a place in the Mansarovar Hostel in the south of Mall Road opposite Khalsa College, I had made other arrangements for my stay. Three of us Tamil students and a Geology student from Odisha took a room for rent in the two-room tenement of an employee who was working at the International Students' Hostel. Guna and I came from Pondicherry. Lenin was from Nilakottai which was in the south of Tamil Nadu. Pujari was from Puri.

It was the month of December. It was freezing cold, around nine in the night. Everyone was trying to sleep on the *razai* spread on the floor instead of sleeping on the cot. Guna and Pujari got into an argument about the sleeping arrangements. The argument was about who was going to sleep on the eastern side and soon it became a big quarrel and soon they were hitting each other. Guna said Pujari had called him by his caste name and he kicked him. Pujari kicked him back. It was turning into a huge fight. Neither would submit and they could not be separated. Pujari was a hefty person. Guna was short. Guna knew better Hindi than me. I got really scared. It was a new place. It was a city I did not know. And the abuses exchanged tore through the night.

The employee in the other room, who was quite drunk, came and separated the two. Finally, the fight came to an end. We decided to ask Pujari to leave the room the next day. He had said that we had lowly minds like our caste. Had he just tried to show off that he was more of an intellectual, we would not have minded. But he had showed his sacred thread and shouted at us in Oriya and his views on caste was reason enough to ask him to leave. But he brought all the other students from Odisha and tried to act smart with us. In order to defend ourselves, we began to bring together all the Tamil students studying in the university.

Thus, Delhi University Tamil Students' Association was born. Those who made it possible were Asghar Ali Patel, Panneerselvam, Gunasekar, Kamalakkannan and Lenin. The then Petroleum Minister at the Centre, Vazhappadi Ramamurthy was invited as a chief guest on the occasion of the inauguration of the association and he donated ₹10,000 on the occasion.

One of my Delhi friends belonged to the Kongu region. His marriage took place in Erode. I attended the marriage. It was a

Tamil marriage with no rituals. There was no holy fire or Brahmin priest. Songs from Thevaram, Tamil devotional poetry, were recited instead of mantras. The marriage took place in a huge hall and one could feel the Kongu cultural influence everywhere. I greeted my friend and shook hands with him. He was thrilled and there was a reason for that. Two months ago, an incident had taken place. I had come home from Delhi for my holidays and had decided to visit him at his house. I travelled a long distance to reach his house. He welcomed me with a lot of joy. He had a big independent house surrounded by turmeric fields, paddy fields and coconut orchards. Close to the house was the cattle of goats, cows and buffaloes. There was also a small cottage industry section to make jaggery. One could smell the melting jaggery in the air.

My friend took me inside the paddy fields. He was staying in the International House hostel of Delhi university. He was my friend from Delhi. I was very happy to meet him after a long time. I had, at times, stayed with him overnight in his hostel room without the warden coming to know. He had helped me with blankets and other winter clothing. Son of the soil of Kongu region.

It was getting to be dusk. His middle-aged mother served us coffee. My friend began to do small jobs connected with the farm. I accompanied him. His father was not at home. It was eight at night. One could hear the frogs hiding in the fields croaking. After finishing some small errands associated with an agricultural family, both of us sat at the table to eat.

My friend's mother was serving us food while chatting with us. The conversation led to my native place and I told her the name of my village. She casually asked, 'Thambi, which caste do you belong to? If you are a Gounder, which clan group do you belong to?' as she was serving food. I was taken aback. I thought my friend would have told his mother my caste. I was enjoying the food and here was a problem. I could feel my heart beating fast. I looked at my friend. Before I could say anything, my friend spoke. 'He is from the Nadar caste. Why do you ask?' he admonished his mother. The room went silent. I did not speak. I could not swallow the food. My heart was heavy. My friend saw my face had fallen and told me while we washed our hands, 'I was so afraid you were going to say which caste you belonged to. I have somehow managed the situation, fortunately. My mother is not educated. Please don't be offended.'

It was not my friend's fault. Caste still is an unchanging factor of rural life. Even today I feel as if the thorn of the fish I ate that day is caught in my heart somewhere. He was happy I attended his marriage under the circumstances. In a city atmosphere, the caste identity and faith in caste does not get revealed openly. It remains there very subtly.

When we talk of love for our native place and love for our soil and so on, it is, in fact, the traditional way of defending the caste system.

****

Taking Life as It Comes

M. Venugopal

I am connected in many ways with caste. It is not true that only the backward castes face hurdles in their life. If an upper caste person is poor the troubles that person faces are many. The problem is the upper caste person cannot remain hungry nor can that person go and beg. This was my experience in my childhood.

I was born into a well-to-do family which had lands and owned a house. Appa, my father, died when I was a child. My mother was from a village and not educated. She was cheated by the agnates of the family. We did have land. But Amma was someone who had not dealt with the world outside the home. There were six or seven children to be brought up. Who could she take advice from? Since she did not know anything about farming, there was no income. And the rains also failed; so the family faced poverty. She was from a well-to-do family. So, the land got sold.

My caste did not bring me any special honour. We were a small group in the village. We were dependent on others for everything. We had a bullock cart and an oxen. But we did not know how to drive a bullock cart. So, there was no other option but to sell it. Boys from peasant families would keep away saying I was from the upper caste and I could not mingle with upper caste children because I was from a poor family. I was filled with an inferiority complex those days.

They would not include me in games that needed bodily strength. 'He can't do this. They eat only rice,' they would say and exclude me. I have won games often with my strong body. But to put me down they would go near my house and yell out my caste name, add an abuse and run away. When the abuses were centred around mothers and sisters, my mother would beat me to a pulp saying, 'Why do you hobnob with low caste boys who speak like this? Just wait and see what I would do to you if you go again!' You were not supposed to cry if beaten. If you cried, you would get beaten more.

Vanniyars, Udaiyars and other castes lived in different areas in Senthamangalam, my native place. This was the situation in the sixties. I belong to the Karuneegar caste which comes under the Other Backward Class (OBC) whose main occupation includes teaching, administration, accountancy and similar fields. There were just a handful of us in our place. My playmates were from other castes. Although the boys may fight, the elders would treat one another in terms of sibling and customary relationships. There are many who are still elder sisters, sisters-in-law and uncles as they were for me in my childhood.

Once I teased a young girl in the next street and Amma admonished me saying, 'Dey, she is like your elder brother's daughter. You should not tease her.' She was an Udaiyar girl and not of our caste. In those days, we used to call all Muslims Mama or uncle. There was a Muslim gentleman who had a meat shop. We used to call him Mama and he used to call me Mappillai or son-in-law. It was this habit that made me address Keeranur Muthlib, whom I knew in Pudukottai when I was there in the Department of Land Survey, as Mama. He used to say, 'But I don't have a daughter, Mappillai!' During college days I very much wanted to marry a Muslim girl who was my classmate. But it did not happen. The reason was that I did not have the guts to marry her. We remained friends.

The game of caste began when I was a small boy. I did not know much about upper castes, low castes and lower castes. Whenever Amma went to the market or to another town or for a wedding, she would come into the house only after having had a bath. I asked her about it once when I was older. She said that people from many different castes would come everywhere and it would be polluting and that is why a bath was needed. Is it possible to believe in such things now? Amma, of course, is no more.

During our school days, we were most attracted to Annadurai and Periyar. Their meetings would take place in the grounds outside the Perumal temple of Senthamanagalam. I did not miss any of their meetings. At least two or three others would join me. By the time I returned from the meeting, it would be after nine in the night. News would have reached home that I had attended the meeting. Amma would blow me up saying how dare I attend a meeting of a party that claimed there was no god. The trouble was that only I had this tendency in our family.

My first love—or should I say first crush or first harmless fun? I had gone to the Mariamman temple festival just to loiter around and have fun. I saw a classmate of mine and smiled at her and my friends teased me saying, 'Having fun, eh?' That was it. Someone saw this and reported to my mother that I was talking to a girl from Mudaliar Street. My mother pounced on me and asked if I had gone to the temple festival to watch girls from all kinds of castes. I got beaten for this too. It never hurt when Amma beat. There were only two agnates of our caste around. So, all my dealings were with boys of other castes.

These caste differences did not really affect me. I moved with everybody. Whoever invited me for food, I would happily go there. Hunger knows no caste, I suppose. Wherever I played, whoever stayed close to that place, I would eat in his house. It was as simple as that. A playmate was a playmate. I would never ask him his caste. But wherever I went, the news would reach home. Only then would I come to know that I had played with boys from Muslim, Mudaliar, Gounder, or Udaiyar households.

I took up a job when I was 17. I wanted to be economically independent. I was greatly influenced by Annadurai and Periyar. So, I wanted to have an inter-caste marriage. I wanted to marry someone from a really poor family. I wanted to uplift her life. I thought it would be nice if I knew the family beforehand. I asked a couple of friends. One told me to avoid it for it would lead to problems later. Another told me that I should go ahead for life was full of problems anyway, and everything depended on how we deal with it.

One of my friends came from such a disadvantaged family. He had been my colleague for a while, and I had helped him. His family was a large one. I thought I could marry the elder daughter of the family and approached my friend through another friend. He asked me if I was in love with her. I told him I wasn't but that I only wanted to help him out since he was the eldest. He said he would like to get his daughter married to me but that the other three daughters and three sons would then find it difficult to find partners in their own caste. He said I was really large-hearted. He continues to be my friend.

I tried a second time with another girl. She was also from a poor family. They were struggling with the problem of dowry. I went till Madurai trying to seek out this girl. She was in Theni or Melur. My friend had promised to take me there to make the proposal. But midway he said that he had to go back because he had to irrigate his tuber field. It was like holding a cat on one's lap while hoping a cat would not cross one's path and bring bad luck. We had given the excuse at home that we were going to Namakkal to see the morning show of a film. This friend spoilt it all. Much later, I came to know that he had been manipulated by my elder brother. He had told him to see to it that I don't get to see the girl. My elder brother was his teacher. His devotion to his guru overthrew all my plans for marriage. So, my second attempt was also a failure.

I remember an experience I had as a small boy. An old man, who was our neighbour, passed away. He was above 70. He had two wives and many children. His first wife was not alive. His body had been kept in the hall. His second wife was sitting at his head and crying. He was a well-known person. There were many women around. Suddenly, there was a stir in the crowd. The lady got up swiftly and tied up her flowing hair and said, 'Who allowed this woman to enter the house? Hey, you elder one, just show her the slipper and send her away!' Her five sons came running and someone took away the other woman. I knew that woman. Her daughter was also standing there shedding tears. The sons of the wife knew it. But the matter was that the woman who had been chased away belonged to a lowered caste and was the old man's mistress in his younger days. The relationship had continued until the end. Everyone knew about it. But nobody would talk about it. They knew yet pretended not to know. In a short story by Poomani, on one such occasion an old man would comment, 'When you slept with the person on the field bund, wasn't caste important then?' Is this going to be the truth forever?

A Gowda caste girl who studied with me was interested in me. She invited me to restaurants a couple of times and for a film once. There were three other friends with me. They would tell me to go because she had invited me. But I couldn't. One of the three was my brother's student. The news would reach from Bangalore to Senthamangalam the very next day. So that love bud got charred even before blooming.

Before this Gowda girl incident, I had met a Kendriya Vidyalaya teacher during my bus journey from Jalahalli to college. She was Vaishanavite. We used to chat and got friendly with each other. It was all very unhurried and days passed by slowly. Friends who used to come along began to tease me. The reason was she had large eyes and long hair and she had a snaggled tooth which showed when she smiled. But she was very short; she did not even reach my chest. 'Hey, do you want to have a family with her or are you going to carry her on your hip? Don't be after her,' my friends would tease. But I wasn't one to give up. One afternoon, I asked her right in the middle of the road in Malleswaram. She was the only person to whom I had confessed my love. She smiled softly and told me, 'We are Iyengars. You are from a different caste (maybe she knew from my skin tone). These things will not work out. Let us be good friends.' Get lost all of you women, I thought, and let go of her. The irony of the matter is that from the age of 17 all the women I went searching for and moved with and the woman I finally married at the age of 26, were all named Vetri, success. How sad!

The government offices are where caste problems reign supreme. Reservations are distancing people. Like the star on the Milky Way, they say, keeps moving away from another star.

I worked as an officer in a bank for two years and later as a manager. There were four of us in senior positions. One of us was from the SC/ST group. Had I wanted, as the manager, I could have found out about his caste. But it did not occur to me. I never bothered to find out his caste. How does caste matter, I thought. Only when he got promoted did I come to know his caste. Even though one is not caste-conscious one cannot avoid troubles arising from one's colleagues. My promotion got postponed twice. The first time it was due to the hatred a colleague had for me; he called me a caste fanatic.

In our office only two persons were of a different caste; another person and myself. I was a Karuneegar and he a Mudaliar. All the others belonged to the same caste, which came under SC/ST, and which was considered lower than mine. When it comes to promotion rules they apply equally to everyone. Both of us were due for promotion. One of the two would have to be pointed at for nursing caste feelings to prevent his promotion. So, I became the caste fanatic. An anonymous letter was written and I lost my promotion. The person who wrote the anonymous letter later came and expressed his anguish. What could I do except wish him well while metaphorically gnashing my teeth?

Another time an officer who had come for inspection wanted me to take him and his family in my car to Tiruchengodu temple and the hill temple with me driving the car. I was not anybody's slave. Both of us were officers. I refused. As I have said earlier, everyone in the office was of the same caste. Someone who had ill feelings for me because I had prevented him from taking a bribe complained that I don't respect people of a lower caste. So, I lost my promotion a second time.

When I worked in the air force I had many friends. I never knew who belonged to which caste. In the air force, they looked down upon those from Salem district. Salem did not have a Tamil dialect of its own like Madurai, Tirunelveli and Kanyakumari Districts. Chennai and North and South Arcot Districts also had special ways of speaking. Salem District was not separated into Krishnagiri and Dharmapuri then. A Salem person would always begin the conversation with, 'How are you keeping?' and his spoken language was also not all that refined. 'So, you are from Salem?' they would say and ridicule him. I wanted to stop that and began to speak in grammatically correct Tamil.

These have been my encounters with caste.

I take my sons to the homes of all my friends. In villages, it is very difficult not to observe caste rules. But I have never asked anyone about their caste affiliations. Nor have I talked about caste with my children. I was hoping at least one of my children would fall in love with someone of another caste and marry them. But I have not given up hope. I have four grandchildren. One of them, at least, must have an inter-caste marriage. I will prepare them for that. But if none of them comes forward, there is not much one can do about it.

******

About the Editor, Contributors and Translator

Editor

Perumal Murugan (1966)

Belongs to Kootappalli in Thiruchengodu Circle, Namakkal District. Has a doctorate degree in Tamil. Professor in Presidency College, Chennai. Has published poems, short stories, novels and essays. Interested in publishing and in lexicography research. Wife: Ezhilarasi, Daughter: Ilampirai, Son: Ilampirai. Email ID: murugutcd@gmail.com

Contributors

N. Arulmurugan (1972)

Belongs to Jegadabi in Karur District. Has a doctorate degree in Tamil literature. Works as District Education Officer. Is a poet and has written books on poetry and other research articles. *Matrup Pathaiyil Sellavum, Nadhikraiyil Tholaintha Manal* (Take an Alternative Path, Sand Lost in the Shores of a River) are his poetry collections. *Samayath Thaththuvap Poaril Neelakesi* (Neelakesi in Religious Philosophical Discourse) is an important research title by him. Wife: Jothimani, Son: Thamizhvanan, Daughter: Thendra.l Email ID: arulnam@gmail.com

K. Anbazhagan (1977)

Belongs to Kovilpalayam in Thiruchengodu Circle, Namakkal District. Has a doctorate degree in Tamil literature. Works as Assistant Professor at a Government Arts College. Has published two books: *Drobadhai Kuravanji* and *Panchali Vanavasam* (Folk Dance Drama on Daraupadi and Panchali's Exile in the Forest). Interested in folk studies and folk theatre performances. Wife: Sheela, Daughter: Oviya.

M. Ananthan (1988)

Belongs to Manjanayakanur in Namakkal District. Working towards a doctorate degree in Tamil literature. Wife: Gomathi. Email ID: elakkiananthan.nkl@gmail.com

N. Ranjan (1984)

Belongs to Kalichampatti in Namakkal District. Has a doctorate degree in Tamil literature. Works as Assistant Professor in a government-aided college. Is part of modern theatre groups performing plays such as Mu. Ramasamy's Nija Nataka Iyakkam and Murugaboopathi's Manal Magudi. Interested in Tamil grammar. Email ID: nsartamil@gmail.com

R. Rajasekaran (1983)

Belongs to Mangalapuram in Namakkal district. Doing his PhD in Tamil literature. Working as Assistant Professor in a self-financed arts college. Has written some research articles and is interested in contemporary writing. Wife: Shyamala. Son: Jana. Email ID: rajasekarjana@gmail.com.

P. Rajeskannan (1977)

Belongs to Periyeri in Aathoor Circle, Salem District. Has an MA, MPhil and MEd in Tamil literature. Works as a senior teacher at a government school. Interested in Education Studies. Wife: Gowri. Daughter: Ezhilmadhi. Email ID: prktamil1977@gmail.com

P. Ezhilarasi (1968)

Born in Velam, a small town near Ranippettai in Velur District. Has a doctorate degree in Tamil. Working as a professor in Queen Mary's College, Chennai. Has published a poetry collection, *Midhakkum Makarantham* (Floating Fragrance). Has published research articles on the description of women in Tamil novels, and an anthropological study of potters in Tamil Nadu. Interested in contemporary Tamil literature. Husband: Perumal Murugan, Daughter Ilampirai, Son: Ilamparidhi. Email ID: spezhilvlm@gmail.com

T. Kalaichelvan (1985)

Belongs to Kumaramangalam, in Thiruchengodu Circle, Namakkal District. Has an MA, BEd and MPhil in Tamil literature. Is on the editorial board of the magazine *Uzhunilam*. Working as an Assistant Professor in a self-financed college. Interested in creative writing. Email ID: kalaitamilma@gmail.com

K. Kasimariyappan (1965)

Belongs to Sivanthipuram in Tirunelveli District. Has a doctorate degree in Tamil. Works as an Associate Professor in a Government Arts College. Interested in Dalit Studies and other studies on life at the margins. Writes poems under the pen name Kombamadasamy. Has written many research articles and participated in many seminars. Wife: Meena. Son: Kapilan. Email ID: meenamariyappan@gmail.com

V. Krishnan (1967)

Belongs to Udumalaipettai, Coimbatore District. Has a PhD in Tamil literature. Works as an Associate Professor in a

Government Arts College. Is interested in researching feminism and modern Tamil literature. Has written many research articles. Wife: Subashree, Son: Siddharthan, Daughter: Sangamithrai. Email ID: sukisangu@gmail.com

P. Gunasekaran (1983)

Belongs to Ramanathapuram Pudur in Namakkal District. Works as a senior teacher in a government school. Interested in writing fiction. He is part of the editorial board of the magazine *Uzhunilam*. Wife: Shanthi, Daughter: Thansi. Email ID: guna83guna83@gmail.com

P. Kumaresan (1986)

Born in Thannirpandhalkadu in Rasipuram Circle, Namakkal District. He has done his post graduation, BEd and MPhil in Tamil literature. Takes part in public elocution competitions and has won prizes. Email ID: kumaresan1470@gmail.com

S. Gopi (1983)

Belongs to Pavithiram in Namakkal District. He has a post graduate degree and a BEd and MPhil in Tamil literature. He is doing his PhD from Gandhigram Rural University. Interested in art and culture studies. Wife: Divyabharathi. Email ID: skopinkl@gmail.com

Govindaraj (1966)

Belongs to Tiruppur. Has been a practising homeopath for the past 20 years. At present, in order to have a valid degree, he is a student in the Homeopathy Medical College. Towards the end of 1980s, he came into the Tamil literary scene as a writer to be taken notice of. Has published many stories in the *Mana Osai* magazine. Has published a short story collection *Pasalai*

(Lovesickness). Has also written many medical articles. Daughter: Vannidhi. Email ID: govindthji@gmail.com

C. Sathiskumar (1986)

Belongs to Veerappan Chathiram, Erode district. Has MA and MPhil degrees in Tamil literature. At present working towards a PhD degree. Working as Assistant Professor in a self-financed college. Has won recognition in writing poetry, essays and in public elocution competitions. Has brought out a poetry collection, *Karaiyil Thudikkum Miinkal* (Fish Writhing on the Shore) under his pen name Kaviyanpu. Wife: Revathi, Son: Makizhnan. Email ID: revathiraagavi@gmail.com

C. Chandiran (1973)

Belongs to Vaikarai in Thuraiyur Circle, Trichi District. Has a doctorate degree in Tamil literature. Works as a senior teacher in a government school. Has written many research articles. Interested in Folk Arts Studies. Wife: Thoni, Son: Nedumidal, Daughter: Pirainudhal.

A. Chinnadurai (1978)

Belongs to Thottapadi in Vizuppuram District. Working towards a PhD in Tamil literature. Working as a Tamil teacher in a government school. Interested in research on Dalit and Folk Arts Studies. Wife: Sarala, Daughter: Yazhini. Email ID: chinnayazhini@gmail.com

P. Suresh (1984)

Belongs to Senthamangalam in Namakkal District. Is a graduate Tamil teacher in a government school. Has published short stories under the pseudonym Senchadaiyan in the magazines *Uzhunilam* and *Uyir Ezhuthu*.

C. Sureshkumar (1988)

Belongs to Siluvampatti, Namakkal District. Working for an MPhil in Tamil Literature. Interested in writing poetry. Email ID: kavisureshkumar1988@gmail.com

M. Senthamarai (1986)

Belongs to Dhathathiripuram village in Namakkal District. Currently working for an MPhil degree in Tamil literature. Husband: Prabhakar. Email ID: senthamarai24@gmail.com

V. Dharmalingam (1979)

Belongs to the village Sarvay in Aathoor Circle, Salem District. Has a doctorate degree in Tamil literature. After working as a professor of Tamil in self-financed colleges, is currently a Junior Assistant in the Department of Registration. Interested in modern literature and criticism and has also written a few research articles. Wife: Sangeethadevi, Sons: Sivageethan, Kapilan. Email ID: dharmalingam_vai@yahoo.com

M. Natarajan (1974)

Born in Bommanpatti in Namakkal District. Has a doctorate degree in Tamil language. Working as a professor in the Government Arts College. Interested in Folk Studies and has published a book on folk stories of Namakkal District. Wife: Rajalakshmi, Son: Rajarajan. Email ID: muthusamynatarajan2010@gmail.com

P. Nallusamy (1974)

Belongs to Puduchathiram Olappalayam in Namakkal District. Has a doctorate degree in Tamil literature. Works as an Assistant Professor in a private college. Interested in Semiotics and has written a few research articles. Wife: Vanthia, Son: Kavin. Email ID: kavinnallu@gmail.com

P. Balasubramanian (1981)

Belongs to Kavedipatti in Namakkal District. Studying for a doctorate degree from Gandhgram Rural University. Was on the editorial board of the magazine *Kalachuvadu* for some time. Interested in contemporary literature and folk theatre. Wife: Yazhini, Son: Gopinath. Email ID: balupkvp@gmail.com

R. Prabhakar (1980)

Belongs to Kolathupalayam in Namakkal District. Working towards a doctorate degree. Works as a junior assistant in a government high school. Writes short stories under the pseudonym Theeran and has published stories in the magazine *Uyir Ezhuthu*. Was on the editorial board of the magazine *Uzhunilam*. Wife: Senthamarai. Email ID: theeran1980@gmail.com

K. Poonkothai (1984)

Belongs to Ilamkarisalkulam, Virudhunagar District. Is working towards a doctorate degree in Tamil literature. Husband: Dravidaselvan. Daughters: Sangamithra, Ezhilmadhi.

R. Mahendiran (1982)

Belongs to Vadukappatti in Namakkal District. Has an MA and MPhil in Tamil and a BEd degree. Published the magazine *Uzhunilam* for some time and attempting to write stories and essays. He is also a painter and terracotta sculptor. Wife: Padmini, Son: Pirainilavan. Email ID: mahendiranr198@gmail.com

P. Muthusami (1975)

Belongs to the village Veppanatham in Aathoor Circle, Salem District. Has been part of the editorial board of the magazine *Kalachuvadu*. Has worked as a Junior Research Assistant at the Central Institute for Research in Classical Tamil. Currently works in the Department of Highways as a Junior Assistant. Runs a blog named 'Theettu'. Interested in essay writing and in research on print history. Wife: Azhagurani, Daughter: Karkuzhali, Son: Neduvel. Email ID: muthusamiga@gmail.com

R.Venkatachalam (1969)

Belongs to Athiveerampatti in Oothankarai Circle, Krishnagiri District. Is awaiting his PhD degree in Tamil literature. Works as Assistant Professor in a government college. Interested in Dalit literature. Active in trade unions and has written a few research articles. Wife: Chennammal.

M.Venkatesan (1972)

Belongs to the small town of Nayakkanur near Singarapettai in Oothankarai Circle, Krishnagiri District. Has a doctorate degree in Tamil literature. Works as Associate Professor in a government college. Has written a book on Dalit writer Bama's novel *Sangathi* and its place in modern Tamil literature from a Dalit perspective. Interested in modern Tamil literature and in research on life in the margins. He was on the editorial board of the magazine *Veru Veru* and is a student of the well-known professor K. Panchangam. Email ID: venkatesanphd@gmail.com

M.Venugopal (1943)

Belongs to Jankalapuram in Namakkal District. Has a post graduate degree in Sociology and has a BGL degree in law. Worked in the Indian Navy for a while, and later in a bank, and has now retired. Writes short stories and poems. Has published a story in the magazine *Uyir Ezhuthu*. Wife: Jeyam, Son: Periyasamy, Daughter: Ulakamudhalvi.

Translator

Dr C. S. Lakshmi has been an independent researcher in Women's Studies for the last 35 years. She has a PhD from Jawaharlal Nehru University, New Delhi, and has worked as a Research Officer in the Indian Council of Historical Research and has also been a college lecturer in Delhi for two years. She received the Ford Foundation Fellowship to work on a project entitled Illustrated Social History of Women in Tamil Nadu in 1981 and in 1992 she received the Homi Bhabha Fellowship to do a project on women musicians, dancers and painters. This research work has been brought out in two volumes by Kali for Women. She is also a renowned author of Tamil literary fiction under the pseudonym Ambai.